ANA

A novel inspired by a true story

ANA

JOANNE LOUISE HARDY

With foreword by
JAMES REDFIELD

INSIGHTFUL LIVING

Although inspired by a true story, this novel is entirely a work of fiction. All names and locales used are fictitious and any similarities to real people is purely coincidental. It may read like a narrative memoir, but it is not one—it is a creation born from the author's imagination inspired by stories told by a person who wished to remain anonymous.

PUBLISHED BY INSIGHTFUL LIVING FEBRUARY 2021
ISBN 978-1-7365149-0-0

Dedicated to Sofia and Lucille.

Shine bright, darling girls.

FOREWORD

Sometimes, a novel is so timely, it is a statement about where humanity is going.

Everywhere you look, we are experiencing a "wake up" call that is challenging, yet historic. This massive awakening is spiritual and global, and looks deeply at all our world's institutions, especially healthcare, governments, news, and increasingly… our own lives.

What we are discovering is an alarming lack of transparency in the world. Yet our reaction represents a breakthrough, as if something has shifted in our tolerance level, so we can now hear and see the raw truth, even if it lowers our idealistic assumptions a little.

Increasingly, we know that truth is more valuable than any attempt to sugar coat reality—because the truth draws us together, and leads to honest reform and reconciliation.

The book you are reading is one of these liberating insights about our world.

In 2017, Joanne Louise began working with us at Celestinevision.com, initially as a writer and then as a key part of our management team. But in the background, she was always working on this novel.

How the book happened is fascinating. As Joanne explained to me, some time ago, a woman came into her life wanting to share her personal journey and offer the truths she had learned as inspiration for a fictional novel.

She felt that her experiences, beginning early in life—which were very difficult—could stand as a testament of awakening for others traveling a difficult path.

Joanne told me she agreed to write this novel, elevating the story she heard into a broader mozaic of time and place, one that anyone could use as a lens into their own lives. The novel has taken seven years, inspirited by the truths Joanne has found, until it has now come fully to life as a story that can be applied to all.

ANA is an incredibly powerful adventure that's nothing if not honest. It begins with a young woman growing up with not enough money, not enough love, and not enough compassion from others. Yet in this challenging world, the protagonist sought to make sense of her life, even as those around her sought to take advantage.

Did she make mistakes? Yes. In her aloneness, she makes every mistake. But in her solitary search for something better, her heart stays true and she finally finds a higher path—something we all yearn for.

Now, through Joanne, this larger story is available, and her muse's intuition has come true. We all struggle with our past, and must come to grips with our confusion, and missed steps. And like the character at the center of this novel, we can all believe that our lives can be a special message.

In that revelation, ANA shows us something eternal: Even if we start in a difficult place, even if we struggle, the only journey that matters… is to the light we learn to give.

James Redfield,
author of The Celestine Prophecy

ANA

JOANNE LOUISE HARDY

2014

Knowing yourself can be one of the hardest aspects of life to master, and being certain of your life path can be just as challenging. My name is Ana, and it's taken me a lifetime to be able to confidently say I know both. While my journey started out so dark I sometimes wished I'd never been born, I have now found a stable state of happiness, and I know my one remaining mission lies in writing to you.

Living in the modern world can be hard, and we can be certain that every human will come to know both physical and emotional pain, as well as pleasure. My childhood in particular was so disturbing I felt constant, indescribable emptiness; my life providing a torrent of events that I've had to endure in my struggle to know freedom. But now that I accept everything I have been through, I can positively affirm that I know peace, and it is a beautiful sensation.

Both my body and mind have been scarred during my time here, but as my spirit prepares to move on to the next dimension, I feel as if I'm being called to share my experiences in an attempt to support others who may have suffered in similar ways.

Whilst there are many unsettling things happening around the world, I see that we are all connected, and while emotions are contagious, they are so draining when not managed properly. Like the ocean, our minds have the potential to house enormously powerful storms, and although we may try to ride the waves and keep our heads above water, when trauma happens, it takes immense strength to regain composure. Life can so easily knock us off balance when its waves come crashing down.

With all the drama I've known in my fifty-six years, I've come to realise that it's impossible to stay grounded all the time, unless you are literally a saint. The life I've lived has led me to what I will term enlightenment, but to get here I also came to know the dark, turbulent side of humanity, and I often suffered at the hands of others.

I grew up with parents who weren't interested in talking about the Big Picture, and I never knew any elders who were willing to tell me about the lessons they'd learned. So, at times, I lived as an island, when I desperately craved the wisdom of others. With this in mind, my intuition is now yelling at me, urging me to share my tale, with an underlying promise that in doing so, I may help to uplift others who are battling their own storms.

My life was a stream of perpetual challenge, but I believe in my heart that I've now risen above the drama. I know that each human life brings its own stresses that must be handled, but I now trust with every atom of my being that we are, by nature, a strong and kind species. And it's when people are unhealthy in their mindset that unhealthy situations ensue.

I recently heard someone say, "We should be kind to those who are mean to us, as they are the ones who need it most." And there is much wisdom in these few words. As I close my life, I refuse the task of judging anyone, for no one truly knows the depths of emotion, nor the twists of the nervous system which drive people to act the way they do.

No matter who you are, nor where you're from, I reach my hand out to you now, to tell you that you are not alone. We are all in this game together. And yes, some of us unfortunately receive awful hands that we must play, and we may fight and struggle against the tide to save ourselves. But, now that I am attuned to inner peace, my struggle has stopped so that I have become the eye of the storm, and from here I can observe all the craziness that's out there without letting it disturb my flow. And if I can achieve this blissful state, I know you and everyone else can too, for we're all made of the same matter.

While many necessary changes must be made to allow peace to ripple through humanity, I choose to trust that the Universe knows what it's doing, and that among the billions of us that reside on planet Earth, there are now those present who will deliver upon their own personal missions to set peace free. It's true that there is much greed currently throwing its weight around within society, but there is also so much love that I know peace and light will continue emerging until greed holds no power over us.

In my eyes, the beauty of the human race is that we are each unique and equally important, and we all bring a special set of knowledge to stir into the melting pot. When we harbour secrets inside, we aid no one. When we bite our tongue and keep things hidden, our skin may grow thicker but the wounds inside never heal.

Although my mother believed you should hide away your darkest secrets, I am choosing to adopt a different manner—and I do so in the name of spiritual evolution.

I would like to share my experiences with you and explain how the Universe has proved to me that there is life after death. For I no longer wonder if the next dimension exists; I have seen it first-hand, and there is no doubt in my mind that our souls endure after we pass away.

In the past, it's seemed to me that people have often been too afraid to share their spiritual stories for fear of being ridiculed or seen as crazy—I know I've certainly felt reticent to tell others of the encounters I've had, fearing that I would be mocked. But, recently, I have been hearing more frequently of other people who too have made contact with the other side.

It now feels to me as if a new age of spiritual confidence is flowing through our societies, urging us to open up to ideas which would have previously been considered eccentric. And, together, when we don't hold back, when we release everything that's inside us, we give each other strength, and we assist the conscious evolution of our entire species.

When we share our tales, we realise that we are far from strange or delusional. We are simply souls encased within human bodies, trying to comprehend the events of our life and the true nature of the world we inhabit.

There are many types of humans on Earth, with our varying personalities and traditions, but I do feel that no matter where we're from, our own personal problems are our highest priority, we all revel in the delight of falling in love, and we each have the capacity to hurt deeply when things don't turn out the way we'd hoped they would. Underneath it all, I know the most important thing that we have in common is our huge capacity to love. And I believe Love is the strongest element we have.

In the following pages, I will air my truth, my story of transformation. With love, I offer you my life. Please take from it what you will.

CHAPTER ONE

nce upon a time, I was a young girl growing up in a family so dysfunctional it barely warranted that title. I lived with my parents and my four siblings in a working-class suburb of Nottingham, England, and every day that I spent in our home brought its own torment.

My dad was Irish Catholic and arrived in Nottingham after serving in the army in the second world war. At the tender age of twenty, he got a job working down a coal mine, met my mum, got married, and got her pregnant, all within a year.

My mum had worked as a servant in an upper-class household before she met my dad. And after becoming a mother at the age of eighteen, she never returned to employment—instead occupying herself with all the demands that running a household brings. But as the years passed and my siblings and I arrived, the relationship between my parents became so strained they barely even spoke to each other.

Now add a big sprinkle of crazy into the mix. My mum was quite twisted; she liked to shame people, and she'd frequently take her frustrations out on us kids. She ran our home like it was an army barracks—as if me and my siblings existed simply to serve our parents—and neither my sister nor I were allowed to go to school regularly.

We were treated as scullery maids, and instead of placing any importance on our education, my mum chose to utilise our time by imposing a fanatical cleaning schedule—we would wash clothes, scrub floors, and polish the house all day, and then, in the evening, our kitchen duties would commence.

My sister is seven years older than me, my elder brother four years my senior, then my two younger brothers are five and six years my junior. So, I grew up pretty much smack-bang in the middle of us all, which I can honestly say felt like the worst position.

Mum seemed to view my elder siblings as more useful, my younger brothers as more demanding, and unless it was to give me an order, I was constantly overlooked. She had no interest in being affectionate with me, ever. In fact, she was scarcely affectionate with any of us.

I was a very gentle girl and my siblings were good kids too, but we grew up knowing the wrath of our mother all too well, and every day one of us would get beaten. I spent my days doing everything she told me to do, trying to blend into the background of our home and avoid conflict, and I would get knocked around the house as payment—although, I always found it much harder to watch her hit my siblings than to take the beatings myself. It was just awful.

Violence escalated quickly and could appear from out of nowhere. Take for example, the day at seven years old when I went to my mum with a splinter stuck under my toenail, and she subsequently pinned me down on the floor and pushed a needle deeply under my nail for what felt like an eternity until she got it out. She used one of the most brutal torture techniques known to man without hesitation or regret to "help" me…

We lived in poverty, scraping by on what our father earned, whilst my mum was addicted to gambling, and every night, she'd venture out to the local bingo hall, then stay on after the bingo to play roulette. Even though we were poor, my mum would squirrel away her winnings (she invariably had a little bit of money), however she was so obsessed with it, she refused to spend any on me. She did buy clothes for my siblings, but I lived in hand-me-downs from Louisa and garments that our neighbours gave me. I spent my childhood feeling so unloved by my mum that I felt hollow.

My dad was nice, but he was very weak in comparison to Mum and he'd never stand up to her for us. I learned very quickly that the only result achieved by speaking my mind was a good hiding, so I shut up and did as I was told, forever dreaming of the day when adulthood would finally arrive.

Our house was incredibly humble. We lived on a drab street of terraced houses, and when I'd peg the washing out in the backyard, I'd hear the dramas of our neighbours shouting their way through their disputes—I knew sombrely that they heard ours too. We didn't have a bathroom inside (we took our baths in a tin tub in front of the fire, all seven of us taking turns with the same water) and our only toilet was outside. We had a dining room with a large table, and two armchairs next to an open fireplace, yet despite there being a total of nine chairs in that room, my siblings and I were always expected to sit on the floor unless we were eating. Although, on rare occasions, my dad would let me sit on an armchair next to him when my mum was at bingo, and he'd say something like, 'For Christ's sake, Ana, don't tell your mum you've sat there, or else we'll both be in trouble!' I loved those nights so much.

I'm sure working in an upper-class household dramatically impacted my mum, and I believe that underneath it all, she was ashamed of her social status. When she'd go out, she would doll herself up in her best skirt suit, her make-up applied beautifully, her hair styled neatly, and around strangers she'd put on a weird, posh accent.

On the rare occasions we entertained guests, we'd sit in the front room of the house (which was reserved for best without exception) and we'd watch our mum play the hostess role, whilst complying with her rule that children should be seen and not heard. However, when guests and on-lookers disappeared, my mum would swear like a trooper. It was the norm to hear things such as, 'By God, I'll teach you!' and 'I'll fucking kill you, you little shit!' yelled at us on a daily basis.

Now, you should bear in mind that although swearing is commonplace these days, back then it was considered very foul language, and I think most of my mum's generation would have been appalled to hear a man use those words in front of a lady—let alone hear a woman directing them at children.

As our mum had no interest in nurturing us, Louisa took on the role of my mother and I always looked up to her—she had such a calming influence. I delighted in how she'd never fail to find something to make me giggle when we were alone. We shared a bed in the attic, and when we went upstairs at night, Louisa would cuddle me to sleep—when we held each other, I knew love. She'd comfort me by telling me, 'Don't worry, Ana. One day, we'll find our way out of here.' And I longed to believe her.

I look back now and wonder why my mum's priorities were set as they were. Why would she pretend to be classy around strangers, but let me live in rags? I just don't get it, even today. I do however realise now that both my parents were simply stuck in survival mode, coping with life in their own way. They'd been stunned by the hardship they'd suffered during their formative years and they'd had no time to heal before starting their family. Whilst my mum knew no better than to enforce the notion of 'spare the rod and spoil the child', I'm positive we should throw out the rod and nourish our children.

To add to the unsettling experiences I knew at home, when I was eight years old, our sixty year old neighbour, Derek, started sexually abusing me. My mum made me take him our dinner left-overs for his dog one evening and I'll never forget how after he'd invited me in, he stood at the back door blocking my exit. I was absolutely powerless against him.

When I said, 'I really need to get home,' he ignored my words, picked me up, and ran his hand up my leg into my knickers. After I'd endured the vileness of the encounter, he put me down, gave me a coin out of his pocket, and I was allowed to leave; only to be ordered to go back around to Derek's again any time we had food scraps.

I wasn't confident enough to tell my mum what Derek had done to me, but after it happened twice, I did tell my elder brother, Jimmy. From that day on, whenever there were leftovers to be taken, Jimmy offered to go in my place and thankfully our mum never objected.

Whilst a part of me wonders if I shouldn't mention such distressing elements of my life in fear that it will be too disturbing for you to read, I will press forward with my honesty. For I know that with all the strength and wisdom I've gained, if it's difficult for me to share my story, it will be near impossible for those who feel more fragile to tell you what's happened to them. So, here, I wish to set an example and declare that it's a positive thing to talk about bad experiences.

If we try to pretend ugly events never happened, and suppress them, they will dwell within us forever. But, if we talk and share what's happened, that hurt is aired and given an opportunity to heal. And with no darkness buried inside, love has the chance to flow through our entire being without meeting any barriers that prevent it from reaching our core.

When I was nine, there was a night when I was woken abruptly by Mum yelling and screaming at my sister downstairs. It soon became apparent that Louisa hadn't been alone when Mum had returned home early from bingo. She had walked in to find Louisa having sex with her boyfriend in the dining room, her hair dishevelled and her underwear discarded on the floor. I was absolutely terrified for my sister's safety.

After her boyfriend was told to leave, I bore witness to the sounds of Louisa's sobbing and her cries of pain from the beating she endured. My mum was so loud I'm sure the whole street heard as she yelled that

Louisa would be thrown out in the morning—there was no place for 'little trollops' in her home! Knowing I couldn't possibly intervene, I had no alternative but to lie and listen, anxiously waiting for Louisa to come up to bed.

She was crying when she finally came upstairs, and we lay together with our bedspread pulled up over us, holding each other while we sobbed. She begged me to bring our little brothers to visit her if our mother did force her to leave, and through my tears, I assured her I would, but I was so full of fear it was terrible. The thought of Louisa leaving our home frightened me to my core—I had no idea how to imagine life without her at my side.

After that night, the days passed, each filled with its own violence and turmoil, but in the end rather than throwing Louisa out, my parents made her boyfriend and his parents come to our house to talk about them getting married—it was such a surprise reaction! Luckily, she got her period a few days later, so she knew she didn't need to marry him. But looking back, I think my dad was probably the one to come up with the wedding idea, as Mum would have most likely relished the thought of throwing Louisa out as a shamed woman (at just sixteen years old, and a year younger than she had been when she'd conceived Louisa).

It took me until I was a teenager to see this episode for what it really was, and to realise that if my mum had only stayed home to look after us in the evenings, the opportunity for Louisa to do what she did would have never occurred. If she had been attentive to us and cared about our welfare enough to watch over us, many regrettable actions would never have been made. But, I guess, our family had to learn this lesson the hard way. And when we see our parents behave in ways that we don't want to copy, our sense of morality develops and we can vow never to make the same mistakes ourselves.

Later that year, while I was still nine years old, there was a horrifying commotion one evening when Jimmy went out to the toilet and found Louisa collapsed on the floor, barely conscious. Mum was out gambling, Dad was downstairs, and I was in my bedroom when Jimmy screamed for us to come outside. With my younger brothers still sleeping, my dad and I ran out the house—I'll never forget the way Dad bellowed with all his might for the neighbours to come and help us. I could see the experience was breaking him in two, tears pooling in his eyes.

Our neighbours were very good to us that night. Within a few minutes, half a dozen concerned adults were gathered in our back-yard, while I looked on, shaking, with tears streaming down my face.

Louisa had taken an overdose in an attempt to commit suicide, but thank God, our neighbour, Mrs Baisley, recognised the symptoms and took control. She managed to rouse Louisa enough to get her to drink salt water, and within seconds Louisa was vomiting violently all over the floor. Thankfully, my prayers were answered. My sister survived.

When I talked to Louisa about why she had tried to take her life, I understood why she'd contemplated that death was a viable escape route from the physical and mental abuse she suffered. However, to temper this tragic episode, I'm pleased to report that Louisa found happiness later that year when she met a young man called William and fell madly in love. They married when she was seventeen and, subsequently, she moved to live in Leicester (a neighbouring city) with her new husband.

My sister beamed with a glowing energy that told the world she knew a beautiful love that filled her heart and soul, and I was incredibly happy for her. It was wonderful to see her gain her freedom, but selfishly, I missed her with every atom of my being. And every night when I went to bed, I longed to feel her embrace—my bed felt too big without her. I was so lonely.

In turn, at ten years old, I took on the responsibility of looking after our younger brothers, Finn and Patrick: carrying out the normally parental duties of reading to them, bathing them, getting them ready for bed, tucking them in, and so on, in addition to my usual chores.

My life as a child consisted of working as a scullery maid and nanny in my own home. It's ironic really, because my mum named me after enjoying the 1956 film 'Anastasia' in which Ingrid Bergman played the beautiful Russian princess. Mum thought my name sounded quite posh and exotic, so she named me after a princess... but then she treated me like a slave. I'm sure she did love me in her own way, but she was so egocentric and cruel that her love was nothing like what I now perceive this emotion to be.

So, my start in life was, all in all, rather horrific. I was a kind, intelligent, pretty child with dark brown hair and big, brown eyes, yet I felt worthless. My thoughts didn't matter; my opinion wasn't invited. I, or rather we, were systematically crushed and broken. But now

I have healed, I can look back on my childhood with compassion and forgiveness—and in this mindset the past holds me prisoner no more.

CHAPTER TWO

To escape the terror of my childhood I loved to read; the experience of losing myself in a novel has always been a joy I've revelled in. Louisa taught me how to read, for which I will forever be grateful, and my dad was always willing to tell me the meaning of new words if I pointed them out. As there were very few books in our house, I rarely read stories that were aimed at children of my age. But I would sneak off to the library whenever the opportunity arose and devour anything I could get my hands on. I'd dive into the story and wish to never come out.

Although I was rarely at school, I passed my Eleven Plus exam with flying colours and was accepted into the local grammar school (much to my mum's surprise). So, my parents did what was expected, enrolling me at the school and signing the contracts for my education. Yet despite this agreement they had made with the local authority, Mum still preferred to keep me at home doing the housework rather than to let me go to school. And when I did go, I found I didn't fit in.

I met a lot of new girls when I joined that grammar school, but many of them thought I had a funny name and would poke fun at my old clothes. Because I was often absent or late, I was always behind with the classwork, and the teachers quickly seemed to view me as a disruption—it didn't take long before I hated going.

The first time truancy officers knocked on our door, I answered and they assumed I was a boy as Mum had cut off all my hair when I had caught head-lice. I remember one of them said, 'Hello, sonny, does Anastasia O'Connor live here?' And I said she did, but she was out. When they walked away, I closed the door quickly, my heart pounding in my chest.

The second time they knocked, Mum answered, and when they told her she was breaking their contract, she asked them, 'Why don't you just mind your own business and fuck off?"

I remember standing next to her as they walked off in shock, and that was the last we ever saw of them. After that, Mum continued to pick and choose when she would let me go to school, but I don't think I was ever there more than two days a week.

On one of those not-so-merry days at the grammar school, I recall a teacher talking to me at the side of the hockey pitch, saying, 'You're like a soldier who's walking in line, whilst looking at everyone else and wondering "why are you walking like that?"' And that was a very accurate observation. The people and the system I encountered at that school seemed so strange to me. There was little kindness shown. Instead, teachers chose to rule with iron fists, and if you so much as spoke when you weren't invited to, you were threatened with a trip to the head-mistress' office.

During my schooling, we were taught to fear the system and those at the top of the pyramid—there was little room to flourish unless it was in the way that was expected of you. No one else in my classes ever questioned the information in our textbooks, and my classmates would always look at me with disbelief when I did. The pupils who got the best results in tests were those who managed to regurgitate the information their teachers gave with the most accuracy, and that was all that was required.

As I analyse the system now, I believe there are significant gaps in the curriculum. And if I was able to enhance it myself, I would include meditation and spiritual studies from primary school onwards—I say this because I have personally benefited more from my spiritual practices than from any formal education or specific knowledge set. When you need to stand on your own two feet and cope with life's stresses, meditation is the most powerful discipline I know.

I once thought meditation was about being calm, but as I've continued in my journey, I've come to feel that it is more about connecting with Love than anything else. It's the realisation that there is Love in the atmosphere, outside of us, that will pour into us and strengthen our spirit if we just open ourselves up to it. When we connect to this energy, our mind dismisses fear and we're cradled in the arms of the Universe. We are loved. We become love—and that's an incredibly fulfilling and empowering sensation.

When I was twelve years old, Jimmy was sent away to a Young Offenders Institution, which came as a *huge* surprise to me. I wasn't told why he was being locked up at the time as our family never discussed anything openly. Only later, when I had the opportunity to ask

Jimmy myself, did I learn he'd hurt someone in a brawl. When he disappeared from our home, I remember thinking he was just a boy, how could anyone want to lock him up and take him away from his family? I needed him, and he needed us.

Jimmy spent eighteen months inside, but do you know what disturbs me the most about that period? My parents never went to visit him, not once. Can you imagine having a child and not wanting to see them? I can't. My mum felt that Jimmy had brought shame on our family, and they wrote him off for the entire time.

I remember the day Jimmy got out of prison as if it were yesterday. I was cleaning the windows in the front room, so I happened to be looking out onto the street when he came walking up to our house wearing the cheap, light-coloured suit he had been given by the prison. I had no idea that he was getting out that day, and I ran like a flash of lightning out the front door to grab hold of him.

What baffles me is that although we had a car (as battered as it was) and my parents would have been informed of his release, they didn't go to pick him up. I can't fathom how, instead, Jimmy's homecoming went completely unannounced, and he was made to catch three buses back across the county. Bless him—he wasn't a bad lad at heart.

I was thirteen at the time, and after running out to Jimmy, I threw my arms around him, holding him tightly with absolutely no intention of letting go.

It was so wonderful to have him home. My head on his shoulder, I sobbed with relief. Then only when I pulled back did I notice that the mascara I had recently started to wear had made black smudges all over his jacket—which I washed clean for him, later on.

When he came into the house there were no discussions about his time inside; there was no party held for him; no gruelling evenings of hard-talk to be endured. He was just back.

My parents accepted Jimmy as much as they accepted any of us and life carried on. Bizarrely, I remember Mum never bought Jimmy any new clothes, and he walked around in that prison suit for weeks until a neighbour took pity on him and bought him a couple of new outfits—it was so strange.

When I was fourteen, I sneaked out one night with my friend Pamela (who lived on the street behind ours), and we went to a party that was being thrown at her boyfriend's house. Well, when we arrived, I couldn't have been more surprised to see his mother handing out whisky sours to the youngsters whilst drinking the stuff herself. It was the first time I had ever tried alcohol, and I'm sorry to say, I proceeded to get terribly drunk.

There was a lad at the party called Daniel, who seemed to take a shine to me—he seemed nice enough— and Pam was desperately trying to pair us off as he was her boyfriend's best friend. I remember us sitting kissing at the bottom of the stairs, but then my head started spinning, and when I went to find Pam, she suggested I rest upstairs in the guest bedroom.

After Pam left me alone, Daniel came in, and when he lay down with me, I told him I wasn't well. But honestly, I was absolutely plastered, and when he made his advances more forcibly, I didn't have the inner strength to make him stop. So, unfortunately, this is how I lost my virginity: weaving in and out of consciousness as he pushed himself inside me next to a pile of coats.

Luckily, I managed to get home that night without waking my parents, so my outing went unnoticed. And I remember doing the laundry immediately after I woke to wash my knickers, as Mum had a habit of checking them for any signs that I'd been doing wrong.

My head was banging, but as scrubbing the floors doesn't take any mental application, I managed to hide my hangover from my mum and survive the day. I felt empty and a little numbed with shock, but I was also bitterly disappointed that I could never take back my first time. It's not a memory that I'm proud of, nor anything I would want anyone else ever to go through, but it was what it was, and there's nothing I can do about it other than accept it.

I've realised now, we are in control of how much we allow our past to impact our present. We choose whether or not we replay moments in our mind over and over again, and we decide how much we let past events drain our energy. I now know the best thing I can do is let go of any hurt, anger, and anxiety, acknowledge what these episodes taught me, and move on, focusing on the positives I know in the present, rather than the negatives I once knew in the past.

CHAPTER THREE

Not long after that party, I decided to run away from home in search of a better life. I got to the point where I snapped; I just couldn't take any more abuse from my mum. There was no way to win against her, so I saw flight as my only option.

Without practically planning my departure at all, I set off one afternoon with just my handbag and nothing much in it. I remember sneaking out the house and immediately feeling enormous relief at being free from its claustrophobic atmosphere.

I had next to no money, and not knowing where to go or what to do next, I walked to the nearest main road and stuck my thumb out. I just wanted to get as far away as possible.

It was no more than ten minutes before a car stopped for me. Peering in through the open window, I saw a balding, fortyish man with white blonde eyebrows and pale blue eyes looking out.

'Where are you heading?' he asked.

'Whereabouts are you going?' I countered.

He told me he was driving to Derby (which was about twenty miles away), so I agreed that was fine and got in. As I settled into the passenger seat, the man turned to me and asked, 'Have you got any money towards the petrol, love?'

Shaking my head apologetically, I asked if I could still go with him. And in reply, he steered away from the kerbside, saying, 'I'm sure we can work something out.'

As we drove, we chatted a little about the weather and the traffic, and after half an hour or so, I was surprised when we seemed to be arriving in a suburb rather than the city centre. We continued past houses and, feeling that the journey was about to end, I asked if he knew how I could get to the city centre from where we were. In return, he gestured behind us to the main road and said there was a bus stop close by.

I asked if he would stop for me before we got too far away, but to my innocent disbelief, he said we would need to work out payment for the journey first. He kept on driving out into an area that seemed quite industrial and finally stopped the car down a small side road next to an old factory. Undoing his seat belt, he turned to face me. The look in his eyes causing a tight knot to form in the pit of my stomach, I watched as he unhooked the belt on his trousers and pulled the leather strap through the clasp.

'What do you want?' I asked, not wanting to hear his answer.

After a moment's reflection, he replied, 'You can suck me off; that should cover your fare.'

Needless to say, the idea repulsed me, and I found myself replying (with surprising confidence for a fourteen-year-old scullery maid), 'If you think I'm putting your thing in my mouth, you must be off your rocker!'

'Sex then,' he slurred. 'Or I could teach you a lesson about what happens when you're rude to people who help you?'

'What do you mean?' I asked, while he started satisfying himself with his hand.

'Well, this is a deserted area—if I leave you in a heap in the gutter, it might be hours before anyone finds you.'

I looked around the empty streets and mocked myself inwardly for thinking any ticket out of Nottingham was going to be better than life at home. I considered jumping out the car, but I had no idea where I was, nor where to escape to, and I didn't believe I would be able to outrun him.

As he continued to pleasure himself, I looked out of the window rather than looking at him, and replied, 'How about we settle on a hand-job?'

I had never actually given anyone a hand-job before, but Pam had recently started doing this for her boyfriend and she'd talked me through the basic steps. Fifteen minutes later, I was dropped off at a bus stop, thinking I desperately needed to find somewhere to wash my hands.

I was horrified and felt sick to my stomach, but despite my journey starting in the most horrifying manner, I had no intention of going home.

After only a few minutes, the bus arrived, so I climbed aboard the double decker and headed upstairs. Taking a seat behind a girl who looked only a year or so older than me, I was pleasantly surprised when she turned around and said, 'I haven't seen you around here before. Are you new to the neighbourhood?''

I told her, 'No, I'm from Nottingham, but I just really need some space from my family, right now.'

With an empathic laugh, she replied, 'Oh god, tell me about it! My parents are doing my head in.'

She told me her name was Hayley, and as I took in her long, blonde, poker-straight hair, blunt fringe, and smoky eye make-up, I thought she looked the bee's knees.

Taking a silver cigarette case out of her bag, she asked, 'Would you like a ciggie?' And although I wasn't a big fan of tobacco, I saw her gesture as an olive branch being offered by the Universe and gladly accepted.

'I like your cigarette case,' I ventured.

She smiled out of the side of her mouth as she lit up. 'Thanks, it's my mum's. She's going to go crazy when she realises it's gone.'

My eyes narrow with intrigue, I asked, 'So, why would you take it?'

I remember being amazed by her confidence as she raised her eyebrows and told me, 'Because she can get fucked, as far as I'm concerned.'

Ten minutes later, we got off the bus in the city centre and, not knowing where to go, I paused. I'd just escaped rape and the entire world seemed crazy. I had no urge to cry. I was just numb. It's like my body could function, but my traumatised mind had completely checked-out.

When Hayley realised I had stopped, she turned around and walked back with an inquisitive smile on her face.

'Where are you going to go, now?' she asked, tucking her hair behind her ear.

I shrugged. I didn't know Derby at all, so I simply said, 'I really need to find a toilet.'

She laughed, at my bluntness I think, then linked arms with me and replied, 'Come on, I'll show you where the public loos are, then we'll buy some booze and hang out for a while. Does that sound like a plan?'

'Sure,' I replied. The beginnings of a smile starting to emerge from the corners of my mouth, I felt a sense of relief begin to creep over me. Hayley told me she didn't have much money, but she knew a cheap off-licence where she could get served, and off we trotted. I can't tell you how grateful I was to have some company.

We walked along the streets of Derby, our chatter flowing, and the comical things she said soon had me laughing. She took me to some toilets and then we went to a shop where Hayley bought a big bottle of cider and twenty cigarettes. She suggested we head to the riverbank to chill, so we strolled down the roads towards the river and did exactly that.

We sat on the steps that led down to the water, the leaves of the horse chestnut trees rustling pleasantly behind us, and the faint hum of city noise constant in the background. We drank our warm cider, watching the ducks bobbing along in the water, and giggled while the sun started to set. Allowing a pleasant interlude of escapism to wash over us, we acted our age for a short while, pushing the realities that hurt too much to the backs of our minds.

After we had been sitting for an hour or so, a group of five teenage boys came cycling along the river path and called out to each other to stop when they reached us. The lad at the front of the gang smiled as he jumped off his bike, leaving it on its side at the top of the steps, and didn't hesitate in making a beeline towards us.

'Evening, ladies,' he said as he sat down on the step up from us with a cheeky grin. He was an attractive young man, maybe seventeen or eighteen at a push, and he had brown, wavy hair that he ran his fingers through while he spoke. His manner was confident, probably a little overconfident in fact, but he seemed quite funny and charming.

His friends followed suit, one by one, leaving their bikes, then dotting themselves around us on the steps. And I must say, at that stage, the evening was turning out to be a welcome respite from my general anxiety— it was far easier to try to suppress my emotions inside than to acknowledge them.

The boys were all fairly good looking, and we happily let them share our cider. We chatted and joked with them as the light of the day faded, and after an hour or so had passed, the boys decided they were off, telling us they were heading to a house party nearby. When they asked if we would like to go with them, we agreed and each took a ride on the handlebars of a bike, indulging a very rare moment of fun.

We ended our journey at a small, dingy flat, on a high floor of an unattractive block, where a young man no older than twenty let us in. There was music playing loudly from a stereo, the atmosphere was smoky, and the lighting dim. After being given a vodka tonic without ice, we were invited to sit on the floor in the living room, so we made ourselves at home, and quickly adjusted to chilling, talking to the boys, smoking cigarettes and tapping the ash onto a plate in the centre of the room.

I remember being in the kitchen at one point later on, and a boy called Steven came in and started sweet-talking me while I sat on the worktop. I must confess after the horror I had experienced earlier that day, it was a nice distraction to receive some attention from a good-looking teenager who spoke kindly to me. I found it enjoyable to flirt with him and it wasn't long before we had started kissing, but then two of his friends walked in and I recall them laughing at having caught him copping off.

Steven suggested we go to the bedroom for some privacy and in my drunken state I agreed. We lay down together on a single bed; he didn't turn the lights on, so we kissed in the dark, and I allowed him to have sex with me while I tried to block any negative thoughts from entering my mind. The sex was OK, I suppose, it didn't hurt physically at least, but I was so emotionally numb, I just gave that boy what he was after—it seemed the obvious thing to do, I was so used to serving people.

We were under the covers when Hayley came in the room with a boy; they were kissing, their hands all over each other and they lay down on the single bed on the other side of the room. There was only one bedroom, so we each pretended the other wasn't there and she had sex with that boy too. I didn't question if what we were doing was right or wrong, it just happened.

After Steven had finished his business, he held me for a few moments and we lay together not speaking as my eyes began to close, my head resting on his chest. Then, out of the blue, there was a knock at the bedroom door and another boy poked his head into the room. He spoke into the darkness when he asked, 'Oi, is it my turn yet?'

To my astonishment, Steven replied, 'Yes mate,' and jumped out of bed. After he left the room, we never spoke again.

The new boy made his way towards me and, truly, I felt like screaming. I tried to talk to him as rationally as

I could, saying that I didn't feel well and I didn't want to do anything with anyone else. I sank into the corner, my back against the the wall, and although I spoke, my words were ignored. He climbed onto me, pressing his body against mine, and when he forcefully parted my knees, Hayley called out for him to get off me, but the boy she was with pinned her down and told her not to get involved.

I knew that Hayley and I didn't stand a chance against all the young men in that flat, and I felt sick knowing we couldn't stand up to them. We were defenceless. We had nowhere to go, no money to get anywhere, and it was the early hours of the morning.

That night, Hayley and I lay wasted in that bedroom as each and every one of the boys took their turn in using our bodies for their own sexual gratification. The situation was so intense that Hayley and I didn't even speak to each other. All I heard from her were the sobs of her suffering and the pleas she made for them to stop.

None of the boys stayed in the room with us after the various rounds of intercourse had finally come to an end. So I waited for the dawn to break and then got up, woke Hayley briskly, and said we needed to leave. When we walked out the room, we saw four of the young men were sleeping in the living room, so we crept past them, headed for the door, and managed to leave without them waking.

We flew down several flights of concrete stairs and ran out across the road. I remember exhaling deeply, thinking I just needed to breathe, to regain some composure and get some clarity on how to deal with my situation. We had very little money—in fact, we only just had enough to buy two cups of tea. So we decided to find a café, and stumbled across one quite quickly.

Walking across the threshold of that place was like finding refuge. It was wonderful to feel the level of security that being in a public place brought, and the staff welcomed us with a smile—for at least as much time as two cups of tea would buy.

The café was busy with labourers about to start their working day; sausage and bacon butties were flying out the door, while a half a dozen men sat around us flicking through tabloid newspapers. Hayley and I took a table by the window to drink our tea, and we quietly watched the world wake up, whilst I wondered what the hell I would do next. With no money and a string of attacks notched up since leaving home, my head was a mess. We discussed what had happened, and our hearts lay heavy in our chests. I was numb with shock from the inside out. As I struggled to process my emotions, Hayley sipped her tea with tears in her eyes.

When she whispered the words, 'I feel so dirty,' I knew exactly what she meant. It was like both my physical and spiritual being had been covered in the most horrific tar.

An hour or so later, after the staff had asked us twice if we would like a refill, Hayley said we should go before they asked us to leave. So, I went quickly to use their toilet while I still had the chance.

I washed my face in their sink, combed my hair and tried to pull myself together. Then, as I walked out, I saw to my astonishment that the police had arrived.

When I saw one of the officers place his hand on Hayley's arm, I knew we were going with them—I could only guess that one of the staff had phoned the police after overhearing our conversation. I remember wanting to feel relief that those officers had arrived. I so desperately wanted them to rescue me and to take me to a safe place. The only problem was they said they would need to call our parents, and I knew there'd be hell to pay when I saw my mum.

With hindsight, it's easy to see that I was placing myself in danger the second I got into a stranger's car. All I had wanted was to escape the abuse I knew, but instead of finding freedom, I found hell.

I thought I was tough enough to look after myself, but I wasn't. I was easy pickings, and within only a few hours, several men spotted that and were rapid in taking advantage of my vulnerability. I was naïve in my nature. My innocence had led me to take people at face value, never encouraging me to consider that they might have had ulterior, sinister motives.

No one had ever talked to me about sexual assault, but if they had, I would at least have had an understanding of the dangerous situations I could find myself in and how I could best avoid them. Awareness may have given me a little more common sense than my life experiences afforded me at the time.

Hayley and I felt so ashamed of everything that had happened to us that we didn't report those lads for raping us—even though the police who picked us up asked us for our story, I couldn't bring myself to tell them what had really happened. So, the boys got away with it, and I can only hope that they never repeated what they'd done to us with other girls.

Whilst my actions had been naïve, I do now realise that I wasn't guilty of anything. At the time, I thought that it was me who had done wrong and that I was in trouble with the police for running away—when really I was very much the victim.

When I consider the subject of sexual attack, I believe educating teenagers in the dangers that exist is paramount. To protect themselves from the darker side of humanity, teenagers have to know about it—as much as we may not want to scare them. As more and more sex crimes are exposed, we see that not only are random strangers a threat to children, but also realise the magnitude of organised child-abuse rings that exist. And whilst I know brilliant work is being done by investigative teams to bring the offenders to light, I also know there are countless victims who don't speak about their experiences, or whose voices aren't heard.

The problem of sexual violence is significant, and I believe that whilst teenagers are particularly vulnerable, there is real value in opening up and discussing this subject with them in order to help to protect them—it illustrates the dangers that exist out there and scenarios they may never imagine.

CHAPTER FOUR

t was my dad and Jimmy who came to pick me up from the police station, an awful experience in itself. I must have looked such a state. Having been too distressed to sleep in that flat, fatigue oozed out of me, and they looked at me as if I appalled them.

Strangely, neither of them said a word to me until we arrived home and, even then, I don't recall them saying much. I wondered if my mum had ordered them not to talk to me, and the idea of her waiting for me filled me with dread.

When we arrived home, we walked around the back of the house, my dad leading the way, with me trailing behind. My head firmly down, I wanted to close my eyes, vanish into thin air and escape my reality.

I walked through the door to see Mum immediately in front of me, and before I knew what was happening, she pushed me hard and I fell onto a stool in the corner of the room. My legs in the air, the stool wobbled, and I tumbled onto the floor. Towering over me, Mum snarled, 'You've been on your fucking back, haven't you? You little whore.' And she tore my knickers off from under my miniskirt.

My younger brothers were thankfully at school, so they didn't have to witness the scene. But with no regard for Jimmy being in the room, my mum sought to inspect my private parts while Dad went upstairs to fetch his 'pit-belt'. When he came back, he whipped me with it. Without saying a word, he lashed at me again and again. Trembling with fear, I said the only thing I could think to say, 'I'm so sorry.'

'Sorry? You're sorry?! I'll give you sorry!' Mum yelled.

It was at this moment that I chose for some reason to look up, and as I made eye contact with her, she slapped me sharply around the face.

'You bring shame on this family, and you think sorry will cut it?!'

She hit me again, whilst Jimmy stood silently by the back door, watching the episode unfold.

'The whole, bloody neighbourhood will know what you've been up to, Anastasia. And, by God, if rumours start flying around, you're going to wish you had never been born!'

With no words to offer, I lay there and took the beating, thinking that not existing sounded rather appealing in comparison to the life I was living.

I slept very little that night, despite my exhaustion. And as I lay in my bed, I tried to comprehend what possible importance my being could have. I felt so insignificant and trapped by my body. I longed to understand the reason I had been brought to life; there was simply no logic behind it that I could see.

I was nothing.

The next day I was in pieces, battered and bruised with welts all over me from my dad's belt. Longing to be somewhere else, I spent the day sitting in the front room—which we were never normally allowed to use.

But as I couldn't bear to be with my family, I took myself in there without asking, and no one came to fetch me out. I stared out of the window for hours watching the clouds, trying to find a comfortable way to rest and contemplating how disastrously wrong my attempt at running away had gone.

In the afternoon, Jimmy came in to see me, and much to my surprise, he apologised to me for not being able to protect me. He told me, 'We all think about running away, you know. The only difference with you is that you're crazy enough to actually do it.'

When he put his arm around my shoulder to try to comfort me with a hug, I winced in pain, so he quickly pulled back and gave me a sympathetic smile. He didn't stay with me long, but I did appreciate knowing that he wished he could have done something to stop the attack I had suffered.

I realise now that this harrowing start was due to nothing more than my mother's own fear. Her wrath was caused by her inability to successfully manage her life. She believed that she was losing control of her family, and this frightened her, which in turn enraged her, for she had no idea what to do to make things right. Instead of taking any responsibility for my actions, she considered that only a bad child would run away and she pushed me away with guilt trips and silence—when what I really needed was for her to draw me closer. She had no idea how to be a mother.

I understand how easy it would be for you to view my mum as the villain in my life story, but I feel it's important to tell you here, that as an adult, I don't view my mother as a monster. I feel she was a woman who had severe mental health issues, and sadly at the time there was no one around who was able to help her in the way she needed.

About six weeks following my attempt to run away, I discovered I was pregnant, and my world flipped upside down. I was totally overwhelmed and I knew I desperately needed help.

Contemplating my options of who to talk to and how to inevitably break the news to my parents, I decided to confide in Jimmy's girlfriend, Yvette, who he had been dating for several months (and who went on to become his future wife). Now, Yvette was always very sweet with me. She was several years older than me, at eighteen, and she had a daughter of her own who was one and a half years old. I considered that out of the few people in my life, she would most likely have some natural empathy for my situation, and knowing the dynamics of my family fairly well, hopefully she would be able to offer some good advice.

When Yvette next came to our house, I managed to get a few minutes alone with her in the evening and told her I was pregnant. She was so compassionate, it was a big relief to confide in her; she assured me not to worry and suggested that she'd go and tell Jimmy for me.

When she shared my news, I know she impressed upon him to be cool about it, and a little while later Jimmy and Yvette came up to my bedroom where I was lying low. My dad was downstairs, Mum was at bingo, and our two younger brothers were already asleep, so we had a little privacy while Jimmy sat on the edge of my bed and Yvette sat cross-legged on the floor.

I shall always be grateful for how Jimmy supported me that night, and how he took control, saying he would tell Dad, and then he would go and meet Mum from bingo to talk to her for me too. He reasoned that if he could speak to Mum during her walk home, it would give her time to cool down a bit before she saw me, and I thought that sounded like the best option I had.

So, I stayed in my room while they went downstairs to talk to Dad, and after a few minutes, Jimmy called for me to come down. Dad was sitting in his armchair and didn't say a word to me when I walked in. Instead, he just looked at the fireplace with silent tears occasionally escaping his eyes and running down his distressed face; in turn, they also fell down mine. I felt terrible, honestly like I was the final straw to have broken my dad. Not long later, Jimmy and Yvette left us—Jimmy saying he would walk Yvette home before he'd go to find Mum.

Surprisingly, I didn't get beaten that night. 'You'll have to get rid of it,' were the first words my mum said when she walked in through the kitchen door. Then, as I stood watching her take her coat off she added, 'Anastasia, unless you want the biggest hiding you've ever had in your life, I suggest you get out of my sight, because everything about you disgusts me right now. Go up to your room and don't let me see you again until morning. I bloody well mean it, Ana! Don't you test me!'

By the time she finished her outburst, I was already half way up the stairs. There was nothing I could say to remedy the situation, and I knew I was lucky she had only threatened me.

Abortion had recently become legal in England, and I knew of a couple of older girls who had had to have one. But coming from a Catholic background, I knew it was considered a mortal sin, and truly, I was broken-hearted. I knew that I couldn't be a mother to the embryo inside me, but I *really* didn't want to have an abortion.

I remember the next morning when the household had come to life after a troubled night's sleep, I walked into the dining room where Mum was setting the table for breakfast and she completely refused to acknowledge me. I said 'Good morning.' But she ignored me. So I made a little fuss of my brothers, and then followed my mum into the kitchen to help her start the day.

There was toast under the grill, and Mum stood watching it like a hawk with her back to me, while I filled the kettle and made a pot of tea. I knew better than to try and start a conversation with her, so I let the silence be.

The first words she said to me, not even looking up from the plates as she buttered the toast were, 'You know I'll throw you out if you don't get rid of it, don't you?'

I quietly replied, 'Yes, Mum.'

And so, it began; my first mortal sin and, according to our religion, a ticket to hell prescribed by my parent. Abortion was something I can't believe I had to do, but I know it was necessary at the time—it was a struggle to look after myself as it was, let alone look after a baby with no support from my parents.

You might think I should have had the child and given it up for adoption, but my mum would never have let me walk around with a bump—all the neighbours knowing that 'I had been on my back'. She would never have tolerated such shame.

Combine all this with the fact that my baby had been made through rape, and, well, I personally think it's clear pregnancy doesn't come with a 'one size fits all' answer. And in my mind, there is no way that episode in my life warrants eternal damnation—just living through it was torture enough.

Unfortunately, my abortion went terribly wrong. The doctors had to fight to save my life on the operating table, cutting me wide open and putting me back together with staples and stitches—the procedure scarring me for life, in more ways than one.

When Jimmy came to visit me in hospital, he told me that my younger brothers had asked him why Mum was behaving bizarrely at home. Apparently, she had been out in the backyard pegging washing on the line and shouting things like, 'Ana, put the kettle on and we'll have a cup of tea.'

Yet while Finn and Paddy may have found her behaviour strange, Jimmy and I both knew it was out of shame that she shouted those things. She wanted the neighbours to think I was at home, so they wouldn't suspect anything was wrong.

When I finally returned home, I had changed inside and felt more like a woman than a girl. I was burdened with far more emotional baggage than any fourteen-year-old should ever have to carry. And sadly, I never went to school again.

At that time in life, I carried so much guilt, it was crushing. I took complete responsibility for my actions and circumstance, as if everything was my fault. I felt judged by my mum, and when she called me a disgrace and told me that I brought shame on our family, I allowed those labels to stick to my heart. The emptiness I felt inside paradoxically consumed me.

When I reflect on this now, I find my teenage mindset so saddening and wish that I could go back in time and visit that version of me. If I could, I would give that girl the huge hug that she so desperately needed. I would tell her that I love her and how worthy of love she truly was. I would assure her that no matter what terrible things whirled around in her head, she was forgiven—and that being raped wasn't her fault. She didn't 'deserve' it and it wasn't her punishment for being a 'bad child'. I would tell her that she's very beautiful on the inside, and that her situation doesn't define her... and it never would.

Although I can't go back in time, I can now call that girl into my mental space when I close my eyes. And through deep relaxation, I can give her that hug that's inside me and pour my love on to her. I've heard people talk in recent years about healing your Inner Child, and this concept, I think, is crucial to our well-being. Where there is a traumatised version of us that exists in the past, we mustn't hide from it, or allow it to follow us as a lonely shadow that we can't escape. Rather we should shower it with love and embrace it.

When we accept and love ourselves completely, we forgive ourselves. Relinquishing any guilt we've held on to, we show ourselves empathy as if we were comforting another person who had experienced trauma, and through regrouping any fragments of our psyche which previously pulled us to dark places, we make ourselves consciously whole. When we let love flow through the very essence of our being and all the versions of us that ever existed in the past or will exist in the future, the emptiness disappears. Through authenticity, we set ourselves free.

Whilst I couldn't escape my turmoil as a teenager, as an adult I have the power to pick up my inner child, nourish her, and carry her away from all the pain that she endured. And as I live in the present, she's inside me, knowing love and being offered a fresh start with every day that dawns.

CHAPTER FIVE

After the abortion, my doctor referred me to a charitable organisation offering mental health support, and I was soon assigned a female counsellor called Linda, who had frizzy, brown hair and wore the biggest spectacles I'd ever seen. Now, Linda was very kind to me; she seemed to have a belief in me that I didn't possess in myself at the time, and she truly seemed to care about turning my life around. Every time I met with her, she was full of positive ideas and comforting advice, and it felt like she was the only beacon of light that I had during those dark days.

However, not long after I started going to counselling, Linda arranged for me to see a psychologist and a set of weekly appointments was made for me with a man called Peter—an arrangement that unfortunately went on for over a month. Rather than stay in his office for my appointments, Peter used to take me for rides in his car, and with my history of misfortune, maybe you can guess what's coming next. When he ran his hand up my thigh during those rides, I just sat there and took it, wondering how the hell he thought that would help my mental health.

I never told Linda, but it confounded me how someone who was employed to help me could then abuse me, and I lost a lot of faith in their organisation and their ability to help me.

You should bear in mind during all this, that the legal age for leaving school back then was fifteen, but the school I went to insisted students must stay until sixteen—so I had stopped going nearly two years early. After a while, I received a fine from the school for my truancy, addressed directly to me, despite still being a minor. It stated that I had broken our contract, but with no money, I ignored their demand and Mum just told anyone who telephoned to fuck off. My parents never went up to the school or took me to visit the headmistress or anything like that; I was simply written off as a lost cause.

It was around this time that my dad was involved in a bad accident at work, and after several weeks in hospital, he was discharged and signed off on long-term sick—not knowing whether he would ever be able to work again. Sadly, my dad quickly became dependent on medication, alcohol, and sleeping tablets to get through each set of twenty-four hours that arrived. At times, he seemed vacant, like he was totally zoned out. And it was heartbreaking as my dad turned into another body in the house that relied upon me.

When I was fifteen, Linda asked me what I would like to do for work going forward, and after reflecting for a few seconds, I told her, 'I might like to be a beautician.'

It wasn't a career that I had ever really dreamed of, but to be fair, there was no career that I had high aspirations to attain. I had very little clue over what I could actually do with my life. Having left school with no qualifications and through knowing such low energy at the time, I couldn't imagine that anyone was going to want me to work for them. I had felt as if I had no choice other than to just keep doing whatever my mum told me to, every day, and there was nothing I could do to escape it. However, when faced with Linda's question, it was enjoyable to briefly contemplate what I might like to do with my time if I had the opportunity. I considered that doing women's make up and helping them feel nice could be a pleasant way to spend my days.

A few days later, Linda told me with excitement that she had got me an interview with a big health and beauty retailer, and she said it could be a fantastic opportunity. She had put me forward for a position as a shop assistant and ventured that I might even be able to work on their make-up counter if things went well.

I agreed to go, but for some reason when the day of the interview came, I decided I couldn't—I didn't have the bus fare to get there. I suppose I could have tried harder to find a few coins, but I think deep down I didn't believe I was worthy of that position, so I allowed money to be my excuse.

After I missed that interview, I cut all contact with the charity. I was so mixed up, I felt awful that Linda had put her trust in me and I had let her down. The idea of seeing her was too much for me to deal with. I couldn't bear to see any disappointment in her eyes. Although, looking back, I realise there's no way Linda would have berated me for not attending. She would have continued to help me if only I had let her, but I was far too afraid to do that at the time. I was ashamed of who I was. A little like my dad, I had checked-out of life mentally, wishing I could just disappear. Even when help was being offered to me, my state of despair was so acute that it forced me to push it away.

After several months of being on long-term sick leave, my dad tried to commit suicide. I guess he felt his life was simply too hard to continue, and the shock I experienced in finding him in his room one evening, slumped over the bed with an empty pill bottle at his side, was so intense it's hard to put that feeling into words. I couldn't let him die. He had to be OK.

Having learned from when Mrs Baisley saved Louisa, I ran to make salt water and then, singlehandedly, I brought my dad back to life. When his eyes regained focus and his breathing steadied, I collapsed onto his knee and buried myself in his embrace.

Traumatised tears of relief poured out of me, and I sobbed angrily, 'Don't you dare do that again, ever, Dad! Not ever! I need you! I love you!'

When I looked into his eyes, I saw he was crying too, and he smiled weakly as he told me sincerely, 'I love you too, my darling.'

The episode didn't attract much attention from the rest of the family nor the doctors; everyone understood why he thought death might be preferable to living, and Dad was put on pills to improve his mood—which I suppose were significantly cheaper than giving him the mental health care he really needed. It seemed like all the doctors could do was prescribe drugs to numb his emotions rather than help us to address the underlying issues.

It was also while I was fifteen that my mum declared, out of the blue, one Saturday afternoon that it was time I earned my keep. I remember her walking in the back door, pulling her nylon shopping trolley behind her, and announcing that she had run into the local textile mill manager in the greengrocers and she had got me a job.

She said, 'Mr Wilkinson's a very decent man, Ana, and you don't know how lucky you are that he's agreed to take a chance on you. You're to start at 8 o'clock on Monday morning and, believe me, you'd better not fuck this up!'

So, I started working at the mill full-time dyeing fabrics, but I can't say I found it an enjoyable experience. It seemed like everyone working there was suffering some kind of low level depression, having resigned themselves to the idea that the world had nothing better to offer them. However, deep down, I knew I didn't want to stay there long-term.

My parents always took the lion's share of my weekly pay packets, allowing me to keep just one note and the coins—but once I started to experience the feeling of having my own money (as little as it was), I felt a glimmer of inspiration begin to light up inside me. I realised that factory job was to be my exit strategy and route to freedom.

I considered that if I saved up for long enough, there would come a point when I would be able to buy a ticket out of Nottingham and go somewhere new... I just had to withstand life until that time arrived and figure out where on earth I would go when it did.

After working at the mill for several months, Jimmy and Yvette came home late one Friday night after my parents had gone to bed. I was still up reading by the fire, and they sat down with me in the dining room. We chatted, listening to the radio, and as we spoke, Jimmy did something I had never seen him do before: taking a small pinch of cannabis out of his pocket, he started rolling a spliff.

I watched curiously as he sealed everything into place. Then, he astounded me when (with a distinct twinkle in his eye) he asked, 'So, little sis', do you fancy a smoke?'

It was the first time I had ever tried marijuana, and we smoked his joint next to the open fireplace—Jimmy telling me to breathe out into the fire, so the smoke would go up the chimney and not into the house. And I have to say I liked it.

Smoking it like a cigarette, I inhaled too deeply at first and endured a coughing fit that I feared would wake our parents. But then I adjusted to the sweet, mild smoke as it entered my body, and I started to feel quite mellow.

Within half an hour, I was experiencing the world from a new, relaxed perspective. All my worries had become a little less intense; it was a rather comforting feeling. It was like my mind was able suddenly to take a step back from the pain that whirled inside me and view my problems as if they weren't really my own.

I was able to detach myself from my memories and allow myself to open up from the defensive position I usually adopted. It gave me space to be, like nothing I'd ever known before.

A little while later, I was in stitches of laughter, I mean I was *really* giggling with big, mascara-ridden tears streaming down my face; I was totally unable to contain myself at the hilarity of our conversation. Then, gradually, in my hazy state, I drifted out of the conversation as we chilled on the dining room floor and I contemplated my life deeply. I decided I believed firmly in the notion that change will always come, and I resolved that I just had to be patient in waiting for my chance to find freedom to arrive. Then, as I continued in my self-reflection, I turned my head, and that's when I saw Jesus.

I had to do a double-take, but when I focused I saw that it was indeed Jesus, and he was standing in our kitchen. He didn't speak to me with words, but the emotion that I felt upon looking at his face was incredible, and his bright, beautiful being felt very familiar. While I stared in shock, I whispered the words, 'Jesus is in the kitchen,' which caused Jimmy and Yvette to look across at me and crack up in laughter.

The apparition still intact, I didn't shift my gaze, but insisted in a quiet, astonished tone that he really was there. So Jimmy got up to investigate what I could be interpreting as Jesus, but they saw nothing and quickly resumed their conversation.

I have no problem telling you that I smoked pot quite regularly during my early adult life, but never again did I experience anything like that first time—and I never hallucinated through smoking cannabis again.

When I saw that apparition of Jesus it didn't freak me out. It was just a wonderfully comforting encounter, which came at the exact time I needed it. And looking back on this memory, I feel very blessed to have experienced this.

As the months rolled past, I saved every penny I could. Having severed my links with the charity, I made regular trips to the doctor to seek help and was rewarded with medication to relax me and improve my mood. I liked those pills, whatever they were, and they certainly helped me to sleep. I felt throughout this time that I was focused on the big picture, and I believed that once I had a bit of money behind me, I would be able to escape and find a way to make a proper go of my life—I just needed some help treading water.

Those months while I saved up are just a blur in my memory really. I kept visiting the doctor and inventing reasons for him to keep writing prescriptions, and I was getting high with Jimmy and Yvette regularly—but I knew deep down that drugs weren't something that I wanted to get into really. My sights were set on leaving town and I would get high just often enough to make the wait a little more bearable.

There then came one night when Jimmy, Yvette, and I were sitting out in the back yard, and Yvette told us how (before she had fallen pregnant) she had hitchhiked her way to the coast and worked for a few months in a holiday camp. She had shared a small chalet with three girls, partying every night after work—and I must say, when I heard Yvette's story, a surge of excitement ran through me, and I felt that living and working somewhere like that—where you could enjoy yourself with new friends—was exactly what I needed.

Suddenly lit up with inspiration, a new ambition settled itself in my being: I decided I would move to the seaside. I imagined myself spending my evenings chilling on a beach, watching the sea, and having fun with other teenagers who had also had enough of family life. And these were images I enjoyed conjuring up. Whilst my body was trapped by circumstance, my mind always yearned to be free.

When the day came that I received what was to be my last pay packet from the factory, it was late spring. As usual my dad was waiting for my board at the dining table, so I paid my dues and then went straight up to my room. I had been hiding my savings in the base of my bedside drawers, taking the bottom drawer out and using the few inches of space underneath to house a small tin, which I took out for the final time that evening. Adding my new money to it, I counted up and decided I finally had enough to leave.

I spent most of that evening up in my room, and I wrote out a note to my family, which, after much deliberation, finally read:

> *I've gone to the coast in search of a new job.*
> *Please apologise to the factory for me.*
> *I love you all.*
> *Ana X*

I had considered writing a lengthier message, but figuring my parents wouldn't care much for deep and meaningful content, I kept it brief. Then I packed the few belongings I had into my old school bag—which you can imagine didn't take long.

The next morning, I got up at 6:00a.m., which was much earlier than my family ever rose. After tiptoeing around to get myself ready, I made a jam sandwich to take with me and left my note propped against the kettle.

After creeping out the house as quietly as I could, I walked quickly down our street. My heart was pounding and my ears were on high alert for any noise coming from our house, but none came. When I turned the corner of our road, I found myself breaking into a run, wanting to get away as fast as I could.

I was finally free.

CHAPTER SIX

After catching a bus to the city centre, I walked purposefully to the train station and bought myself a ticket on the first train heading to Skegness—the closest coastal town to Nottingham and only a little over two hours away.

I did have a fairly long wait on the platform before my train pulled up, but when it did, it was like my white stallion had arrived to carry me away. My adrenaline racing, I climbed aboard, found a vacant seat, and sat with my bag on my knee as I gazed out the window. Seconds later, the train set in motion, and I watched curiously as Nottingham gradually disappeared behind us.

I was so excited, that journey flew by. I had taken a book to read, but I was so spellbound by the experience of travelling, I don't think I read more than a couple of pages. I must confess though, I really did enjoy the experience of treating myself to a cup of tea from the buffet carriage. Despite the tea being weak and overpriced, I felt very grown up and independent in my travel! The train felt like a much better and safer option than hitch-hiking.

When we arrived at Skegness, I skipped off the train and walked in the only direction that called me: towards the sea. The heat from the morning sun was strong and the salty aroma of the North Sea clung to the air. Seagulls cawing overhead, I fell in love with the atmosphere immediately.

Within minutes, I saw the sea appear ahead of me for the first time in my life and I was awestruck. Shimmering with the sunbeams which danced upon it's waves, I found it utterly entrancing.

I decided the first thing I wanted to do was to take a walk down the pier. And, minutes later, the wooden boards were bending under my feet, while the breeze blew strands of hair into my mouth. I felt absolutely high as a kite!

Tucking my unruly locks behind my ears, I looked out to the sea in front of me, contemplating its vast complexity and wondering at all the life that existed out there under the waves. Breathing in the fresh sea air, I longed for this to be just the shake-up in life I needed. On that day, everything was possible. My future was no longer just an idea in my head. It was real. It was beneath my feet, above my head and all around me.

I turned and looked back at Skegness and all the people who were busying themselves in the town, and thought it all seemed quite incredible. I saw the Pleasure Beach with its helter-skelter and big wheel, children riding donkeys, families making sand castles together; the parents with smiles on their faces. Everyone looked happy.

I think seeing the sea was the first moment of my life that naturally gave me a taste of inner peace. I must have stood on that pier for over an hour, and during that spell no one came up to me; no one desired my time. There was only the sea to interact with, and it gave me its energy in abundance.

I had escaped the draining undercurrents of living with my mum and was able to glimpse how amazing freedom felt.

I stood at the very end of the pier looking out and saw a few thin clouds stretching out towards the horizon—it was like they had been painted in the sky. I closed my eyes, inhaled deeply, and raised my arms up. Stretching my whole body, I opened myself up to the Universe and my new beginning. I consciously breathed in the sea; the fresh air seeming to cleanse my every pore. I was so ready for change.

I had wanted to get as far away from Nottingham as I could, and that pier felt like the furthest I could have possibly gone.

I leaned over the railings to watch the waves roll around the stilts that propped up the pier, and then I watched them lap onto the shore, wetting the sand and leaving strands of seaweed behind until the next wave arrived to pick them up. And suddenly I knew I had to get down there. I needed to feel the sand in between my toes and the water rushing against my legs.

With this urge sweeping over me, I skipped joyfully back down the pier and out on to the beach. I took my sandals off and, as my feet sunk into the warm sand, I was immediately in heaven.

Not having a swimming suit, I knew I couldn't go very far into the sea. But with a huge smile on my face, I ran out over the firmer sand and let the experience of feeling the cool waves ripple over my feet consume me. The sea wasn't very deep immediately, so with my bag on my back, I held my skirt around my thighs and waded in up to my knees.

Walking forward, the sea was so cold! But it was so exhilarating and refreshing, I couldn't help but laugh with the waves as they playfully lapped up against me.

I stayed on the beach all day. Watching the waves, the birds, and the people come and go. I didn't get hungry and I felt no desire to be anywhere else.

When the sun lost its strength, giving way to the evening, the beach began to empty as the tourists gradually left to wash and change for dinner. But I still sat, marvelling at the sky as it took on pink and orange hues and how that altered the colour of the sea at the horizon. Only when a chill arrived in the breeze, did I decide the time had come to venture into town and deal with the reality that I had nowhere to stay.

After batting the sand off my feet and calves, I headed along the main road running parallel to the sea, wandering past the various buildings and businesses. I gazed upon the closing souvenir shops with their displays of postcards and buckets and spades. Looking for job adverts pinned up in windows, I saw positions available in a chip-shop, a newsagent's, and a café, but not feeling drawn in, I kept walking.

The first place that really appealed to me was a rather large hotel; it was a long way from being five-star, but to me, it seemed incredibly elegant and refined. Three storeys high, the building was rendered white, it had large bay windows, and an assortment of flags flew proudly from the rooftop. A raised patio area sat adjacent to the hotel lobby, and several guests sat enjoying the early evening, sipping cocktails decorated with tiny umbrellas and wedges of fruit—I thought it looked like the height of sophistication!

Seeing a notice in their window advertising a waitressing vacancy with a live-in option, my inspiration surged, and I stared at that hotel, wondering what life might be like inside. Deciding there was no time like the present to act, I walked up the steps and into the lobby with all the confidence I could muster to apply for the job.

Finding the lobby area busy, I awaited the receptionist's attention at the side of her desk, looking around at the classy decor and fancy paintings on the wall. Once the hotel residents had all been served, the receptionist (a girl only a few years older than me) smiled in my direction, and I suddenly realised how beautiful she was—stunning, in fact. She had huge, brown eyes, long, dark-brown hair, and a smile that could have seen her on a toothpaste commercial.

'Can I help you?' she asked.

Reading her badge which pinned the name 'Deborah' to her blouse, I smiled, stepped up to the desk and asked (with a tone which I hoped was both polite and friendly) if their waitressing vacancy was still open.

The way she looked at me altered slightly as she took in my appearance, clearly trying to assess if I might fit in. Then, offering me a smile, she replied, 'I'm pretty sure it is. If you give me a minute, I'll check for you.'

I thanked her and watched as she dialled a single digit on her telephone. My heart pounding with nervous anticipation, I listened to her briefly explaining my arrival. But after only a few seconds, she looked up at me, gave me the thumbs up, and promptly ended the call.

With a smile on her face she told me, 'You're in luck! Gavin, our restaurant manager, will be down to see you shortly. Would you like to take a seat while you wait?'

She gestured towards a row of red velvet armchairs that stood to the side of the lobby, so I agreed and thanked her profusely. Then, just as I started to turn away, she added, 'Good luck!' which struck me as incredibly kind —and not something I was used to at all.

I waited for ten minutes, silently admiring the grandest building I had ever set foot in, and then a man dressed in a white shirt, black tie, and smart trousers appeared on the staircase. He came straight over, introduced himself as Gavin, and offered me his hand to shake—which I have to say, I did find a little on the limp side.

I guess he was about twenty-six or twenty-seven, and his short, wavy hair was styled into place, looking almost wet with the amount of hair cream he had used. He had a slim build; his eyes were dark and heavy-lidded; his nose a little on the large size, and his skin was marked with scars from the acne he had clearly suffered as a youth. Thinking he was neither attractive nor ugly, I introduced myself and tried to judge his book by its cover, as he did the same to me.

Gavin offered me a quick tour of the hotel and promptly led the way to the busy bar with its wood-cladded walls and countless spirits stacked behind the smartly dressed bartender. Every table was filled with guests smoking and drinking, and no one paid us the slightest bit of attention as we stood at the side of the room. We continued through to the lounge, and then completed the tour by arriving in the restaurant, which proved to be a room Gavin was very proud of.

The dining room was much larger than I had imagined it would be, and the small team of waiting staff looked very professional as they prepared for the evening service. Gavin suggested we take a seat in the corner of the room and led the way once again as we weaved between the tables covered with starched, white cloths. Journeying across the room, it struck me how attentive the staff were to their tasks, polishing the wine glasses and setting every table with precision. I couldn't help but think of how impressed my mum would have been—she would have been in heaven dining there!

Gavin beamed with pride as he told me that they had an excellent reputation for both high-quality food and service. Then, when he asked me to tell him about myself, I almost didn't know where to start. But I think I held myself well as I explained I had left home in search of a new life by the sea.

I told him, 'I think I would suit the role as my mum has very strict standards at home.' And I described how I had always helped in the kitchen every day and served our family meals.

To my surprise, he seemed to find it amusing that I would compare my family life with that of working in a restaurant, so I politely tolerated his condescending expression, but knew there was no way he could work me as hard as my mum had. Letting his chuckle pass me by, I reassured him that I believed I woud be very competent in the role.

I knew, without a doubt, I would be able to take on anything the restaurant could throw at me, just as long as they kept a roof over my head and gave me a reason to stay by the sea.

It appeared my face fitted, and after fifteen minutes together, he smiled and suggested we do a trial week to see how we got on. I obviously accepted with delight. So, after we had shaken hands on the offer of employment, Gavin walked me back to reception, asked Deborah to organise a room and a uniform for me, and twenty minutes later I was down in the restaurant starting my first shift.

I found working in that hotel very easy, and I don't think I'm boasting when I tell you that I was naturally good at waitressing—it was something I had been training for my whole life. Looking after people, taking their orders, bringing them food, laying the tables, polishing the cutlery, and clearing away the plates, seemed like a piece of cake in comparison to what my home life had been—it felt like a blessing that the hotel didn't want me to scrub the floor at the end of my shift! It was also a plus point that the customers were generally very nice to me and grateful for my service; the majority even tipped me, so that seemed like a real step up in life!

The bedroom I had been given was small and simple, but it was plenty big enough for me. I felt like my heart now had space to beat and my mind was free to contemplate the life I had and, moreover, what I should do with it. I didn't have a sea view from my room (those were reserved for paying guests), but when I woke in the morning, I could be out the hotel and on the beach within seconds.

I would work the lunch and evening shifts; I was given every Tuesday off, and I spent very little time in my bedroom other than to sleep. I gravitated towards

Deborah in my free time, and she soon told me I should call her Debs. She always wore bright yellow nail varnish, and I liked that very much. She fascinated me, seeming to find me and my ways rather amusing, and we laughed together a lot.

At the end of an evening, when the night porter took over reception, Debs and I would head out to the beach and drink whatever we could afford to buy, giggling and staring up at the night sky, wondering what life was all about. Some nights I went to bed with bites on my legs from the sand-flies, but every night I went to sleep with alcohol in my bloodstream.

I would wake up in the mornings with a hazy, aching head and make a cup of tea from the Teasmade on my bedside table. I'd take a bath in the shared bathroom across the hall, wanting to fall asleep in the warm water rather than make a move to start the day—thank God they never asked me to work the breakfast shift!

The other waiting staff were pretty dull, a couple of them were a bit sour in the face, and there were certainly no strong characters to bounce off other than Debs. Anyway, after a few weeks, Gavin seemed to have developed a crush on me, and I noticed the way he looked at me started to change. I would be taking a table's order and he'd be speaking to customers across the room, but he'd look over their shoulders at me and watch me as I worked.

Now, let's be clear, I know your boss is meant to watch you to make sure you're doing things right, but the way he looked at me was different. There was a smouldering desire behind his stare that began to make me feel slightly uncomfortable.

Debs noticed it too; in fact, I think all the staff noticed the way he stared at me. In team meetings, we'd stand around in a circle and somehow Gavin would make me feel like I was the only one he was talking to. Sure, he was friendly enough with everyone else, but the way he smiled at me wasn't platonic, and I'd feel incredibly self-conscious when he'd cast his eye down over my body while he spoke.

The situation came to a head one night after we had closed the restaurant and were cleaning up, preparing for the next day. As usual, Gavin had taken the money up to the office to be counted and deposited in the safe, leaving two other waiting staff and me to clean the restaurant. I had emptied the ashtrays, taken the tablecloths to the laundry room and was in the process of restocking the wine fridge, when Gavin reappeared to help us finish up. He asked how we were getting on, and my colleagues said they were almost done, whilst I just needed to make one more trip down to the cellar.

As I walked downstairs, I heard Gavin tell the others they could go, so I quickened my step a little, not relishing the idea of being alone with Gavin at the end of the night. The cellar light was still on, and I headed into the concrete room which smelled heavily of damp. I walked promptly to collect a case of wine—we needed Chardonnay, I remember that as I've been unable to drink Chardonnay without recalling this night ever since—and as I picked up the crate, I heard Gavin's footsteps start to descend.

'Ana? Are you still down here?' he called.

I replied, 'Yes,' thinking it was a stupid question as he knew damn well I was. And then I almost walked straight into him as he arrived at the bottom of the stairs. I've always been short, and with Gavin standing about six feet tall and a step higher than me, I looked up at his face as we stood no more than a foot apart with just the crate of wine between us.

He stepped down into the room, so I took a step back— which was the complete opposite to the direction I wanted to go—and I had absolutely no idea what I should do. Smiling gently, he took the crate from my hands, placed it on the stair behind him, and sighed, 'Oh Ana…'

I swear, at that moment my mind went blank and words completely esacped me. There was no question as to what he was after; it had just been a matter of time before this situation would play out—and I had known that from the first time his eyes focused on my bust rather than my face when we spoke.

Without force, Gavin blocked my exit, and when I looked into his eyes, I saw his passion rising to boiling point. I didn't fancy him at all; there was nothing about his blemished face, his strong jawline or his unruly eyebrows which made me want to consummate our working relationship. There was nothing I wanted to offer him on any level.

I watched his eyes look at my mouth then rove down my body to my legs and back up again, where he met my stare. I could see his chest rise and fall with his apparent excitement, and I recall he whispered something about how long he had wanted me.

'I know,' were the first words that finally fell out my mouth. And with that he lunged in for the kiss; his large hands holding my face.

While I was rather numb and didn't return his kiss in the slightest, I must say I did feel affection behind his lust. I wouldn't want you to think of Gavin as a brute raping a young girl, for that wasn't the situation at all. He had feelings for me, mostly sexual, I believe. But I know he liked me as a person too and the emotions that he felt were intense.

I let him kiss me, and I gave him what he wanted as he tried to seduce me in that damp cellar, with the case of wine sat next to us on the stairs—I didn't possess the ability to say no. I accepted it and went through the motions as he undid his trousers and picked me up so my back was against the wall and my legs were hoisted around him.

He groaned as he pushed his way inside me, while I wished the wall wasn't so cold. I immediately wondered how long he would last—surely he wouldn't take more than a couple of minutes?

My suspicions were right and the climax of his built-up desire took around sixty seconds to come to a head. As he came, he buried his head into my neck and called my name, once, twice, and then a third and final time, as if Ana was spelt with a dozen A's at the end.

When his wave of euphoria finally began to diminish, Gavin eased himself out of me and I pulled up my knickers, straightening myself out as quickly as I could. I'd given him what he wanted and now I wanted to go.

It was as he tucked his penis back into his white, Y-front underpants that I noticed there was blood seeping through his underwear and forming a bright red wet patch that was rapidly increasing in size. I knew it hadn't come from me, and I couldn't help but stare momentarily (out of concern) as he zipped up his high-waisted trousers.

'Gavin, you're bleeding,' I quietly stated.

He didn't reply, and I remember watching him, slightly bemused, as he looked down to the floor and fastened his belt into place. With no desire to stick around, I picked up the wine and turned to go upstairs. But then he called out for me to wait, looking at me with eyes like a lost puppy, and he asked me not to rush off. He said that it just happened to him sometimes, and he wasn't sure why, but it wasn't anything I should worry about. With little sexual experience, I didn't fret too much over that aspect of the encounter at the time, but as my life carried on and I had more sexual partners, it was something that I never came across again.

I should mention that a few weeks later, I did decide to get checked out at the doctor's, just in case I had caught anything, and thankfully everything came back clear—so life never did give me an explanation as to what was actually wrong. But on the rare occasions I'm offered a glass of Chardonnay, I do think about Gavin and wonder if he was alright.

CHAPTER SEVEN

The morning after the cellar incident with Gavin, I awoke to the sound of someone knocking on my bedroom door. Reluctant to wake from my slumber and with no desire to speak with anyone at that time of day, I initially ignored my visitor. But seconds later, my skin crawled as I heard Gavin's voice whisper, 'Ana?'

He knocked again.

Pulling my sheet up over my head, I closed my eyes, wishing for him to just take the hint and go away. I didn't say a word, and thankfully he didn't knock again, but when I climbed out of bed ten minutes later, I saw he had pushed a note under the door, which lay folded in half upon the carpet. I groaned and walked over to pick it up, thinking I would rather not read anything he had written. But there was no way I could avoid him long-term, so I breathed in deeply and read:

Ana, last night was amazing. I can't stop thinking about you. Meet me in the laundry room in ten minutes. xxx

My stomach churned at the mental image of an early morning sexual liaison with Gavin, and I ripped the note in half, then into quarters, and dropped it into the rubbish basket in the corner of my room.

'Ugh,' is the only way I can describe my feelings towards Gavin that morning. He hadn't used a condom, but I didn't think there was any way I could be pregnant after the mess the hospital had made of my reproductive organs, and I was right not to have worried on that note.

I worked my shifts that day speaking to Gavin only when my work required me to, and I avoided eye contact as much as I possibly could. When my eyes were forced to meet his, I saw a man filled with docile affection and raging hormones; it was like he was chomping at the bit, just waiting for the opportunity to be alone with me again. It was a very odd situation to be in. He was, after all, my boss—so, let's just say, after getting my bum squeezed several times during the busy evening service, I wanted out.

The next day, I woke up to the sound of a knocking on my bedroom door once again, and in my grumpy, early morning state, I simply said, 'No, Gavin!' loud enough for him to hear, but hopefully not so loud that my voice would travel down the landing.

Thankfully, the only response I heard was Debs' familiar laugh and she called out, 'Ana, it's me! Do you fancy coming to the beach?'

Debs lived in a bedsit not far from the hotel, and without mobile phones the only way she could invite me out was to come to the hotel and physically knock on my door. Honestly, there could have been no better start to my day, and I jumped out of bed with a wave of relief rushing through me: it was Tuesday and the day was my own. I hadn't smiled since Gavin had done what he did to me, so wearing a much needed, daft grin I poked my head out the door.

'Morning!' Debs beamed. 'Are you coming out?'

I replied, 'Yes!' with an abundance of enthusiasm. 'Just give me a few minutes to get ready, and I'll meet you outside.'

Ten minutes later, I trotted down the stairs so fast I felt my feet were barely touching them. The familiar smell of bacon and eggs was heavy in the air, and I dashed quickly through reception to Debs, who I could see sitting on the wall opposite the hotel smoking a cigarette. Crossing the lobby, I saw Gavin clock me from the restaurant where he was already at work, and I chose to pretend I hadn't seen him. Hurrying down the steps and over the road, I didn't need to turn around to know that he was watching me from the restaurant window. It was so obvious to me—I could feel his eyes on me until we had skipped over the first dune and out of view.

I spent that whole day with Debs, relaxing on the sand, talking through my situation with her, and it was such a welcome break. Her company was delightful.

We paddled in the sea, walking down the beach with our feet just covered by the water and our toes sinking into the soft, malleable sand. We took lunch in a beachfront café as our weekly treat and let boys try to chat us up for amusement. We were young, attractive, and I suppose we looked like fun as we sat laughing together, watching the world go by.

As was usual on Tuesdays (providing we had the cash), Debs suggested we head to the cabaret club that evening, and when she offered to lend me an outfit, I was easily convinced. After our day on the beach, I nipped back to the hotel to wash the sand off, but when

I walked into the lobby I saw Gavin standing near the restaurant door, so I darted upstairs, praying he wouldn't come up to find me. I got ready quickly, and before long I was ready to head back out.

Knowing Gavin would still be loitering around downstairs, I wanted to fly out of the hotel window rather than go back through the building. And as I made my way across the lobby, I saw him leave the restaurant and rush towards me.

'Ana!' he called, as I pulled open the front door.

I couldn't ignore him; he was right there behind me in a nanosecond. So, I turned back and looked him straight in the eye as he said my name once more.

'Yes?' I asked bluntly, with little interest in knowing what he had to say. It was my day off, and I felt no obligation whatsoever to deal with him on my own time. His face clouded over as he saw my eyes were not filled with passion but rather showed the storm which brewed behind them. Although I had felt unable to say no to him in the cellar, my suppressed anger at feeling powerless to control my own life was simmering in the depths of my being.

'Can we talk? I need to talk to you,' he said, placing his hand on my arm as if to try to stop me from taking another step. He seemed to have absolutely no regard for anyone else seeing his behaviour.

'No, Gavin. Not now.'

Pulling my arm away from his, I walked through the door I was still holding open, and I didn't look back.

I walked hastily down the streets that led to Debs' place, and five minutes later, knocked on the door of the three-storey house which Debs shared with a handful of other twenty-somethings. Immediately, Debs leaned out of her bedroom window and called down, 'Come on up, babe! The door's open!"

Despite the regular parties that often filled their house, that Tuesday evening I went straight up to Debs' room without seeing a soul. We smoked a joint together and chatted, with Cat Stevens playing on the record player, and Debs fetched what I thought were beautiful clothes from her wardrobe, laying them on the bed for me to try on. She didn't have a lot of money, and I know all of her clothes would have been cheap, or maybe she made them herself, I'm not sure. But her style was enviable, and I loved spending time with her.

Before heading out into town, we drank warm cider straight from the bottle, laughing and joking around, dressing up in spectacularly odd combinations of clothes—pretending we might go out dressed in such a strange fashion. I remember laughing so hard, tears were streaming down my face. My laugh no longer came out vocally, it went silent and took hold of me in my gut, so I ended up doubled over, shaking and crying with delight.

The cabaret club we went to that evening was quite a big venue and it was popular with residents and holidaymakers alike. Walking into the foyer you were greeted with black walls, a rather stylish ambience, and hefty metal, double doors, which led to the bar. Then once inside the club, there was a seating area, a large dance floor, and a stage where the cabaret acts performed. Circular tables dressed with white cloths and little lamps lined the edge of the dance floor, and sometimes the artists would come down off the stage and walk around the front row of tables. It was one step up from a working man's club, I suppose, but I thought it was fabulous.

There was a balcony on the first floor where two rows of tables looked out over the stage, and it was the norm for most tables to be filled each evening. It catered to hard-working folks who wanted to let their hair down and have a good night out, and I felt very much at home amongst that crowd. Despite being two years under the legal age for entry, no-one ever asked me for ID.

That evening, Debs and I sat at a table on the ground floor and watched a young lady with a good voice belt out some modern classics, followed by a comedian whose humour wasn't really our cup of tea, but he was amusing enough. It was fun, and I was happily drinking away my problems (using alcohol as my coping device for covering up all the emotional pain I had ever suffered). And suddenly, I saw Debs' eyes light up by an idea that had evidently struck her.

'Why don't you ask if they've got any jobs here? This would be a fab place for you to work!'

I had to agree that it did sound like fun, so feeling taken with Debs' positivity (and fairly merry from all the booze), I made my way over to the bar and waited for the good-looking bartender to give me his attention. When he had finished serving his customer he raised his eyebrows at me, smiled, and asked, 'Hey, what can I do for you?'

Sensing his tone was flirtatious, I pressed forward with my advantage and inquired if they had any vacancies. Ten minutes later, I was upstairs in an office being interviewed by the club's manageress.

Lydia, an attractive woman who was probably in her early forties, had bleached blonde hair styled just like Farrah Fawcett, curled back and away from her face as if the wind had blown it perfectly into place. She wore a lot of make-up (I think to hide a bad complexion), her lips were paled out with pan-stick, and she had heavy, false lashes framing her eyes. She told me about their waitressing vacancy and asked me about my experience, so I told her about my duties at the hotel, and before long she asked me why I wanted to leave. Unable to think of anything to say except the truth, I blurted out the reason of sexual harassment from my boss, and Lydia immediately looked empathetic, saying she knew all too well how tough those situations could be.

At the end of our chat, Lydia told me I could start the next day, but that I would need to provide a reference from the restaurant and complete a trial week before she could formally confirm my position. I thanked her, believing (correctly) that Gavin would be good enough to give me a decent reference, and then I made my way back downstairs to Debs—only to find she had been joined by two young men. I sat down, interrupting their laughter, and Debs told me the boys reckoned they were sailors, but then whispered to me that she was convinced they were just spinning her a line.

When I told Debs about my new job, she whooped with delight and hugged me tightly, grinning from ear to ear. Then, picking up one of the piña coladas the men had bought for us, she handed it to me and proposed a toast, 'To new beginnings and freedom from Gavin!'

We clinked glasses as if the sailors weren't even really there.

'Now all I need to do is find somewhere to live,' I ventured, remembering the practicalities of life.

And to my delight, Debs replied, 'Well, that's an easy one to fix—you can stay with me for a while!'

Over the course of the next few weeks, I settled into my new life as a waitress in a cabaret bar, and crashed with Debs, having agreed to pay half her rent until I found somewhere more permanent to stay. My existence then morphed into a constant stream of partying. I would drink at work, party after work, sleep in late, briefly worry about money or finding a place of my own, and then I would go to work and at some stage start drinking again.

That club was a strange place to work really. Lydia was normally there each evening, but she preferred to spend her time liaising with the acts and working in the office, rather than supervising the bar and table service. So, we carried on downstairs, feeling a certain degree of freedom in our work, while every Tom, Dick, and Harry offered us 'drinks on them'—which no-one explicitly forbid us from accepting.

All the waitresses wore a uniform that was a royal blue pencil skirt, a white blouse, and a blue chiffon scarf tied around the neck—it was quite smart really. Though I must tell you how shocked I was on my first day, when Lydia gave me my uniform and told me she would dock my first week's wage for the cost of them! I think my jaw must have dropped, as Lydia, noting my surprise, explained that it was standard protocol to charge staff for their uniform and everyone else had paid for theirs. I remember nodding in silent reply and taking my new outfit to the staff toilet to get changed.

I, therefore, started my new job, finding myself unexpectedly in debt. I went from having virtually no money, maybe a few coins in my purse, to even less than that. It hadn't really occurred to me before then that it was possible to have less than nothing, and I found it an unsettling concept.

Lydia told me that I should always make sure I was well presented for work; I should do my make-up nicely and my hair should be neatly styled (preferably pinned up). I was told to flirt with the customers—that they enjoyed it—but never to fraternise with them outside of the club or engage in any sexual relations. She said I should be under no illusion, my employment would be over in an instant if I did.

So, I worked there waiting tables, fetching drinks, and flirting with the single men when they were seated in my area. They offered to buy me drinks and I accepted without issue. I would have gin, vodka, beer, or anything else they chose to buy for me; I wasn't fussy. They bought it, I drank it, and then I'd have a giggle with them, making sure their glasses were kept topped up and that they all had fun.

As well as flirting with the customers, I also found it very easy to flirt with the two guys who worked behind the bar each evening, Nick and Tom, and they seemed to enjoy the banter with all the waitresses just as much. They would pour us drinks on the sly, all of us getting steadily intoxicated each night, and that's how we earned our keep.

A month on, I was still crashing at Debs' bedsit and was showing no real signs of moving out, but thankfully, Debs didn't seem to mind too much. She'd grumble every now and again when the place got too messy, and would comment under her breath that the room wasn't really big enough for two. But other than those throwaway remarks, she never forced classified ads under my nose, and for that I was very grateful.

Then came a night when I was at work doing my usual duties, waiting tables, smiling, and accepting any drink I was given, when a real drama kicked off. The cabaret had finished, the club was less than an hour from closing, and I was fetching a crowd of six big men another round of lagers from the bar. More than merry and much louder than the usual guests, they were filled to the brim with testosterone—so much so that a group of women sitting in their area had asked to move tables, not wanting to overhear their crude jokes and belly laughs any longer.

Nick was at the bar and he had given me a nudge when the group were first seated in my area, telling me they were considered 'heavies' in town. He had told me to keep them happy and stay attentive to them, and I'd thanked him for the advice. Then, when he poured two shots of tequila and passed one to me, we knocked them back while no one was looking.

I don't think I'd drunk much more than any other night, but when I walked back with their order of drinks, smiling as I approached their table, I didn't notice that the woman sitting to my side had stretched her legs out across my path. I went flying—and so did my tray of drinks. Six pints of lager flew out of their glasses and straight over the two men who sat closest to me.

The glasses shattered and I was sprawled all over the floor, my hair and clothes covered in beer. The noise of my commotion roused the attention of the entire club, and I cringed inwardly as some men around me applauded sarcastically whilst I pulled myself to my feet.

At that point, I think the tequila must have gone to my head, because I unexpectedly found myself stumbling back over from a head-rush. The world seemed to spin around me. My brain sloshing inside my head, I put my hands out to catch myself as I fell back down to the floor and then shrieked as a piece of glass pushed straight into my hand.

I remember the words, 'Oh shit!' coming out my mouth and Nick running over from the bar to help me.

But as he arrived at my side, I simply could have died when the large bloke next to me announced loudly, 'She's DRUNK!'

Nick apologised profusely for me as I tried to straigthen myself out, and when I cast my eyes over the two men nearest me, they looked like they had been caught in a downpour of ale. They were absolutely soaked and looked livid to boot.

I apologised, but as my hand was hurting so much and my head was still spinning, I probably didn't give them the level of grovelling they had expected.

Nick told me to go upstairs and said that he would deal with the mess. So I stumbled my way to the staff toilet and thrust my hand under the cold tap. The mirror over the sink showed me that I looked an absolute state: my hair dishevelled, and my wet uniform clinging to my skin.

The cut on my hand was small but deep, and blood had quickly dripped down my arm as I had run upstairs—so now it was all over my uniform, along with the beer.

I picked a shard of glass out of the cut, washed myself as best as I could, and then tried to bandage a hand towel tightly around my palm. Putting pressure on the wound with my other hand, I gazed into the mirror again while I waited for the bleeding to stop. Straggles of hair stuck to my face, and I didn't know why my eye make-up was smudged all around my eyes. Had I cried when I'd fallen to the floor or was it just from the beer? I had no idea.

My heartbeat seemed to thump through my head, and I knew I needed water—water would bring me back down to Earth and help me to find some composure. Bending over the sink, I thrust my head under the tap and drank. Unable to get the stream fully into my mouth, I gulped what I could while the rest spurted out and trickled down my chin.

I drank at least a pint of lukewarm water without coming up for air, and every time I swallowed, I felt it helping to counter the alcohol in my blood stream.

I knew I needed to sober up sharpish…

It was while I was hanging over the sink, gulping down water (which I'm not even sure was safe to drink) that the door flew open, and I turned to see Lydia standing in front of me wearing an expression so furious she looked set to erupt.

She looked me up and down as I wiped my mouth with the towel that was still around my hand, and she said in a tone that was low and so very stern, 'Get into my office now and stay there until I summon you.'

So I did. I sat at Lydia's desk like a bag of nerves, anxiously swivelling from side to side on an office chair, and I waited. Occasionally, I unwound the towel around my hand to make sure the bleeding was stopping, and

I wished I had a change of clothes at work so I could freshen up. But with nothing but the uniform I sat in, I had no choice other than to remain uncomfortably in my wet, bloodied clothes.

Downstairs, Lydia resolved the situation with my table of men by giving them all free entry for the rest of the month, and the club emptied abruptly when the lights had been brought up. The incident settled with all but the staff, Lydia had called everyone to gather around the bar and sent one of the waitresses to fetch me.

I walked down to find my colleagues all stood in a small crowd with Lydia at the helm, awaiting my arrival. Recognising a bad atmosphere when I saw one, I joined them feeling like no one wanted to stand next to me or be associated with me in any way.

Lydia fired me on the spot in front of everyone. I'd obviously figured this was coming—why wouldn't you sack someone who had drunkenly thrown beer over a table of customers? But what I hadn't expected was the wrath of fury that was cast on me as Lydia yelled in a raging outburst that she would NOT TOLERATE STAFF STEALING FROM HER BAR! I was made an example of in front of the whole team, as they all stood watching, at least half inebriated themselves—knowing it could have easily been any one of them who'd made the mistake of tripping over someone's feet.

I had never seen Lydia so red in the face. She told me I disgusted her and she couldn't fathom how I could steal from a company who had so willingly given me a job when I'd needed one.

She declared to the team that she wasn't stupid and she'd noticed the stock of alcohol depleting at a quicker rate than the till receipts showed. She said she had been waiting to catch one of us in the act and asked the group to name any others they knew to be involved in the theft.

All eyes immediately looked from me down to the floor. No one was willing to name anyone else—we were all as guilty as each other. And no one was willing to stick up for me either. It was simply an opportunity for Lydia to address a situation with the group, and she held me up as a case in point for all to see. She said I was lucky she wasn't going to phone the police and that I shouldn't expect a pay packet—she would keep the money to cover my 'tab'.

When the public humiliation was over, I grabbed my handbag and jacket and walked silently out of the club, never to return. As I left, I was watched by all my old workmates as if I were suddenly a stranger to them, and it was only Nick who ran out the door after me once Lydia had gone back upstairs.

He called out 'Ana!' as he ran across the forecourt of the club to the street where I was starting my walk back to Debs' house. But I didn't stop.

'Ana!' he called again.

A few seconds later, he arrived at my side, whilst I kept walking. The wind was stronger than usual, and I crossed my arms in front of my chest, wrapping my jacket around me, wondering what on earth I was going to do next.

I asked Nick what he wanted, and he replied, 'I want to apologise. I'm sorry I gave you the tequila… Even though drinking shots with you has always been highly amusing.' He smiled with distinct flirtation, then added, 'And thank you for not dropping me in it with Lydia.'

I stopped in my tracks and looked at him curiously. 'Well, grassing people up really isn't my style. But I could have done with someone sticking up for me in there, rather than letting me take the rap all by myself.'

He shook his head with regret. 'Oh God, Ana, you know I would have lost my job too, right? I'm sorry I didn't say anything, but I just couldn't afford to become unemployed.'

I knew that was true; he would have been sacked on the spot too, and thinking logically, there would have been no point in that. I breathed deeply and concluded it was what it was; I was just going to have to come up with a new plan.

To my suprise, it was at this point that he put his hands on my arms, holding me quite tenderly, and told me, 'You know, I'm going to miss you, Ana. I've had a lot of fun working with you... And it's always been a pleasure to watch you walk around the club in that tight, blue skirt of yours.'

He smiled a sexy smile and then to my surprise he kissed me. It was initially quite a hard kiss, but then his lips softened—and I have to admit, it was rather nice.

Knowing what a state I looked, I couldn't fathom why he wanted to kiss me that night. Maybe he saw it as his last opportunity to make a move, or maybe he just fancied his chances of getting lucky, I'm not sure. But a few moments later, he pulled back and asked with a cheekily raised eyebrow, 'How would you fancy coming back to my place for a nightcap?'

I shook my head and told him, 'Thanks, but I think I've already had enough alcohol for one night! Plus I'm exhausted, I really just want to go home and get to bed.'

With a twinkle in his eye, he replied, 'Well, that sounds good to me. How about I come with you?'

I couldn't help but smile at his persistence, but still, I was in no mood for late night promiscuity, so I shook my head again and replied, 'No, Nick, not tonight.'

He kissed me once more, quite gently, as if to suggest he might want more from me than just sex. Then he took my hand, kissed it lightly and bid me goodnight, saying he would hopefully see me around.

When I got back to the bedsit, I discovered Debs was out. She'd met a new fella named Doug and had been stopping at his house a few nights each week. So, with the room to myself, I dropped onto her double bed in despair, and whilst shedding tears at my downfall, I fell asleep with my uniform still on.

I didn't stir until Debs arrived home at 7 a.m. to get ready for work. She breezed in the door with a smile that told the world she was falling in love and chirped, 'Morning! Ana? Are you awake?'

'Mmm... I am now,' I murmured, opening my eyes and pulling myself up to sit on the bed. Images of the night before immediately came hurtling back to mind, and I winced in the realisation that I had slept on top of the blankets in my dirty clothes all night. 'Sorry... Good morning,' I replied. 'Did you have a nice night?'

Debs' warm, glowing smile then faded and was replaced by a concerned expression, as she focused on me and realised what a mess I looked.

'Jesus, Ana! What on earth happened to you? You've got blood all over you!'

I explained as briefly as possible that I had tripped over, cut my hand, soaked a load of heavies with beer, and that I had been fired for stealing shots from the bar. But before I had a chance to explain my story fully, Debs interrupted with audible shock, 'You were fired for stealing shots? Ana, what the hell came over you?!'

I told her everyone had been drinking and that it was Nick who had been giving me the tequila—trying to explain that I was the scapegoat for a much larger situation. But when I got to the point that Lydia was withholding my pay packet to cover the missing alcohol, Debs' concern for me turned into concern for herself, as she realised the full implications of what had happened.

'So, you're not getting paid this week?'

I shook my head regretfully. 'No, I'm so sorry Debs.'

'And what about our rent? You need to pay half!'

'I would if I was getting paid,' I countered in defence. 'I'm so sorry. I really never meant for this to happen.'

'Well, we're buggered then, aren't we?' Debs concluded. Her eyebrows narrowed. 'I haven't got enough to pay the whole month by myself.'

Since I had moved in, Debs had been going out a lot more (especially since she had started seeing Doug), so I understood immediately why she couldn't bail me out. She asked me if I could get some money together by the end of the week, but I had no idea how I could, so I said I could try but I couldn't promise and apologised again for the trouble I had got us into.

I had never seen Debs angry until that point, and honestly, it was a horrible experience. She went silent for the next five or ten minutes while she got ready for work; busying herself around the room, she changed into her uniform, brushed her hair and rapidly applied her make-up. Her eyes refusing to look at me, she began to chunter under her breath about how unbelievable the situation was.

Not knowing anything sensible I could say to make things better, I started to babble. I blurted out a string of excuses held together with a hungover need to talk, to say something, to explain that it wasn't my fault—although, looking back, it undeniably was. But Debs just shook her head, looking at me briefly through the reflection of her handheld mirror as she faced the window to apply her lipstick.

When she finally turned around, she glared at me, frustration oozing from her pores and told me, 'Ana, I'm not joking, you need to sort your life out. I am *so* angry with you right now.'

I nodded, it was the only thing I could do as I sat there dumbfounded by life's latest turn of events.

She continued, 'I don't have the money to pay all the rent at this short notice. I was counting on you—and this is definitely on you to sort out, because I sure as hell can't do it for you.'

I took what she said without question. I understood everything that Debs was feeling; I had messed up, there was no question of that. Unable to see a way out, I let the only words I could think of slip out of my mouth once again. 'I am so sorry, Debs.'

As soon as I heard myself say it, I saw her face change and a look of bemusement wash over her.

'Do you really think "*Sorry*" makes any difference?'

She pulled her denim jacket on over her uniform, and as she continued to speak her volume increased. 'You are so selfish, Ana. How the hell do you think "sorry" is going to pay the landlord? You need to think about someone other than yourself for a change and do something with your life. How am I meant to get your share of the rent in three days and make everything magically OK? I've given you so much over the last few weeks: I've given you friendship, support, a bed when you needed one. And what have you given me? A bloody headache by the looks of it and the situation of dealing with a fuming landlord.'

She looked at me, filled with disappointment, and still I couldn't think of anything more to say. Everything felt beyond repair, and there were no words I knew that could remedy the situation.

'I've known you for what, a couple of months? And during that time, you've had to walk away from two jobs? I know you had to leave the hotel as Gavin kept trying it on with you, but now, with job number two already over, I'm wondering what's really wrong with you, Ana? Why can't you hold down a job?'

She stared at me awaiting a response I didn't have. What was wrong with me? I had no idea. What was right with me? My entire life existed as simply a quest to try to escape the suffering I had forever endured. I felt I was failing every which way I turned. Even my ability to tread-water had now vanished, and I was simply sinking. My head beneath water, I had disappeared into a state of hopelessness. And honestly, I'd never expected such retribution from someone who I thought of as a sister.

I had no idea what to think of myself, let alone what to say; I was speechless. After several seconds of silence passed, Debs huffed and headed towards the door. Bringing the drama to a head, she stated, 'I need to go to

work now, Ana. I haven't got time for all this bullshit…
I'll be late as well at this rate. You need to sort this out,
or else leave and find somewhere else to live.'

She picked her handbag up off the floor and turned
her back on me. And with that final condemnation, she
walked out the door and slammed it behind her.

I remember sitting there feeling so baffled by life.
I felt hurt, really hurt, and I had no idea how to make
any money in just three days—even if I did find a new
job, I knew I wouldn't be able to earn enough to cover
the rent.

Suddenly feeling like an unwelcome visitor in someone
else's abode, I pulled myself up from the bed. I washed
my face and looked at my reflection in the mirror,
wondering what I had become. All I saw was a failure
with no self-control. The shame I felt was crippling.

I washed what was left of the previous night's make-
up off my face and changed into fresh clothes. With
no job to go to or anyone desiring my time, I gathered
up my belongings and placed them into my canvas
rucksack. This small task complete, I opened my purse
and counted up how much money I had. With a few
pounds, I figured that I would probably just have
enough for a coach ticket back to Nottingham, and if I
didn't, I would have to go as far as a bus would take me
and then hitchhike the rest of the way.

So, I left and headed back to the life that I loathed in
so many ways, but which offered a degree of normality
that I thought might feel quite comforting after the
shocks I had encountered in my few months away—
if nothing else, the idea of seeing my siblings brought
warmth to my heart.

CHAPTER EIGHT

hen I arrived back in Nottingham, the grey skies and chilled air matched exactly how I felt inside. And the mundane yet hostile energy of our home hit me the second I walked in through the back door.

Mum was in the kitchen cooking and when she saw me, she rolled her eyes, exhaling a short burst of air through her nose.

She scoffed, 'I see the wanderer returns!'

'Hello Mum,' I ventured, immediately feeling the weight of the family atmosphere fall upon my shoulders once more.

'Your dad's in the dining room. Take him a cup of tea when you go through.'

'Yes, Mum,' I replied. Dropping my bag on the floor, I walked over to fill the kettle which sat waiting for me on the stove. While I made the tea, Mum continued reeling off chores I could make myself useful with. And as she spoke I wondered had she missed me at all, or had she just been inconvenienced by her scullery maid going AWOL? I felt no emotion from her whatsoever, and after just five minutes, I was already back into the same old routine.

Only the look on my brothers' faces when I burst into their bedroom told me that my time away had been real. The way they hugged me assured me that I was loved, and I immediately felt a pang of guilt for having left them alone with my parents for so many weeks.

On a positive note, I do think that evening when I arrived home from Skegness was the loveliest evening I ever had with my dad. He was clinically depressed at the time without a doubt, but after my mum left for bingo, we chatted freely, and it was nice that although I had run away, I wasn't actually in trouble with him.

I asked Dad what had been happening over the summer, and he talked a little about the boys, then told me that Mum was stressed, and added, 'But what's new there?!' And we both laughed.

From the way Dad spoke, I believe he had missed having me around, and in a weird way, just for that one evening, it was suddenly wonderful to be home.

Dad told me of how Jimmy had left Nottingham with Yvette and he had no idea where they had gone. He said Louisa was visiting occasionally, but he hadn't seen a great deal of her; he commented, 'I can't say I blame her, who would want to hang around here?'

When my dad grew tired, I said I would let him rest, and covered him with a blanket, before stepping outside for some fresh air. Looking to the stars, I contemplated my life. I had no idea what I was meant to do next, but I knew I needed to find a new job and a way to permanently leave home—staying with my parents could be nothing but a pit-stop whilst I came up with a new plan.

I spent the first few days at home scouring the newspapers for job adverts and sending off applications for waitressing positions. But I was young, with no reference from my last job, no qualifications, and very little experience, so when I phoned to enquire about vacancies, nobody jumped at the chance to employ me.

After several days, I caught the bus into town to search for a job in person. I walked around the department stores, shops, and cafés, politely asking if they had any vacancies. Yet, I was told the same thing again and again: 'No, sorry. Come back nearer Christmas.'

After spending all day in town, my hope was disintegrating with every minute that passed. Once I had ran out of businesses to enquire within, I lit up a cigarette next to the clock tower and sat down on a bench. I knew I had to try to make a go of my life—if only fate would provide an opportunity…

I looked up to the sky filled with clouds threatening rain. Then, as I looked back down, gazing at all the buildings around me, I spotted the Army Recruitment Office. I surprised myself by experiencing a glimmer of hope when I saw it, and I couldn't suppress the thought, 'Surely, the Army would have me?' when it lingered in my mind.

After stubbing out my cigarette, I surprised myself even further by walking straight over the road and opening their door.

Joining up was never an option I had ever considered before, but with no other opportunities presenting themselves, the Army seemed like an interesting possibility to pursue.

The office was active with several interviews in progress, and as I hovered just inside the door, a uniformed staff member called me over to his desk and invited me to sit down. He asked his questions and noted down my details in an incredibly formal manner, whilst I spoke only when I was invited to, silently reading the posters on the walls and feeling intrigued by their slogans:

NEW ARMY, NEW INDEPENDENCE, NEW YOU.

THE NEW ARMY: THE CHALLENGE YOU NEED.

Once my interview was complete, the officer explained I would need to sit a basic aptitude test and took me to an office where I sat alone and did the paper.

Despite having very little exposure to education, I felt I had done well when I finished the test, and after the officer checked my answers, he smiled at me, congratulating me for my high score—and I must say it felt really good to have been successful at something!

I distinctly recall it was the first time I had ever received congratulations in my entire life, and it felt amazing! The officer told me I should await details of my basic training coming through the post, and then he patted me on the back, before calling the next waif and stray up to his desk.

As soon as I got home, I told my dad and he signed my consent form without issue, seeming proud of me for joining up. Giving me his blessing to leave, he said, 'It'll do you some good to experience the focus of being in the Forces. And really, you're best off out of here, you know, love. This is no place for a young lady.'

When I told Mum I was joining the Army, she literally laughed in my face. Her eyebrows lifted high into her forehead, she ridiculed me with the line, 'Ha! You won't last two minutes in the Forces!'

Although that was crushing to hear, the most difficult part of joining up was, by far, leaving Finn and Paddy again. I was genuinely so sorry that I had to leave them, but staying at home wasn't a long-term option for my sanity. I needed to go. When I told them, both boys understood with wisdom beyond their years and laid no guilt trip on me—looking back, I've always thought that was incredibly strong of them.

Within a month, I was on a train and leaving Nottingham once again. My dad had given me the train fare, bless him, and I had kissed him on the cheek before leaving the house. Paddy and Finn were at school, and Mum was out—although I had no idea where.

CHAPTER NINE

oining the Army at sixteen years old, I worked initially as an Inventory Clerk, before progressing to Staff Clerk, and I spent the majority of my days in an office.

I was so used to taking orders at home that the Army mindset was easy for me to adopt—do as you're told, don't think too much, keep your shoes polished, and you'll be OK.

I continuously tried hard and did my work well, but still an underlying void of meaning niggled at my soul. Every evening, I used to go to the NAAFI where folks would take a beer and try to relax. Regularly, I would play cards or dominoes, whilst some played drinking games—and everybody smoked. But the hours I spent there were never anything more than a way of passing time. I'd simply try to distract myself from the emptiness I felt inside with anything that resembled fun.

As far as having boyfriends was concerned, you weren't allowed to have sex with other staff, but relationships weren't forbidden. So, I did date a few young men during my three years serving the country, but I didn't meet anyone special who gave me a reason to be.

My self-confidence was still in tatters from my raw start in life—it's like I was alive in body but not particularly stimulated in mind or spirit, and that was about it. And, I must say, while working in the Army was indeed a chapter in my life, the concept of war always went against every atom of my being.

I recall a time I had to do an inventory of an ammunitions store, however, once I had been left to look around, I quickly started to feel violently sick. Thankfully, I didn't vomit, but, I swear, walking around that store was one of the most unpleasant things I've ever done.

All the time I was in there, I felt a heavy, negative energy on me—as though I was swimming through mud. My stomach churning, I looked at the stock and saw graphic visions in my mind's eye of how the ammunition would be used. I saw buildings reduced to smouldering rubble and people running in anguish, covered in dirt. I felt the emotional pain that would be the domino effect of the physical destruction, deaths and injuries—the suffering that would ripple through the families of the fallen. I felt never-ending sadness when I looked around the room, seeing grief associated with each and every weapon.

One good thing that did come from being in the Army, was that I was allowed to sit my O-level exams (which were the qualifications I should have gained at school at sixteen). I remember hearing that a few other privates were taking their O-levels, and I decided to ask one of the sergeants if there was any way I would be allowed to sit the papers too, even though I hadn't studied for them.

I recall him looking at me with a puzzled expression and clarifying, 'Do you want to register to take a course?'

But I shook my head and replied, 'No, I'd really just like to sit the exams and see how I do, if that's possible?'

I think my request intrigued him and he kindly agreed. So, a few days later I sat exams in Maths, English, and General Studies and I came out with two B's and a C, which really pleased me—I finally had three pieces of paper which proved I was bright.

At the age of nineteen, I had been doing some admin for a sergeant (who was a nice enough man) when he told me he wanted me to pose for an Army recruitment poster. He said in a very serious, professional tone, 'You're the most beautiful girl here, so it makes sense for you to be photographed.'

So, I replied, 'Yes, Sergeant,' as I would with any other command. But I couldn't help but look at him differently once I knew he thought I was beautiful.

When the photographer arrived for the shoot, he asked me to stand between two of the tallest, broadest soldiers we had in our barracks. One of them was to hand me a leaflet, and I was to look up to them and dutifully take what I was offered.

When I saw the finished poster, it seemed very macho and symbolic. My sergeant seemed very pleased with it and told me it was something I should be proud of—but personally, I didn't see anything I liked in it. Pride was a long way off how I felt. I thanked him for his compliment nonetheless, and it wasn't long after this that we started dating.

His name was Ian, and he was married but had separated from his wife. She worked in our barracks too, but I didn't really know her, and he assured me they were no longer together, nor still in love. So, I accepted his situation, and I did enjoy his company for a spell, but unfortunately this short affair was to be my undoing.

After we had been dating a few weeks, there came an evening when Ian and I went out for a drive in the countryside with another sergeant and his girlfriend. We had all been drinking, and we were singing along to the radio, laughing, when Ian took a corner too fast and came off the road.

I can still recall how time instantly changed pace to ultra-slow motion, and our car tumbled down the bank until we came to a stop, the car upside down. The engine still running, I squeezed out through my window and saw smoke coming out from the crumpled bonnet. I shouted at the others to get out—they were barely conscious but thankfully Ian came around quickly, and together we pulled the other two out of the car as it lay smouldering on the field. It was incredible that no-one was seriously hurt.

The incident had been reported by someone who'd witnessed the car going off the road, so the police turned up rapidly and took us back to camp. I don't remember much about the rest of that night, other than going straight to the NAAFI and having another drink to calm my nerves. Yet while I carried on with my evening, I had no idea that the accident was being reported to the Military Police by the officers who'd dropped us back.

The next day when I reported for duty, I was taken to an office and put in front of the Platoon Sergeant as he read aloud the incident details which had arrived on his desk. He told me of two married men in a car with two women who were not their wives, who were intoxicated, and who, as a result of reckless driving, had caused damage to a farmer's land. He said he had been left no choice but to report the matter to the Platoon Commander, and following another short meeting they decided to discharge me.

I couldn't believe the injustice of what was happening; there was no way the accident had been my fault. Yes, I had got in to a car with Ian, but I hadn't forced him to drive, nor done anything to provoke the accident.

When I tried to put forward my objections, the Commander replied by saying it was clear that one of us would have to go, and it most certainly wasn't going to be Ian—and that was the end of my time in the Armed Forces.

When I look back at that time in my life, it makes me think that sometimes, when you're heading in the wrong direction, life has a way of taking the navigation controls out of your hands, and making the decision for you. I wasn't made to be in the army, so I'm grateful that I was forced to leave. Quite simply, I believe in peace, and I have never understood the notion which insists warring can achieve it.

When I think of our world today, I'm certain that world-peace is possible, and that the trigger for us entering this state will be when the human race collectively finds inner-peace. I trust Conscious Evolution is the answer to all of our problems.

CHAPTER TEN

t was 1978 when I returned to Nottingham once again; I was nearly twenty, and life at home had changed, although the mentality of the household was much the same. My dad was still unable to work, and my little brothers were now not so little at fourteen and fifteen; Mum still gambled and was out the house most of the time, and the relationship between her and my dad remained ever strained. Louisa, who was now twenty-seven, had a baby—a beautiful girl they'd named Daisy. And Jimmy and Yvette were back in town, living in a flat close to the city centre.

With a few years' work experience and a handful of certificates to my name, I got a job as a purchasing clerk for a firm in Nottingham city centre. I paid board to my parents and did the household chores whenever I was at home.

At that stage, life was the best I'd had it for a while, but the sense of emptiness inside never left me. And so, as many young people do, I let my hair down at the weekends and partied. I spent a lot of evenings with Jimmy and Yvette at their flat, and if they'd had a spare room I would have moved in with them for sure, but they didn't, so I slept at home—and like my mum, I spent as much time out the house as I could.

Then came one evening when I went round to Jimmy's, and as I let myself in through the unlocked front door, I knew instantly that Chloe was with her grandma and they had the place to themselves. I could hear music and laughter coming from the lounge, and the familiar smell of marijuana filled the air. I walked in to find Jimmy and Yvette sitting with half a dozen friends, chilling together in the lounge and enjoying their Friday night.

Saying hello to the group, I quickly realised that I knew everyone except for one man, and I swear my heart literally seemed to skip a beat as I took in this guy who sat on my brother's floor. His long legs stretched out in front of him, crossed at the ankle; he held a joint in one hand and a beer bottle in the other. And when he smiled at me, I felt like I melted a little inside—my cheeks suddenly burning as I felt myself blush.

Straightaway, Jimmy introduced me to his friend, David, and explained that they had done time in the Young Offenders together—at which point David laughed and interrupted to say, 'You know, my stint inside doesn't need to be the one defining factor you introduce me with!'

Placing his joint in the ashtray, David stood up to shake my hand, then, as our hands touched, I felt an intriguing energy race through me. He had a firm yet gentle grip, and the skin-to-skin contact with this man set my heart pounding.

Feeling myself blush even more, I could only hope he didn't notice. And when I said it was nice to meet him, the look in his eyes lit a fire inside me like I had never known before.

Yvette suggested I should take a beer from the fridge and join them, so I did just that. Then, when I returned, I sat in the only space available—which, as luck would have it, was right next to David. As conversation amongst the group continued, David passed me the joint and asked me about my life.

He was tall, with broad shoulders and a toned, slim build. His dark blonde, wavy hair was fairly long, and his beard and smile reminded me a little of Barry Gibb, but he was less toothy and far better looking in my opinion. He wore a tight-fitting, pale blue T-shirt, bell-bottomed jeans and a gold chain around his neck, and I have to say, I liked his style, and I wondered where the hell my brother had been hiding him all these years!

David told me he worked as a labourer on a construction site, rented a small house across town in a place called Sneinton, and he rode a Vespa scooter which he polished every Sunday. I learned he'd been inside for GBH, but he explained he was a teenager at the time, and it had all been a lot of fuss over a brawl between a gang of lads that had got out of control.

He assured me, 'Don't worry, that really isn't my style any more.' Then he added with a smile, 'Nowadays, I'd rather be a lover than a fighter.'

I remember grinning as he delivered that line, and I fancied him without any doubt. *He was gorgeous!*

So, I guess you could say that was the first time I'd ever been truly sexually attracted to a man—and I never expected to feel how I did. His presence undid me.

As the hours at that party passed, I sat next to David all night and as I got to know the person behind the attractive face, I knew very quickly that I liked him.

I was drawn to him, and I felt so comfortable with him—he was unlike anyone I had ever met.

We talked all night, with neither of us having any desire to leave the few square metres of carpet that we shared. It was delightful.

When it was time for me to catch the last bus home, David offered to walk me to the bus stop—so you know I said yes! Then, as we stood waiting for the bus to arrive, he asked if he could see me again, and, I swear, I felt elated like never before. I remember smiling, feeling in awe of the energy between us, and told him rather demurely that he could.

He asked if he could call me, so I gave him my parents' phone number—the first time I had ever given it out to a man. I wrote it on the back of an old receipt using my eyeliner pencil, and he placed it in his wallet, appearing to be rather pleased by our surprise encounter.

Shortly after, the bus appeared at the top of the road, and I waited, wondering if he would try to kiss me. But instead, he took my hand, brought it up to his face and kissed it gently, before looking into my eyes and asking with a cheeky grin, 'So, I'll see you during the week?'

With joy radiating from my core, I replied teasingly, 'Well, I'm sure I should be able to find a window in my diary.'

A few moments later, David put me on the bus, and I took a seat near the back, smiling a smile that stayed in my heart, unshakeable for the entire weekend.

Over the next few days, I nervously anticipated the phone ringing and frequently imagined what David might be doing during his day, trying to work out when he would call. We both worked full-time, so I knew he would only ring in the evening, and I was sure he'd ring before nine o'clock, as no one ever phoned after nine unless something was wrong.

On the Monday, the phone rang at 7p.m. and I dashed to answer it as if my life depended on it. With butterflies raging up from my stomach and into my mouth, I said hello, only to find it was one of my mum's friend's ringing for a gossip, and Mum went on to hog the line for over an hour! I wanted to yell, 'Mum, get off the phone! David might be trying to call!' but of course, those words never came out, and the phone didn't ring again that evening.

The next day the phone rang at 8 p.m. and Paddy picked it up. You should bear in mind that our Paddy had grown into a very self-assured teenager, and he took immediate delight in hearing a male voice on the other end asking for me. He bellowed, 'Ana! Your *boyfriend*'s on the phone!'

Thank God, my mum was out at the time, but regardless, I could have clobbered him for how he shouted for me that day—knowing full well that David would have heard! My face flushed bright red as I flew down the stairs, and I snatched the phone from Paddy in a lovable way that let him know he was in for it when I hung up!

As soon as I heard David's voice, my insides seemed to turn to goo. While I was ecstatic that he had called, I tried my best to keep my excitement in check, and after a couple of minutes making the most delightful small-talk, David asked if I would like to go out for dinner with him. Of course, I agreed I would love to. And I can tell you, hand on heart, I had never worn such a humungous smile. The energy he created within me made me feel so high, it was thrilling.

After we had spoken for a couple of minutes more, David asked for my address and told me he would be round at 7.30p.m. on Thursday to pick me up. Putting the phone down, I ran back upstairs to my room, closed the door and danced with delight to let out the abundance of happiness I felt.

When the day of my first ever *real* date arrived, I looked like the Cheshire Cat all day long. I remember my mum asking me what the hell I was so happy about, like there must be something wrong with me, and I shrugged my shoulders, keeping my news to myself—suspecting she would only find some way to spoil it if I told her.

Thankfully, Mum had gone out by the time David was due to pick me up, so I only had to explain my outing to my dad, and he seemed genuinely pleased for me when I told him. He said that when David arrived I should bring him in for a minute, so he could meet the man who wanted to date his daughter.

So, at half past seven when David came knocking, I did just that. I opened the door with a smile and quietly apologised that my dad wanted to meet him, but he just grinned, said that was no problem and came straight in.

Dad was sitting in the front room, and as we walked over, I watched my dad's face with intrigue as he stood up and began to take David in. Trying to judge the man before him, he cast his eye over his bell-bottomed trousers, his roll-neck jumper and his unruly, blonde hair.

Dad stared for a moment before any words came out of his mouth, so David quickly delivered a humble,

'Good evening, sir,' to break the ice, and offered his hand to shake. I watched the two of them firmly shake hands, with my dad clearly assessing David's grip and sizing him up, while wearing a look of what I think was pleasant surprise.

'So, Ana tells me you know our Jimmy?' Dad said, a little in the style of a policeman interviewing a suspect.

'Yes, sir,' David replied. 'I've known him for a fair few years now, but I live on the other side of town, so I don't tend to come over to this neck of the woods that often.'

'And what do you do for a living?' my dad continued in his investigative tone.

'I work on a construction site across town, for J.H. Milner's. I've been labouring with them for about eighteen months now.'

My dad nodded his head in reply. 'And where are you planning on taking Ana, this evening?'

'I thought I would take her to The Wheatsheaf pub for a meal, if that's OK with you?'

Dad looked across me with a smile starting to creep behind his solemn face and said, 'OK, David. Well, it's been nice to meet you. Have Ana back home by eleven o'clock, please, she's got work tomorrow.'

'No problem at all,' David agreed. 'Thank you for letting me take her out.'

I kissed my dad on the cheek and said I'd see him later, and then as I started to head towards the door, Dad added, 'Now, you look after her, you hear? Or else you'll have both me and Jimmy to deal with, OK?'

It surprised me that my dad, who was clearly so ill, would make such a statement. But with a smile on his face, David replied, 'No problem at all. I promise I'll look after Ana and keep her safe.' I remember thinking he was the first person I had ever known to profess they could do such a thing.

When we left the house, I saw his scooter parked outside and two helmets placed on the seat awaiting us.

'Do I really have to wear one of those?' I asked, thinking the helmet would squash my hair. But he assured me I did and keeping me safe was rule number one. So, despite my playful objections, David took a helmet and placed it on my head, and I stood still as he fastened the strap under my chin—my knees already feeling weak in his presence. He then climbed on the scooter in front of me and told me to hop on the back, and my stomach somersaulted as I placed my arms around him and held on for the ride. He felt amazing. His body was toned in all the right places, and 'Wow' is the only way I can sum up how I felt about him.

We rode to a pub a few miles out of town in the countryside, and the smell of the cooking floated out the building, making my stomach rumble from the second we arrived. I had never been to that pub before, but when we got inside I instantly fell in love with the ambience: there was low music playing, exposed beams running across the ceiling, and a candle lit on each table. Romance was certainly in the air, and I delighted in it.

As the evening passed, we chatted, we laughed, we ate some *really* good food, and I was utterly captivated by his company. We gazed into each other's eyes, and I studied his mouth as he spoke, imagining his kisses would feel divine.

At the end of the meal, David paid the bill—not entertaining the idea of splitting it for even one second—

and leaving the change on the table as a tip, we walked out into the car park and chilly night air. I linked my arm into his for the short distance it was across to the scooter, and after we had donned our helmets, I hopped on behind him once again.

I remember spending the entire journey home feeling exhilarated as I held on to him, thinking nothing except how amazing it felt to touch him. It was as if my brain no longer dominated my body: my thoughts subsided and the energy created when two bodies connect physically and mentally consumed me entirely.

As promised, I was back by 11 p.m. (in fact, we were ten minutes early to boot), and when we had taken off our helmets, we walked up to my front door, and I waited with anticipation to see how David would say goodbye. I remember standing on our doorstep, not wanting to go inside, and David taking my hands and holding them as he thanked me for an amazing evening.

I said I'd had a lovely time too, and then he asked if he could see me again at the weekend—while I continued to wonder if surely a little kiss wouldn't be inappropriate before I went in? However, instead of his lips meeting mine, he briefly held me in his arms, kissed me lightly on the cheek, then told me I should get inside before I made myself late.

Not wanting to part from him, I reluctantly agreed and went in to find my dad waiting for me in the dining room. The first thing he did was check his watch, then seeing I was on time, he asked if I'd had a nice evening.

I cooed, 'I've had a *lovely* time, thank you.'

Planning to go straight up to bed, I went to the kitchen to fetch a glass of water, and as I filled it up, my dad called through to me, 'How does David know our Jimmy again?'

This question caught me off guard, and I didn't quite know how to respond, so I skirted around the issue and just replied, 'Oh, they hang around with the same crowd.' Then I took myself off to bed, making the excuse that I was tired and needed to get a good night's sleep before work—when really I was walking on air.

David and I started seeing each other twice a week (it seemed the week was just too long to meet up any less) and all our dates went the same way: he would ride across town to pick me up, and then he'd take me out somewhere nice. Maybe we would go to a pub or a restaurant, to the cinema, or for a walk along the riverside with an ice-cream...

Simply put, I fell in love, and the depth of emotion I felt intensified every time I saw him.

It took David until our third date to kiss me, and when we kissed it was like I had never been kissed before. Feeling his lips on mine and the tenderness behind his embrace, I sensed he was falling in love too.

After we had been dating several weeks, we were invited over to Jimmy and Yvette's one night for a party, and after a few drinks, I found myself alone in the kitchen with David. We had both refilled our glasses with gin and tonic and then out of nowhere I kissed him, I just couldn't resist, he was so gorgeous that I couldn't do anything else. As my lips touched his, I felt passion fill my body and my entire being was aroused.

I knew that if kissing him made me feel so good, then sex was about to transcend to something I had never known before. So, being the horny little minx that I was that night, I suggested to him that we should go back to his house and spend the night alone rather than staying at Jimmy's party.

I had yet to visit his place and the timing seemed right to me, so I raised my eyebrows and gave him a cheeky smile. However, to my surprise, David pulled back and replied, 'No, Ana, not like this.'

I hadn't thought for a minute that he'd reject me, and my face must have fallen, because he looked deep into my eyes with a reassuring gaze and said, 'It's not that I don't want to. I'd obviously love to take you home with me—what man wouldn't? But I think we should wait and do things properly. I really like you, Ana.'

I probably shouldn't have said what I said next— there would have been so many fitting things I could have said in response—but in my initially confused state I replied rather flatly, 'I'm not a virgin, you know.'

Thankfully, he laughed and replied, 'Neither am I, and that's not what I was implying. It's just that I don't want our relationship to be some fling we rush into. I really like you. In fact, I should probably tell you that I'm falling in love with you, I know I am. And I'm pretty sure you feel the same way?'

I nodded, trying to comprehend that him turning me down was an honourable thing to do. Then he kissed me again and said, 'I mean it, I want to do this the right way, OK?'

I agreed that was fine, and after disappointment had given way to clarity, I realised that he must have really loved me—he loved me so much he wanted to give me the respect he believed I deserved.

When I understood he was treating me like the lady I had the potential to be, I fell in love with him even more.

CHAPTER ELEVEN

As the weeks passed, David and I kept seeing each other—without sleeping together—and I lived in a bubble of euphoria, until one Saturday morning, when at half past nine, there was a knock at the front door. I had got up early that day, so I had already washed and dressed. I'd eaten a bowl of cornflakes and was scrubbing the kitchen floor when we all heard the knock. Mum was washing the breakfast dishes and Dad was in the dining room reading the paper, while the lads drifted around the house, bantering as they did. None of us had anywhere to be, but we were all busy in our own way.

When we heard the knock, we all paused to look at each other in puzzlement, and Mum asked my dad, 'Who's that?' as if he should be able to tell from just the sound alone.

'How the hell should I know?' Dad retorted, giving my mum a glare that told her he thought she lived in cloud-cuckoo-land. Then he told Paddy to make himself useful, and Paddy, of course, did as he was asked.

As Mum chuntered under her breath about how it was a little early for visitors, I continued scrubbing the floor. Then a few seconds later, we all heard Paddy shout, 'Anaaaa! Your boyfriend's here!'

It seemed like an incredibly bizarre time for David to come calling as I had only seen him the night before, so I genuinely had no idea why he was there.

I jumped up and dashed to the door, aware that Mum had immediately started giving Dad the third degree, saying, 'Boyfriend? What boyfriend? Did *you* know she's got a boyfriend?' But I was out the room and at the door before I heard Dad's reply.

Despite having been dating David for several months, Mum had always been out when he'd picked me up, and I had never brought him up in conversation with her. We never chatted together, and I didn't care for her constant negativity, so I hadn't told her—and it quickly became obvious that Dad hadn't either.

Anyway, sure enough, there was David standing on our doorstep, wearing a suit (of all things!), and holding a bunch of flowers in his hand. I tucked my hair behind my ears, pulled my frock straight and, with an embarrassed smile, I asked him what he was doing.

'I'd like to talk to your parents, please, if that's alright? I'm sorry to come knocking so early, but I wanted to try and catch them before your mum goes out.'

At that moment, Mum burst into the front room ready for a bit of drama, and when David saw her, he asked if he could please come in, so I stood back to allow him through. Before Mum could say a word, he walked up to her, gave her the flowers, and told her, 'It's lovely to finally meet you, Mrs O'Connor.'

Now, I think my mum was dumbstruck to see a tall, good-looking man in our front room, wearing his best suit and proffering flowers at half past nine on a Saturday morning. I know for sure, like me, she'd have wished she'd put on her make-up earlier that morning—I felt a bit awkward for her, knowing she would have been inwardly cringing at how she looked, with her apron over her dress and a headscarf covering her hair.

Mum looked stunned, so David took the lead in the conversation by saying, 'I'm sorry to interrupt your morning, but I have a very important question to ask you and your husband, if you can spare me a little time?'

I had never seen my mum stuck for words before, but David's charm and insanely good looks seemed to make her revert to the lady who put on a posh accent. Realising she must play the role of the hostess, she then clicked into character and invited David to sit down, thrust the flowers at me and instructed, 'Ana, go and fetch your dad, make a pot of tea, and get these beautiful flowers in some water.'

I asked no questions aloud, but I looked to David to ask with my eyes what was going on, and I remember him holding my gaze momentarily—I couldn't help but smile. Doing as my mum had invited, David sat down on the armchair by the window, and he told my mum what a nice house she had, as she perched herself down on the settee, her legs crossed at her heels, her hands in her lap, and suddenly on her best behaviour.

It turned out that I didn't have to go and fetch my dad, as before I got to the door, it opened in my face and Dad joined the party. I watched as he took in the scene, and David launched into action once again, getting up from his seat while apologising for the disturbance and shaking Dad's hand.

Knowing Mum expected the tea made promptly, I nipped out to put the kettle on, trying my utmost to hear the polite chit-chat they made while I was out the room. I heard Dad ask David whereabouts he lived, then Mum asked what he did for a living. And the whole time, Paddy and Finn stood in the dining room, watching the bizarre visit unfold through the crack in the doorway, while occasionally looking back at me to make eyes and poke fun.

Once I had prepared a tray with a teapot, cups and saucers, milk, and sugar bowl, I was ready, and I returned to the front room shaking with adrenaline. I remained silent (so as not to interrupt the conversation), placed the tray on the coffee table and started to pour the tea while they spoke about David's job.

As I filled the second cup, David concluded his point and then said, 'To come to the reason for my visit this morning, I need to tell you that I've fallen in love with your daughter, and I would like, with your permission, to ask Ana to marry me.'

My goodness, at that moment my heart somersaulted; my whole being jolted, and I poured the tea straight onto the table completely missing the cup. I looked up at him with the teapot still in my hand. I had no idea of what to say, apart from, 'I better fetch a cloth,' and David grinned in response to my clumsiness.

I'm sure he was as nervous as hell, but he maintained his composure beautifully throughout the whole encounter—he was simply lovely on all levels. Anyway, as I'm then mopping up the spilt tea and my parents appeared to be stuck for words, a second unexpected knock came, this time from the back door. Life paused as we collectively wondered who was now arriving to join the moment.

'Jimmy's here!' Paddy called, unbolting the door.

Then we all heard Finn say, 'They're all in there with Ana's boyfriend.'

A second later, the dining room door pushed open and I watched Jimmy (in a bit of a shell-shocked daze really) as he laid eyes upon David, in his suit, drinking tea with our parents.

'Oi, oi! What the bloody hell's going on here?' Jimmy asked with a laugh at the apparent hilarity of the scene.

'David's just come to ask if he can marry our Ana,' Mum replied in a lacklustre voice—and I swear she looked like she had seen a ghost, she was so pale.

Jimmy raised his eyebrows at David and asked, 'Really?' to which David nodded, and I was relieved to see that Jimmy looked absolutely made up by the idea. I was so thankful that my big brother had arrived at exactly the right moment to keep things calm.

'And I hope you said yes?' Jimmy asked, beaming with intrigue as he looked towards our parents.

'We haven't really said anything yet, duck,' Mum confessed, her normal Nottingham accent momentarily resumed. 'David asked for our blessing, then Ana spilt the tea, and then you knocked at the door... and here we are…' She trailed off, then looked at me and quipped, 'Ana, are you going to finish pouring the tea or are you just going to stand there like an ornament?'

I clicked back into motion, muttered something about fetching another cup for Jimmy and walked out of the room, thinking it was the most bizarre and wonderful thing that had ever happened to me.

Once I was back on the other side of the dining room door, I found Finn and Paddy stood grinning, still glued to their vantage point at the crack of the door, and the three of us couldn't help but overhear the conversation naturally start back up in my absence. Walking through to the kitchen, I recall briefly leaning against the worktop, feeling like my heart was beating a little too fast. David had come to ask for my parents' permission, not mine. But with a few deep breaths, I steadied myself and wondered, regardless of my parents' opinion, did I want to marry David?

YES was the answer which filled every inch of me. Yes. Yes. Yes, I did.

No more than a moment later, as life was picking me up and lifting me to the highest high I had ever known, I overheard my dad ask my brother and my apparently soon-to-be-fiancé how they first got to know each other.

And after an initial pause, David replied, 'Jimmy and I met in the Young Offenders Institution.'

I entered the room just in time to see my mum's face drop and her eyes narrow. 'You mean you were locked up together?' she scoffed.

'Well, I wouldn't put it like that, we were only kids, and that was a long time ago now,' David replied. But before he had chance to say another word, Mum cut him dead.

'Oh! Well, that's just bloody lovely, isn't it? That's just what we need, another criminal in the family!'

I finally finished pouring the tea and stood back at the side of the room, leaving my own cup untouched on the table. I watched David try to reassure my mum that he had changed a lot since he was younger, and his offence was simply a mistake he had made when he hadn't known any better.

Jimmy interjected that they shouldn't hold the past against him; he assured them he knew David very well and that he'd definitely give his permission for David to marry me. But Mum saw it differently—she didn't like his past one bit— and she was up and out of her chair, snapping back into Mum mode, yelling, 'You kids bring me nothing but shame and now you want to add another good-for-nothing into the mix! I've heard enough!'

Starting to walk out the room, she bellowed, 'You come around here before we're even ready for the day, asking for Ana's hand in marriage and you're a bloody convict! No! No way! That is my answer to you, young man. Not over my dead body. You can go now, David, thank you very much!'

The room fell silent as Mum slammed the dining room door shut, then David solemnly replied, 'Well, it's a real shame she feels that way. I'll leave you to your morning.'

He headed to leave and as I watched him start to turn the door handle, I knew I couldn't let him go.

'David! Wait!' I called, as my dad and Jimmy looked on. Then, when his eyes met mine, all I felt I needed to say was, 'Yes.'

At that moment, David's forlorn look turned into a grin, and Jimmy cheered with delight as my mum came back in the room and started ranting all over again. It's funny really, because I know she was mouthing off, but her words washed over me like I had Teflon shoulders. And I knew when I looked deep into David's eyes that I desperately wanted to marry him.

I did hear my mum tell me I was no longer welcome in the house if I chose to disobey her, but at that moment all that mattered was that I had the opportunity to be happy with this wonderful man and for us to one day have a beautiful family all of our own. It was at that stage I think we can say I stopped living in fear of my mother and became a woman who could take on the world. All I had to do was look at David and the love I felt for him gave me the courage I had never had before to stand up for myself and address her as an adult.

I believe I was very calm as I told my parents, 'Mum, Dad, I want to marry David, and if that means I'm no longer welcome here, then that's a real pity. But I'll go with him now regardless, rather than stay here shaming you any longer.' I looked to David for reassurance, and he nodded, so I went upstairs to pack a bag, while he went outside to wait for me.

As usual, it didn't take me long to gather up my things, and within a few minutes, I was out of the house and on the back of David's scooter with a rucksack on my back... My Prince Charming had finally come to rescue me.

I can't tell you how fast my heart was beating when I arrived at David's house. It was the first time I had ever been to his place, and I had never imagined that my initial visit would coincide with moving in.

Within the space of ninety minutes, I had got engaged, walked out on my parents, and moved house. My emotions were soaring, yet at the same time I felt stronger than I had ever felt in my life.

My new home was a lot like my parent's house. It was just smaller and at the end of the terrace row, but the street carried an atmosphere that felt very familiar. I imagined most people who lived in the area were struggling to make ends meet, and when I heard yelling coming from a house a little further down the street, I smiled wryly to myself, thinking that somethings didn't seem to change no matter where I lived.

David pushed his scooter down the alleyway, locked it up in his yard, and then opened the back door, standing aside for me to enter first. With a broad smile on his face, he told me, 'Your castle awaits you, m'lady.'

So I replied playfully, in my finest English accent, 'Why, thank you, kind sir.'

Walking in to the kitchen first, I was pleasantly surprised by what I found. The house was simply furnished, but it was tidy—and to say he hadn't been expecting me to visit, there was no sink full of pots or dirty coffee cups lying around. It pleased me to find out my husband-to-be clearly took care of his home.

Taking in my new surroundings, I quickly assessed there was nothing wrong with how the house was kitted out—it was just a little sparse on décor, that was all.

I walked around visualising how much cosier it could feel just by adding a few things here and there. With a couple of rugs, extra cushions, maybe a few ornaments and a shelf of books, the house would soften, and I easily imagined it could become our perfect home.

After David had made us a cup of tea, we sat together in the lounge, on his tired sofa—which I must confess didn't look like it had its cushions plumped very often—and I poured my heart out to David, trying to come to terms with my mum's reaction to our surprise engagement. We talked at length, and no matter how rude I said my mum had been, David assured me that he could understand her point of view.

We drank our tea, side by side. And after our tea was gone, we sat holding our empty cups, as if we weren't quite sure what we were meant to do next.

The atmosphere was incredible to me. We were both clearly in shock from the abrupt fashion our engagement had taken, but it was lovely nonetheless.

When the clock struck 12:30p.m., David suggested we could probably swap tea for a beer, and I thought that sounded like a plan. So, I followed him as he fetched two bottles from the fridge, and we stepped out in to the back yard to have a cigarette, get some fresh air, and settle into our situation.

After a few moments outside, David announced, 'So, babe, I'm thinking that until we're married, I'll sleep on the sofa, and you can take the bedroom.'

Although I thought it unnecessary, I was very flattered, and I admired the gentleman he was proving to be. However, when I considered it was a two-bedroomed house, I asked, 'Hang on, why don't I just sleep in the spare room?'

At that point, I watched David's expression fall as he came face to face with a situation he could no longer avoid. Instead of giving any reply of substance straight away, he simply said, 'OK,' then stubbed his cigarette butt out in a plant pot and told me, 'You better come with me and I'll show you upstairs.'

I followed him dutifully through the house and when we arrived at the top of the stairs, he opened the first door we came to and stood back for me to look inside. My mouth then instantly fell open and my eyes just about popped out of their sockets. The room was filled to the brim with cannabis plants.

Looking at his crop (which appeared to be thriving), I mentally processed his set-up of lamps, cables, and hoses that trailed across the floor.

'Wow… This is quite an operation you've got going here…' I remarked—unsure of anything else I could possibly say.

David apologised profusely for how I was only just finding out, explaining, 'I never knew how to tell you before, but this is a real passion of mine… It's a hobby, I suppose, like gardening? I look after my plants and I really care about them, you know?'

I don't think I said much else, but rather I looked around, studying everything. I guess I was a little surprised by just how attractively healthy his plants looked—their energy was vibrant!

After spending a few moments digesting the revelation, I suggested we go back down to the lounge. Then, once back on the sofa, David reassured me he really did work full time as a labourer and explained that growing weed was just an interest of his… which had ended up earning him more money than his real job.

Suddenly the penny dropped as I realised how David could afford to treat me the way he did, paying for everything all the time; it all made sense. I considered for maybe all of ten seconds if I was willing to accept that the love of my life grew dope in his back bedroom, and I quickly decided that I was. Life without David was unimaginable, and at the end of the day, I liked to smoke the stuff myself.

As we came to the natural end of that topic, David took my hands and looked deeply into my eyes. I think he was searching for answers to the questions he had racing around his brain, and when he found what he was looking for, he dropped down on one knee in front of me. To my amazement, he pulled a ring box out of his pocket, opened it to reveal a very pretty, diamond solitaire ring and asked, 'Anastasia O'Connor, please will you marry me and make me the happiest man alive?'

I grinned, feeling a lot like crying at the prospect of getting to keep him forever, and obviously I said yes.

It was the happiest moment I had ever known when he slid that ring onto my finger and told me, 'This doesn't stop here, you know. I want the whole shebang with you, Ana: kids, a dog, even a cat maybe… everything.'

And that's when I did cry, as the idea of having a family as well as a marriage was everything my heart had ever yearned for—a proper family who would love and cherish each other exactly the way a family should.

Desperately wanting to share the same bed, but holding to our promise to wait, we got married very quickly; just five weeks after I had moved in. We had a simple ceremony at the local registry office, with Yvette and Louisa as my bridesmaids, Jimmy as best man, and David's parents witnessed the marriage for us on our certificate. Afterwards, we hosted a party at the local pub, and aside from my parents and younger brothers being absent (which left a gaping hole in the event), it was the most wonderful day I could have imagined.

I had bought my dress—nothing fancy, not like a real wedding dress or anything, but just a smart cream dress from a department store in town—and that was all David would entertain me paying for. I had had very little money when I had lived with my parents but after

I moved out I quickly found I had a lot more disposable cash. However, David insisted he would pay for the wedding and that it wasn't even up for debate.

He said if I bought myself a nice dress to wear on the day, he would sort out the rest. And he did, bless him. He bought the wedding rings, the cake, the flowers, paid the registry office fees, and even ordered the first round of drinks and a tray of sandwiches at the reception.

That night, my first night as Anastasia Philips, we went home and David picked me up as if I were made of feathers to carry me across the threshold. Shutting the door behind us, he carried me upstairs to the bedroom where I made love to someone for the very first time. That night, I discovered the gift of the orgasm that Mother Nature gave us all and I delighted in it.

I discovered that when two people are in love and they share their bodies, sexual intercourse is beautiful. It felt absurd to me that previous generations could have allowed sexual pleasure to be viewed as immoral, as there was nothing sinful about what we did together, no matter how we did it. Our love was so deep it made me feel high. I was high on David, and I was finally high on life.

CHAPTER TWELVE

The next year passed quickly. We continued to live at David's place, and with some loving attention the house quickly became a lovely home. I made new curtains and cushion covers, and over time, I bought rugs, books, and trinkets to place on our shelves. Our house was easily transformed into a cosy, little love nest—which just happened to have a copious amount of cannabis growing upstairs.

We both worked hard at our full time jobs, leaving home by 8a.m. each morning and returning by 6p.m. to spend our evenings together. And we would begin and end our days by making love. David always wanted to make love in the mornings—he said it was the best way to start a day, and I have to say that I agreed. Feeling his body intertwined with mine was the perfect way to greet a new dawn. I would then make my journey into work sat on the bus each morning, feeling pleasantly sore between my legs—a gentle physical reminder of how in love we were.

We were both eager to start a family, so we never used contraception. And every month, I would wait for my period with bated breath, regularly counting the days since I had last circled the date in my pocket diary. But as the months went by, I failed to fall pregnant, so I just tried to accept that (like many people) it might take a while to conceive, and I tried to push any worries over my fertility to the back of my mind.

In turn, we passed our weeks and months pleasantly, living in a state of newly-wed love, and when the weekends arrived, we partied. Friends would come over to our house, or we'd meet them down the pub. And everyone we knew bought their marijuana off us.

David was a real connoisseur of cannabis, growing it like an avid gardener might tend to their allotment—diligently ploughing his energy into caring for his plants. He had read book after book on cultivation, and the various strains he produced were all of high calibre—the result of his painstaking research and desire to grow the best crops he possibly could.

In the evenings, David might leave the house for an hour or so, to deal to his acquaintances, and (with nothing better to do with my time) I would often go with him on the back of the scooter.

However, it was during these trips I came to see a weakness in my husband for the first time. When I watched him, I saw that he was rather clumsy when he met people in what were meant to be discreet locations—and I thought he looked far too obvious in every deal I saw him make. His talent was in growing, but in selling he clearly let himself down. If anyone drove or walked past us when he was dealing, his anxiety would cause him to freeze up, and it would be a real giveaway that he was up to something.

After watching David deal on several occasions, I decided he should let me take the lead in the physical exchange. I knew I could swap pot for money with a lot more finesse than he did—I considered it a better option than my husband needlessly getting unwanted attention and ending up back inside. So, I would tell him to wait with the scooter while I nipped into a park or walked down an alley at the side of a shop to meet whoever was buying.

I got a routine going, where my customers would pass me their money via a handshake, we would talk for a moment about what they were getting, and then I would hug them as if saying goodbye, sliding the weed into their pocket or hand, and that would be it. I would trot back to David, happy that no one would have suspected a thing if they had happened to see. And we made a fair amount of money that way.

We were by no means financially wealthy, but we were comfortable. I could afford a new dress if I wanted one, we ate out at restaurants, went to the cinema, concerts, and even occasionally saw plays at the theatre.

We partied frequently with Jimmy and Yvette, and we knew a lot of people who took all kinds of recreational drugs. Some took LSD, most sniffed coke, and we all smoked a lot of weed. You got high however you wanted to, but not in a dirty-drug-den kind of way—we all held down full-time jobs and functioned well at work, but at the weekend we let ourselves go.

David and I were happy with our lot, but with every month that passed and every one of my periods that arrived without fail, I began to lose hope that we were going to be able to make a baby. We were young and healthy (aside from all the drugs), we made love every day, and I felt sure I should have fallen pregnant—I suspected David thought that too.

After eighteen months of marriage, my health played on my mind constantly—although it was a subject neither of us really wanted to acknowledge, it was much nicer to go on believing that I might be pregnant this time next month than to discuss other possible realities. When the subject of having a baby did come up in conversation, I found it too difficult to say my concerns aloud (it would have made them too real) and I would change the subject quickly, forever side-stepping the topic with David, while it niggled away at me every single day.

Our relationship started becoming slightly strained through my inability to talk about the fear that possessed me. So, deciding it was time to face the music, I booked an appointment with my doctor. I didn't ask David to come with me; he had to go to work anyway, but talking about my fertility was something I wanted to do in private. It was something I felt I needed to cope with by myself. I was so scared that my abortion at fourteen had damaged my reproductive organs, I wanted to ask the doctor my questions honestly, without feeling ashamed in front of David that my past had ruined everything for our future.

Many months went by, during which I underwent a multitude of tests. I was put on a fertility treatment, then, after we had been married for just over two years, there came a month when my period went three days late. Filled with adrenaline, I went to the chemist to buy a pregnancy test after work, thinking I'would use it the next morning if my period still hadn't arrived.

My God, I can't tell you how nervous I was when I went to bed that night! I was so scared of the potential disappointment, I found I couldn't even tell David what I was contemplating.

The next day, I woke up and still hadn't got my period, so I did the test. My heart pounding violently, I stood at the sink in our bathroom, watching that little, plastic stick—I could barely bring myself to breathe, let alone think. Then, as the seconds passed, the two thin, blue lines my heart yearned for started to appear.

I shouted out for David from the bathroom, and then I ran into the bedroom where he sat on the edge of the bed rubbing his eyes and wondering what the hell was going off. When I showed him the test, he grinned with amazement and tears quickly started running down my cheeks.

'Really?' he asked, looking wide-eyed from the stick to my face, 'A baby?'

'Yes,' I nodded. Then David pulled me down onto our bed, encompassing me in the biggest hug I had ever known. He was wearing pyjama bottoms without a top, and I happily snuggled into the warmth of his chest, running my fingers lightly over his skin. Looking into his eyes, I asked, 'Darling, are you happy?'

And he laughed, grinning at me as he replied, 'Can't you tell?! Of course, I'm happy. I'm over the moon!'

I lay there feeling the most wonderful combination of shock and euphoria, and we let the minutes roll past until David's kisses stole my attention and we made love, gazing at each other, wearing really big, daft smiles. The embryo that had nestled into my womb completed us. Any elements of our relationship that had become strained vanished instantly—we suddenly had everything we had ever wanted.

David promised me that when the time came he would sell off all his growing gear, and we'd turn the back bedroom into a nursery. He pondered if he might do another crop of cannabis or two to help to pay for all the things a baby would need, and then he'd stop. And I knew when he said that, our baby would be our saving grace. With parental responsibility, we would be able to settle down, stop all the partying which we had used to escape our fears, and we could be happy living a normal life.

I stopped using drugs the second I found out I was pregnant (it went without question that I wouldn't have dreamt of polluting my baby's home), while David refused anything stronger than cannabis, which didn't concern me.

He would normally have a joint when he got home from work in the evenings, stood outside in the backyard so as to keep the house smoke-free. But I would always stand at the back door and natter to him from just inside the kitchen, always reluctant to pause our conversation just because he was going outside.

We dropped out of the party scene completely— although, I did regularly tell David I didn't mind him going out without me, he said he didn't want to and that he had everything he needed just being with me.

When we were sat on our sofa together, he would often lift up my top and unbutton my jeans (which rapidly started to become a little snug) and he would kiss my stomach, talking to our baby which lay beneath my skin. He'd say he would be the best dad in the world, and that the child would have more love in their life than anyone had ever known before.

We dreamt up names, making up hysterical suggestions that would have us crying with laughter, enjoying every second of it. We were back on track and (aside from the part-time drug dealing) we were a very happy, ordinary couple in our twenties.

I went three months before I miscarried.

That morning, I woke up with what felt like intense period pain and my whole being froze as I realised the sheet I was lying on felt wet. When I jumped out of bed, my life disintegrated in front of my eyes as I saw a pool of blood where I had lain. I screamed a horrible, heartbroken scream and shook uncontrollably as David got me dressed, called a taxi, and rushed us to the hospital, him holding me like a fragile china doll in the back of the cab. I was numb, and there were no words I wanted to say.

I was seen to immediately and when the doctor spoke to us, his clipboard in one hand and his reading glasses in the other, he confirmed what we both already knew.

The time after we lost our baby was incredibly hard. I managed to keep breathing all day long and that was as much as I could hope for. I was devastated—we were devastated—yet as hard as losing our baby was to comprehend, I knew the road didn't end there. I would need more tests to establish if having a baby was ever going to be an option for us.

A few weeks after the miscarriage, I had an appointment with the specialist at the same hospital where I'd had the abortion all those years before, and after another round of tests and examinations, I was told the odds were stacked against me being able to conceive again. They said even if I did, it was very unlikely I would be able to carry a baby to full term.

Boy did we spin out after that news. I became a real wild-child. I felt our marriage slipping away from us as I knew I could never give David what he really wanted— what we both wanted in life. We didn't really speak much during the weeks that followed. We were together in body but distanced in mind, and gradually I found it hard to look at David without recollecting how he had proposed to me on one knee and told me he wanted us to have the 'whole shebang' together.

I felt incomplete; like I had a huge gaping hole in my core that I would never be able to fill. And knowing there was nothing wrong with David's fertility just made things worse. Our future, or rather the lack of the one we wanted, was entirely my fault.

We disagreed frequently and would end up arguing over trivialities, taking opportunities to let off steam at each other. I genuinely believed that I could feel David starting to let go, starting to distance himself from me— or maybe I was the one forcing the distance between us. I honestly don't know, but I felt I was losing my mind and best friend at the same time.

We would be at home chilling together in the evenings and David would look at me; I didn't need him to speak to know what he was thinking. I had no desire to hear the words come out of his mouth, and I wouldn't let them come out of mine. I didn't want to hear that our relationship might come to an end; it all hurt too much.

I felt I was watching our relationship fade, and it was far too painful to process. My head told me to let David leave to find happiness with someone else, but my heart could never really consider that an option—I was still head over heels in love with him.

While David was compassionate and put up a pretence that everything would be alright, the distance between us grew. Instead of stopping the drug scene, we fell deeper into it, using all the drugs we could to try to forget our problem, or at least cover it up for another night. My work suffered as the result of too many come-downs and hangovers. And those journeys into work on the bus turned into a half hour of inner turmoil each day, where I was alone with my thoughts and had nothing to distract me.

David started sleeping on the sofa, not in any dramatic way, but in the way that I would go to bed before him at night and he'd stay up late, fall asleep watching TV and never follow me up. I would then come downstairs in the morning, rouse him for work with a kiss, and ask if he'd like a cup of tea. We didn't stop kissing during that time; it's just our kisses weren't at all passionate, they were never leading anywhere. We seemed to have no desire to merge our bodies beyond our mouths.

We said 'I love you' every day, and I knew he meant it, and I honestly loved him desperately. I just felt like fate had totally screwed us over, and the mental effort it took to try to comprehend why this had happened drained me to exhaustion. My energy level was so low at that point, just getting out of bed was hard.

We were still in love but I came to strongly doubt whether that was enough to keep us together, and there were many times during those days when I cried—although never in front of David. Instead of openly sharing how I was feeling, I bottled it up inside me, and only released my emotions into my pillow when I would go to bed alone at night.

At the weekends, we would fill the house with people, trying to get a buzz off their energy. And with all the alcohol and drugs we took, sure, some nights were fun, but after our friends left, the sticking plaster covering our wound disappeared.

Six months or so after the miscarriage, there was one Friday evening when we had a bunch of particularly comical folks round for a few drinks, and an impromptu gathering turned into a really fun party. David and I were both in good moods (well, as good as they got back then) after pleasant days at work, and when we were asked if we wanted to go in on some cocaine, we happily agreed.

I guess you could say we were letting our hair down for the night, and the hours flew by with someone making lines every half an hour or so. There was banter and laughter flowing around the house, while empty beer bottles gradually accumulated in the kitchen.

David and I hadn't spoken to each other much that evening—not in an adverse way, it was just that I had been nattering with the girls in the kitchen while the blokes had congregated in the lounge—but we did all mingle and I was certain that everyone was having fun.

You can imagine my surprise when, at midnight, just as I thought the party was in full swing, our visitors announced they were all leaving to go and meet some other friends, and for some reason they didn't invite us to go with them. It seemed really bizarre timing, but sure enough they all started getting their coats on and thanking us for having them over. A few minutes later, we closed the door behind them.

With music still playing on our stereo, we found ourselves suddenly alone. But the atmosphere was nice between us and neither of us had any desire to go to bed at 12 a.m.—we were *wide* awake.

So, I'm pleased to report that we stayed up all night, properly talking for what felt like the first time in ages, and I revelled in my husband's company. It was wonderful. After a while, we stopped drinking alcohol and started drinking tea, our conversation flowing easily and rapidly, it seemed we were suddenly once again back on each other's wave length.

Around 6 a.m., when the new day was starting to break behind our drawn curtains, I watched David as he inhaled on his cigarette and blew a fresh cloud of smoke into the room. It seemed as if he was deeply considering something, so I asked, 'Darling, what's going through your mind?'

He then turned his head to look into my eyes and replied, 'We really need to get out of here you know, babe. We need to get out of Nottingham.'

I remember looking at him as if a bolt of lightning had struck the room, and the energy of the suggestion washed over us like a new era had just been born.

Oh my God, did I love that idea!

You know I had often tried to run away from my problems in the past, but leaving Nottingham didn't feel like I would be running away from a bad situation at that time—rather it felt like we had found a new door that could be pushed open in the matrix of destiny, offering us a fresh start and a new adventure.

Inspired energy surged within me, and honestly, it was the first taste of real happiness that I'd felt in a long time. I deduced that if David wanted to leave Nottingham with me, it meant that he wanted to stay with me, in our marriage, and to try to find a way to make it work. And that's exactly what I wanted.

As daylight grew outside, David continued his theory, saying how he thought a complete change of scenery would do us a good—we could just leave and see where fate took us. He said that if we stayed in the house in Sneinton, he would constantly be reminded of the cot that he was never going to build in the back bedroom and said that it was simply too hard to bear.

I remember welling up, not wanting to cry and spoil the conversation with tears, but it was a very emotional situation. Despite the inner sadness that still dwelled within us, I felt we were finally finding a way to get back on track; our conversation was sparked with new-found positivity, and it was such a welcome change.

I told David I would go anywhere with him. I was all over the idea, and when we finally came down from all the cocaine we had taken that Friday night, we went to bed and made love until it was Saturday afternoon.

During the days that followed, all I talked about was where we could go or what we could do. I pointed out that we would need to give notice on the house and at work (which we had both still managed to hold down despite the roller coaster of life), but the options seemed endless. We could go anywhere; we could hitchhike across the continent, or move to London? Paris? Ireland? This is how I spoke to David in the evenings as we mulled many ideas over.

I would nip into travel agencies during my lunch break and come home laden with as many glossy brochures as I could carry. We could get a flight to a Spanish island, or a ferry across to Holland or France; we could try southern Italy or the Black Forest—I was full of ideas and I would have given any of them a go in a flash if David had bitten.

Then, one evening a couple of weeks after our epiphany, we were at home having a coffee in the kitchen after dinner, and there was a good, positive energy between us. We'd shared nice food, we'd done the pots, and cleared up together, and all the while we'd been chatting and really vibing off the possibilities that could lie ahead.

So, there we were, sitting on the worktops, chatting and sipping our coffee, when David told me of a commune he had heard about that was setting up near Norfolk (about a hundred miles east of us and a little south). He said that one of his workmates had told him about the place, thirty-odd miles from the coast, where 'some eccentric dude' in his fifties was letting people live in his run-down stately home. Apparently, it was a fairly hippy scene, and if you sought freedom and could pay your own way, you were welcome. It only took David a couple of minutes to tell me all the details he knew, and then he paused to roll a cigarette and asked me (with a distinct sparkle in his eye) what I thought.

'It sounds interesting,' I replied, and I meant it. I had never contemplated life in a commune before, but the idea definitely grabbed my attention. There were said to be people sleeping in tents and building their own dwellings on this bloke's private land, and there was a community market where the residents exchanged the things they made or grew—all done in the name of Peace and Love. David said they had the ambition of creating a free community that made its own laws and lived outside the rule of the government. And when I thought about it, the idea of dipping out of normal society did sound appealing.

There was nothing about continuing life in Nottingham with our humdrum jobs set against the mundane, urban city backdrop that inspired me. Without a baby, all we did was run the rat race and pass time at the weekends. Life had seemed so unfulfilling.

We discussed how the idea of the commune resonated, and at one point, when I went all tingly with goose-bumps and the thrill of the adrenaline that was building between us, I suggested it was time to give notice on the house and at our jobs and just go.

David cautioned me that it would be a long drive on the back of the scooter, but said that he was game, if I was. So, as fate weaves its magic throughout life, that evening, all our talks of 'what if?' turned into 'why the hell not?' And we started making plans for the next chapter of our lives. We would leave Nottingham and head to Norfolk.

CHAPTER THIRTEEN

By the end of the month, all our loose ends were tied up, and we set off to Norfolk with a case full of belongings strapped to the back of the scooter. I was so full of excitement for the adventure that lay ahead, it's hard to describe that feeling with words. But I guess that it was hope that fuelled my excitement—hope that David and I could find a way to enjoy married life together, without needing children to fulfil us long-term.

We stopped at a roadside café for a cup of tea to break up the journey; we ate lunch at a service station, and we drove across miles and miles of narrow country lanes, winding our way across the flat landscape. By late afternoon, we finally saw a large, stone wall surrounding the area we were looking for; majestic trees towering above and masking the stately home which lay beyond.

Slowing down the scooter, we pulled up outside a set of weathered, wrought iron gates and saw a long, sandy driveway meandering through a thick forest, while an impressive, white house was only just visible a few hundred yards ahead. Finding the gate unlocked, we walked through and read a large, wooden sign nailed between two posts at the side of the path. Ban-the-bomb signs, flowers, and intricate artwork surrounded its message:

WELCOME TO ARCADIA
The common laws we uphold here are:
No weapons. No violence.
No cars. No stealing.
If you are willing to abide by these community rules,
please continue your journey.

After a moment admiring their sentiment, David looked at me with a cheeky smile and asked, 'Do you think you can stick to those rules, babe?'

'Oh, I should think so!' I replied with a laugh.

After we had closed the gate behind us, we parked the scooter, and started our walk up the drive. Hand in hand, we were completely spellbound by our surroundings. The atmosphere of Arcadia felt magical from the second we arrived. There was an energy about the forest that shone, and in the late afternoon, with the warm sunshine sparkling through the leaves, it was stunningly beautiful.

Nestled amongst the trees, we saw campervans, dozens of tents, and many small cabins dotted around with several more being constructed. Only parts of the land were cultivated and the rest was left to nature to design, so wildlife grew abundantly; every dwelling seeming as if it had been erected in perfect harmony with the nature around it.

I was soon to learn that this is the very meaning of the word Arcadia: the state where humanity exists in perfect balance with the Earth.

There were people milling around dressed in a distinctly bohemian fashion. The women mainly wore long skirts or jeans, a few had scarves tied around their hair, and all the men had beards—as if they had collectively decided shaving was a waste of time.

We walked towards the main house without anyone asking us what we were doing. We got several smiles, a few pleasant hellos, but other than that, no one paid us the slightest bit of attention—everyone was consumed with their own tasks. I would describe that walk as feeling similar to when you've just arrived at a campsite and you're surrounded by other holidaymakers. The buzz of the place was just delightful.

There were acres to the estate and so much to take in. The outbuildings that had once been servants' quarters and stables had been transformed into functioning community services, and there was the most awesome treehouse built high up in the branches of three beautiful oak trees—it was astounding.

So intrigued by it all, we strayed from the path and wandered across the grass to pass directly underneath the treehouse. I looked up to see the coolest, most chilled-out scene I had ever laid eyes on. There were two levels of decking, hammocks stretched between the branches, and people were relaxing in what I can only describe as an outdoor lounge, constructed so high, it lay where normally only the birds would get to rest. There was a rope ladder hanging down one of the trunks, and the living space above was decorated with wind-chimes and all kinds of eclectic knick-knacks.

I kid you not when I say *everyone* up there looked happy. We could hear someone playing the guitar, others were laughing, and even the birds were singing at the same time—it was so peacefully refreshing—I felt a million miles away from Nottingham.

After wandering across the grounds for another two hundred yards, we arrived at the ivy-covered manor house (its rendering clearly having been dropping off for years) and we entered the building, not really knowing who we should try to speak to. But oh my goodness, what we saw inside blew our minds! There was a large, sweeping staircase which landed directly in front of us in the hallway and marble floor tiles under our feet. All the walls had been spray-painted with the most incredible artwork: scenes of large trees, rainbows, stars, fairies, and toadstools took my breath away.

The rooms were alive with the Arcadian community; people dotted around, all seeming totally at ease with life. It was extraordinary, like walking into the most wonderful nightclub you could ever imagine. I soon learned that was the mentality there twenty-four hours a day.

Having asked a passer-by who we should talk with about becoming residents, we were told we would need to find Alfred, who owned the land, and were pointed in the direction of the drawing room, where he had last been seen. Carrying on in our adventure, we ambled through the corridors, admiring the art that covered the walls, until we arrived in the most amazing room I had ever set foot in.

There was no real furniture of substance in the drawing room; the space was instead filled with groups of people who sat barefoot on the floor, scattered amongst blankets, cushions and rugs—everything looked invitingly comfortable. Old, floor-to-ceiling drapes hung at the windows, tied back with tired, golden-thread ropes, and candelabras lit up with multi-coloured candles were dotted around the room. The air smelled of both joss sticks and marijuana; while a shisha pipe (amongst other things) was being passed around.

Soon enough, we found Alfred and introduced ourselves, and from the second I saw him, I decided he had a kind face. There was something about his wildly unruly, grey eyebrows and bright white, curly hair that made me warm to him instantly.

After we had said hello and shaken hands, I couldn't help but compliment him on his flamboyantly patterned shirt, and we were invited to sit down. Taking off our shoes, we got comfortable, and soon the time of day became irrelevant as we learned the history of the Arcadia Freetown.

It was Alfred himself who told us how the estate had been passed down to him through his family trust, and how he had gone bankrupt after years of struggling to keep up with the maintenance of the property. He said the bailiffs had taken all of his personal possessions to recover his debts, and he had been left with the shell of the building, land, and a desire for a different way of life that wasn't controlled by money. We talked at length about his political views and whenever he used the word Freedom, I felt shivers running through me, as if I was momentarily vibrating at a higher level in response to his big-picture thinking.

Alfred told us how he believed land should be free to occupy and said he didn't believe in mortgages and having to work your whole life to pay off the roof above your head. He explained how he had felt his large, family home was being wasted as it sat occupied by only one person, but that his bankruptcy had led to his enlightenment and spiritual growth. He now understood the true game that money is: realising that money itself is worthless and only human effort has value.

With nothing but land to his name, he knew his life mission was to create Arcadia in his own back garden. So, he had spread the word by all means he could, opening up his home, and allowing a society based on individual contributions to consciously evolve.

He spoke as a revolutionary, telling us he didn't believe we should serve the government if they no longer served us; that we should all be free to live and contribute to society however we wanted—without economic policies which favour the rich and impose poverty on the poor. He talked of how he saw an oppression that was stretched out all across the western world, and he wanted better for our country's future.

Over time, Alfred really helped me to develop my views on the fundamental flaws in the world's economic system; encouraging me to reflect deeply upon alternative ways in which societies could operate to better promote equality and become more enlightened.

While the conversation was incredibly profound, I have to stress that I had never met anyone as welcoming as Alfred. His manner was friendly and approachable, his energy magnetic, and his being so very animated as he actively engaged the minds of all around him.

A few warm beers later, Alfred reminded us of the common laws they lived by and told us if they resonated, we could stay in one of the dormitories upstairs until we found a more private area that we liked. He told us that we would pay board weekly to contribute to the running of the community, and we would need to find a way to make our own income as this was a community to contribute to, not sponge off.

Having sold off a crop of marijuana before we had left Nottingham, we'd arrived with enough money to set ourselves up in communal life without stress, and from that moment on, we slotted very naturally into Arcadia.

Surrounded by the most creative people I'd ever met, we spent our time effortlessly mingling and made a lot of friends very quickly. One of the things I loved best about that place, was how everyone was so productively busy with purpose to their days. While a chilled vibe rippled through every atom in the air, there was a hustle and bustle about daily life that inspired me. It was wonderful.

There was a daily market held in the old courtyard, where residents could sell things they had grown or made; a health centre was running out of the old servants' quarters, where you could take a shower and get basic sanitary products. 'The Rainbow Bakery' operated out of an old workshop; a cannabis factory was sited in the old stables, and dozens of allotments were dotted around the grounds. In the manor house there was a communal kitchen, a large dining area, the drawing room, the dormitories, and even a laboratory on the second floor where they made their own LSD tabs. It was a very comprehensive and organised set-up, and we spent several months living in a dormitory, where sheets were pegged between the walls on washing lines—an attempt to offer each mattress a little privacy.

With David's affinity for weed and a passion to grow seeds he had brought with him, he was welcomed into stable life with open arms. And whilst David was at one with nature and entranced by his work, I started looking for something I could do myself.

I wanted to get creative and do something independently. So I pursued an idea I had to make 'Happy' cakes, and I asked the baker, Anthony, if there was any chance I could use his ovens.

Well, Anthony turned out to be completely charming and welcomed my suggestion—he even offered to source my ingredients for me, if I gave him a list and the money. I was delighted! I quickly started making all kinds of cakes and treats on a daily basis. I would bake during the day, then, in the early evening I'd take up a stall at the market and sell what I had made.

From the first batch, my cakes sold out. I made carrot cakes, cookies, and coffee cakes—but nothing sold better than my chocolate fudge-cake. The depth of the chocolate complimented the sweet, almost floral flavour of the cannabis like a dream combination; the cake was rich and moist; the icing gooey—I can still recall the taste now. Living in Arcadia was definitely the period in my life when my culinary skills hit their peak.

After work, we would relax in one of the many amazing venues on offer and we would often get high. There seemed to be so much to life that I needed to figure out. I had big questions in my mind that I assume everyone contemplates at some stage. Why am I here? What purpose do I have? Are we just balls of meaningless energy, created by accident, floating around in space, or is there a higher meaning? At the same time, I struggled to comprehend what I was meant to do with my life if I couldn't have children.

Whilst the scenery surrounding me was incredibly peaceful, inside my head I was far from calm. I had endless questions, no answers of any substance, and a deep-rooted desire to understand Life.

It was at this stage in my life, I got into reading tarot cards—I had always been interested in Spirituality and the mystical side of life, but I had never had an opportunity to really get to grips with it or study it until living in Arcadia. My Tarot teacher arrived in the form of a young lady named Rose, who was about my age, and her husband, Harry, worked in the stables with David. They had been living in the dormitory too (while they were constructing their own cabin), and we got on incredibly well—Rose was such a giggler!

Several months into our stay in Arcadia, there came one night when I was chilling with Rose in the treehouse having a lovely, girly natter, and she mentioned she had a deck of tarot cards in her handbag. She told me, 'You know, I find the cards absolutely incredible. I draw one card from the pack for myself most days—just for daily guidance—and the cards I draw never cease to amaze me. They're just too spot on to be anything other than spiritual messages.' She asked me, 'Have you ever had a Tarot reading before, Ana?'

I shook my head, 'No, never. But it does interest me. Would you do one for me?'

Rose grinned as she replied, 'Absolutely! It would be my pleasure.'

Placing the cards on the table between us, she lit a candle, and then gave me the cards to shuffle while she said a prayer to the Universe. She asked that we meditate silently for a few moments, so I sat cross-legged on a cushion, utterly captivated, awaiting her next move. After several minutes, Rose calmly guided me in focusing my energy on the cards whilst contemplating my life. Then, when the time felt right, I cut the pack, and Rose dealt out ten cards in the formation she said was a Celtic Cross. As each card was turned over, I shivered with resonance—just the images alone triggered a heart-felt response deep within me.

I had drawn cards which showed Lovers, Death, and cards of the Wands suit (which I learned symbolise creativity, but also impulsiveness, a lack of direction, or feeling meaningless) were abundant before me.

Whilst Rose and I had become close during those early weeks, she knew nothing of my marital problems. I had no desire to discuss those with anyone, so there was no way she could have put any bias on the interpretations she gave—she knew very little about my past. As Rose explained my cards, she spoke of Lovers so infatuated with each other they had cut themselves off from the outside world, and then Death, which she said didn't need to mean actual death but could just be the end of a stage of my life. Her words rang so true. She then spoke about a new sexual energy entering my near future and I didn't really know what to think.

I guess you could say the reading spooked me, but still, I wanted to hear more.

In the evenings that followed, I quizzed Rose frequently about her experiences with the Tarot, and she also gave me a book on Numerology which I read from cover to cover in only a few hours. I found that the more I came to understand these subjects, the larger my appetite grew to learn. So, in turn, doing tarot readings and writing numerology birth charts became a regular feature of my evenings.

In case you aren't familiar with Numerology let me steal a moment here to explain, it's a philosophy of spiritual mathematics which has been studied for centuries. But it was denounced for many generations as a dark art because it didn't align with the church's interpretations of the scriptures. I understand there are several theories of Numerology, but the method I learnt had been determined by Pythagoras, who was as much a spiritual guru as he was a mathematician.

Numerology teaches us that numbers are so much more than just symbols used for counting, and that each number has a vibrational frequency and a certain emotional energy associated with it. According to its theories, human life moves in cycles of nine years, with each year aligning to a number, and because of this, you'll experience a slightly different vibration each year, running in perfect order from one to nine throughout your entire life.

The energy perpetuating your life is destined to change constantly. With every day, month and year that passes, our lives will spiral in cycles, and we'll constantly experience the varying subtle energies evolving and leading us towards fulfilling our life's purpose.

Numerology tells us that the numbers contained in your date of birth and name (as all letters have numeric values) carry significant meaning, and the characteristics of our personal numbers will reflect what kind of person you are and the kind of life you are here to live. When certain formulas are followed, you can uncover the life plan you made for yourself before your birth. The underlying essence being that each of us is a spiritual entity currently living a human experience, and that we've come to Earth to develop our souls—while Life itself is underpinned by mathematical programming.

Studying the book that Rose lent me, I was able to create my own birth chart within one evening, and the interpretations I read were so stunningly accurate, I was blown away. The concept of the afterlife, reincarnation, and birth visions explained through Numerology gave me goosebumps from the outset, and the spiritual connection I developed during that time in Arcadia is still very much present in me today.

I think once your spiritual switch is flicked on, there is never an option to go back; you can't 'un-know' things once you experience them to be true. So, if you've never seen your own birth chart, I suggest you think about looking into this further—I'm sure you wouldn't be bored by its contents.

During my time in Arcadia, I filled notepads with sums creating birth charts. I first studied my own, then I did David's, and after that, I would write a chart for literally anyone who asked—every chart I did fascinated me. It was as if through adding up someone's numbers, you could view them from the inside out, paint a picture of their existence, and maybe even help them to better understand certain elements of their journey.

Life truly amazed me at that time, and I fell in love with life, living in Arcadia as a Free Woman. Having copious amounts of free time to indulge in pursuits that energised my soul was a privilege life had never afforded me before.

There then came a night when David and I were chilling by a bonfire and Rose and Harry asked us a really lovely question. After many weeks of hard labour, they had finished their cabin, and they asked if we would like to move in with them until we had made something for ourselves.

I was amazed by their generosity. I remember looking at David to check we were thinking the same thing, and we quickly accepted their offer. Taken by surprise, we were both beaming with appreciation. Then, just after we had finished gushing gleefully about how we would move in immediately, Rose told us, 'We've built a two-bedroomed cabin as we're trying for a baby, but you're more than welcome to stay until we need to turn the room into a nursery.'

I remember Rose grinning at having shared their exciting news, but when I looked at David, I saw an old, familiar weight had fallen straight back on his shoulders. I think my face dropped, and I adopted a forced smile as words came out my mouth to say how happy I was for them.

The look that appeared on David's face hit me like the lowest emotional blow possible. If a facial expression could physically hurt you, David's would have kicked me in the stomach and left me winded on the floor.

CHAPTER FOURTEEN

We moved in with Rose and Harry the very next day, and before I knew what was happening, David had distanced himself from me once again. We shared our new bedroom in the cabin in the woods and continued to share our bodies with each other most days. However, since Rose had mentioned the word Baby, it was like David had tumbled down from the temporary high that living in Arcadia had given him. Just like that, he had nothing to say to me again—nothing apart from 'I'm fine,' or 'I'm just nipping out,' or 'Don't wait up.'

He did my head in! We were so happy if we were allowed just to be us, living in the Now; if a future without children didn't have to exist.

Every time we kissed, I would give him everything I had to let him know that I still wanted him more than anything. I gave him my body, my heart, my soul. He had all of me: my joy, my pain, my smart mouth, and the ditsy moments when my common sense let me down. I offered him friendship, companionship, a hand to hold, and a shoulder to lean on.

I tried to be everything a good partner should be, and I loved him with every cell that I possessed. But I couldn't give him a child.

I tried to discuss adoption with him a few times, but he would just laugh and look at everything around us and say things like, 'Who's going to give us a baby?' or he would venture, 'It's not the same.' He was playing a game that I couldn't win and it tore me apart.

He started chilling away from the cabin—and me—in the evenings, and when he told me he was going out, I knew there wasn't an invitation there for me to go with him. He would go up to the main house, take LSD or whatever, and he would come home in the mornings on a completely different wavelength to me.

Rose had stopped taking drugs any stronger than weed as she was intent on getting pregnant, so we often spent our evenings chatting at home together, listening to music, or we would go and do tarot readings in the treehouse. I felt very comfortable with her; she had a warm, nurturing disposition, and the way she looked at the world and her spiritual views always fascinated me. So, after a while, I shared my concerns with her of how my life was spiralling downwards and I didn't know how I was ever going to bring it back up.

Unsurprisingly, Rose told me I should speak to David directly, find out exactly what was going on in his head and face the music. She confirmed what I already knew internally—the problem was that I was terrified to hear what David had to say. I didn't want to risk finding out that our marriage might be over.

Then came an evening when Rose and Harry announced they were heading down to the allotments, and suddenly I felt as if the right moment had arrived. When David said he would join them, I stopped him and asked him to stay home with me. Looking briefly into my eyes, he saw that I was serious and soberly agreed. I recall Rose and Harry pausing in the doorway as they sensed something was about to go down; Rose giving me a look that wished me luck before they slipped out the door.

With the cabin to ourselves, David stood in the middle of the room looking as though he was about to drown. It was like his head had disappeared beneath water, and I could tell he had no clue what to do.

I ventured a smile and told him, 'Don't worry, I only want to talk. Why don't we sit and have a beer together?'

He nervously agreed, and we sat down on floor cushions in that simple cabin in the middle of nowhere; the birds singing the evening chorus, whilst reggae music played on a small cassette player in the corner of the room.

We sipped from our bottles and I knew he wouldn't start the conversation, so after a few strained moments had passed, I bit the bullet and asked, 'David, what's going on between us?'

To which he shook his head and replied, 'I'm not sure, babe.'

I told him I knew the baby issue still hung heavily over us and that moving to the commune hadn't solved our problems. I said I knew that he wanted us to have a family of our own and that I wanted one too—but that it wasn't an option for us. Summoning all the courage I could muster, I asked him what he wanted to do.

'I don't know, Ana,' came his reply.

I told him that my love for him wasn't in question, but I was going out of my mind not knowing where I stood with him. I asked him if loving me was enough, whether I could really give him all he needed. But frustratingly as hell, he once again said, 'I don't know.'

Now that's when my temper began to flare. I resented him for not having an answer for me. Suddenly, my tone of voice elevated and I yelled, 'You can't keep treating me like this, David! I need more! I don't need a shell of a broken man as a husband. I need the love we used to share and a relationship that gives me light and hope—not one that makes me feel guilty for a situation I can't change!'

I told him, 'You're punishing me for something I have no control over and I can't live like this! I don't know how long I can hold on, waiting for everything to be OK, when you give me no indication that it ever will be!'

Instead of arguing with me or giving me any of the reassurance that I needed, David simply stood up and told me, 'I'm going out... I need to clear my head.'

I watched in disbelief. Without so much as another word, he crossed the room, walked out the door and let it fall shut behind him.

I didn't get up to call him back. I just sat where I was, listening to the sound of his fading footsteps crunching the leaves as he walked down the pathway, and I cried for our marriage that was nowhere to be seen.

David didn't reappear until the next day—I didn't know where he had slept, and I didn't really care. He wasn't willing to talk, and he had left me with an inescapable feeling of emptiness that he seemed to have no intention of filling.

In the days that followed, my contempt for David (and his lack of any apparent backbone) was soaring.

If it wasn't for the wedding rings we wore, you wouldn't have known we were married. He spent more and more time in the stables, and I started to hang around the bakery a little more than I had done before.

I think I've told you before that Anthony, the baker, was very sweet to me, so when I asked him if I could shadow him in the kitchen to learn more about baking (without needing to make everything 'happy' all the time) he agreed without hesitation and was very willing to teach me anything I asked to learn. We made bread together in the morning and I found kneading dough very therapeutic; it seemed to offer an outlet which released a lot of tension. Despite the anger and resentment that I pushed into that bread, everything we made turned out delicious, and Anthony was a very good teacher.

Spending all our working days together, our minds were on the same wavelength, and when we laughed, it felt rather invigorating. Anthony was a young guy, in his mid-twenties, classically good looking with olive skin, dark eyes, and a gorgeous smile—and if I'm honest with myself, he had flirted with me since the first time we met. I've no doubt that the time I spent with Anthony was no good for my marriage; however, when my marriage was invisible, the attention Anthony paid me did, selfishly, feel good.

After weeks of this kind of carry on, and no positive developments with David, an afternoon came when Anthony asked if I would like to go round to his cabin after work and chill together—he said he had been given a bit of coke and offered to share it with me, if I was so inclined. Despite the ring on my finger, my mouth said yes before my brain was allowed to comment; under the notion that we would just be workmates chilling together after hours, I agreed.

When I arrived home from work that evening, I found David was out, and Rose and Harry were relaxing in the lounge. So, I chirped hello and went immediately to my room to change, wondering how I would explain my outing. Half an hour later, when I told them that I was going out for a stroll and that I might pop up to the treehouse, I knew I was up to no good. But regardless, I walked across the land to Anthony's cabin and was relieved to end my journey with no one around to see me go in.

His studio was in a secluded area, surrounded by wild foliage, and when I knocked on the door, it creaked open. I called, 'Anthony?' poking my head into the room that wasn't much more than a large shed, and there he was. He stood up, and if I hadn't been married I think he would have kissed me immediately. The look he greeted me with was so obviously filled with nerves, I could sense his heartbeat had elevated—and he had the same effect on me.

His room was sparsely furnished, there was just a mattress on wooden slats, a few cushions, a shelf filled with books, and his clothes neatly piled up on a table in the corner. As there was no electricity, candles were lit all around us, illuminating the cabin in the dusky evening, and the ambience was incredibly seductive. I knew from the outset that my self-restraint was set to be tested.

Anthony invited me to take a seat, and with nowhere to sit but the bed, I sat on the end of his mattress with my legs crossed, holding my ankles, my back straight and comfortable. Suddenly, I was flooded with an overwhelming sense of relief to be in a place where I could just be me, even if only for one evening.

I was twenty-four at the time, and having lived through so much heaviness for so many years, it felt liberating to be in a situation where my fertility wasn't an issue. That night I was able to be a version of me who knew how to have fun, and I gradually allowed myself to relax.

As I watched Anthony rack up lines of cocaine on the back of a book, I tried not to let myself think about how devilishly handsome he was and instead told myself just to enjoy the conversation—that nothing sexual had to happen between us just because I was in his cabin, sitting on his bed. A few moments later, he offered the book across to me with a rolled-up note, so I inhaled, and I quickly began to feel an enormous weight lift off my shoulders to be temporarily away from my torment with David. Just for a few hours, I felt free.

The two of us nailed that bag of coke quite quickly. With the magnetic force that seemed to exist between us, the suggestion, 'Shall we have another line?' kept giving us another thirty minutes of relaxed conversation before the dynamic between us might have to change in some way. I know you might think badly of me for how I behaved that evening—trust me, I've spent my fair share of time beating myself up over what I did— but honestly, I think there was a huge part of me that needed to remember what having fun felt like.

I continued pretending to myself that we were just friends hanging out for as long as I could, but as the night wore on, we became more and more tactile with each other. Then, the time came when Anthony looked at me with his deep brown eyes, touched the side of my face, and told me I was beautiful.

I didn't know what to say, so we just looked at each other, our minds blown by the obvious heat between us, until he leant in closer. I stayed still initially, but when I felt his breath on my skin and the slightest touch of his lips on my neck, I tried to push any feelings of guilt to one side, telling myself I spent too much time carrying that burden.

When he kissed me, it felt tender and incredibly sexy. And I know it was wrong under the laws of marriage, but I suppose monogamy only works if you've got a partner who wants to be intimate with you—I didn't have the strength to resist. When he gently pushed me back onto his mattress, I lay down with him, and gradually our hands started to explore each other's bodies; it felt natural to want more. So, guilt aside, I stayed with Anthony all night, and he made me feel passionate, wanted, and temporarily unshackled.

I left his place just after dawn and got back to hear the sounds of lovemaking coming from Rose and Harry's bedroom. David, however, was nowhere to be seen. Our bed looked untouched, and I couldn't have been more relieved to have made it home before he did. Where was he? I didn't really care, but then at the same time I had felt wracked with guilt since the moment I'd stepped out of Anthony's cabin. I was a walking contradiction.

My fling with Anthony carried on for a couple of weeks, until people began to talk and brought the situation to a head. Although I lived in a community where love was meant to be free, I heard two women gossiping that you would think having one good-looking man in my life would be enough. And when I heard this coming from just outside the bakery, said just loud enough for me to hear, I knew we had been rumbled.

I guess we had flirted too much as we'd worked, or maybe I'd been seen going into his cabin at night, I'm not really sure. But the word was out, and it was only a matter of time before David would know.

When I arrived home that evening, David was waiting for me in the living room. He said he had asked Rose and Harry to give us some space and that we needed to talk. I obviously knew what was coming, but what I hadn't expected was the intensity of his anger. Boy, did we argue that night! It was a battle of words and emotions as he accused me of the affair, and I accused him of having left me psychologically a long time ago.

I told him, 'Yes, I've messed up! But what do you expect when you do nothing but push me away and make me feel terrible about life?! Where's our marriage gone, David? Where have you disappeared to? You've become nothing but a ghost of a husband!'

I know calling each other names is no way to solve anything, but we blew the roof on that cabin that night. If our neighbours didn't already know our business, they certainly did by the time we went to sleep, exhausted from the drain and struggle that our relationship had become.

The next morning, I got up for work and left David sleeping in the living room, where he'd been all night. I told Anthony the second I walked through the door that David knew about us, and only moments later,

David marched in and pinned Anthony up against the wall. Holding him by the throat with just one hand, he growled, 'If you ever dare touch my wife again, you'll be a dead man…'

David didn't punch him, he just held him there with his hand firmly around his neck as Anthony stood motionless, not even trying to push him off.

When he let go, Anthony didn't move, and David told me, 'Ana, it's time to leave—you won't be working here anymore.'

I didn't argue. For the first time, I saw David fight for our relationship, and I liked it. Now, you should know that I don't mean that I literally liked his style of throttling Anthony against the wall, but I did like the passion I saw in him, and I really liked that he wasn't willing to let another man come between us.

When David told me that I wasn't to socialise with Anthony if I wanted to stay married, I respected that. We could afford to live on the money David made (as we had very basic needs in Arcadia), and so, we resumed our life together and it seemed that David did want me after all—it was amazing to feel that again. Don't get me wrong, we argued often (and I knew he hadn't forgiven me for the affair), but we seemed to have turned a corner, and it felt like we were finally heading back in the right direction. Every time we argued, we would end up in bed together at the end of the night, having wild and passionate sex that released our many pent-up emotions—it felt like we were finally winning our relationship back.

Two months later, we were still living with Rose and Harry when they discovered Rose had fallen pregnant, and although that was a reminder of the children we couldn't have ourselves, a little of their happiness rubbed off on us. Despite the odd argument when David would throw the subject of Anthony back in my face, we were content, and we were regularly laughing together again, which I took as a very good sign.

Then came a morning when I woke up with a strong acid taste in my mouth that water wouldn't fix, and I suddenly felt exceptionally nauseous. The more I woke up, the sicker I felt. A few seconds later, I jumped out of bed and flew out of the cabin just in time to vomit behind a tree. Crouching over, I held on to that tree for dear life, trying to remember what I had eaten the day before that could have made me feel so bad.

A moment later, David was by my side, rubbing my back and asking if I was OK. But when I stood up, he said I was so pale, I was green and insisted we go to the medic.

Following David's lead, I walked across to an outbuilding where a man called Hamish (who had previously worked as an army doctor) ran a simple medical office equipped with everything he needed to offer an efficient first aid service.

We found Hamish alone and he immediately stood up from his desk to come to my side. He felt my forehead, then asked me to sit on the foldaway bed that was made up at the side of the room. My head was spinning, so Hamish told me to relax, then quietly suggested to David that he leave me with him and come back in half an hour.

When he asked me to lie down, I went horizontal with stars whirling in my eyes. He said to describe my symptoms and to tell him if it was painful anywhere while he pressed my abdomen with his hands.

Thankfully, there was no pain or discomfort, so he said I could sit back up, and I watched as he walked over to a cabinet that stood across the room. Taking a small plastic pot out of a drawer, he told me he'd carry out a pregnancy test if I'd go and collect a urine sample.

His suggestion felt like a waste of time, so I confidently stated that definitely wasn't pregnant, and briefly explained my history. Yet with empathy, Hamish recommended that we do the test regardless, so I did as he asked, then lay back down on the bed to rest while we waited for the result.

Several minutes later, I heard the words, 'Ana, if you would like to sit up now, your test is complete.'

I pulled myself up to sit on the edge of the bed, ready to hear yet another reminder that I was infertile. But instead, Hamish smiled and said, 'Ana, I'm happy to tell you, you're pregnant. Congratulations.'

My goodness, I was speechless. I had absolutely no words to say, all I could do was smile a very nervous smile, as my brain tried to process what this could mean. The world seemed to have flipped on its axis, and I really did struggle to get my mind around the revelation. Sensing my astonishment, Hamish asked if I would like to discuss the pregnancy with David present, and I agreed I would. He then asked when I had last had a period, and I had no idea—it seemed like an age since I'd circled dates in my diary.

When David arrived to pick me up, Hamish asked him to take a seat and proceeded to announce my news whilst I sat silently consumed by shock.

David asked if the test could be faulty and Hamish said he thought not: tests sometimes gave false negative results, but he had never known a positive result to be inaccurate. He advised that I needed to visit a doctor in town as soon as possible, then a moment later, a resident arrived at the door with a deep cut on his finger—blood trickling rapidly down his arm. Appropriately, Hamish drew our appointment to a swift close and ushered the man in, while wishing us both the very best.

We walked out into the sunshine and before I knew what was happening, David's hands were around my waist and he lifted me high into the air. He spun me round (which really did nothing for my desire to vomit!) and then he smiled the biggest smile I had seen on his face in a long time.

When he placed me back down, we stayed locked in each other's embrace and he kissed me as if the distance between us had finally vanished. In that moment, we were the only two people in the Universe and only our love existed. The way he held me expressed clearly that David felt we now had everything we could ever need. And although I loved absorbing his ecstasy, I couldn't help but try to force myself to remain calm; the words from the doctors of my past circled in my head, telling me that even if I did conceive, I would be unlikely to ever carry full-term.

I knew we were far from safety, but I must tell you, finding out I was pregnant completely filled my soul with joy.

CHAPTER FIFTEEN

Despite my worry of miscarriage, David and I spent the days that followed our surprise turn of events, living in a blissful bubble. I obviously stopped using any recreational drugs immediately; David once again vowed not to take any stronger than cannabis, and with a baby on the cards, we found ourselves living in complete harmony with each other.

With nowhere else to buy bread, I did still see Anthony when I nipped into the bakery, but our conversations were always to the point and I never hung around after I had paid. I knew Anthony respected my decision to make my marriage work, and at the end of the day, he was a really sweet guy, so he never gave me cause for friction nor drama to worry over.

As I no longer had a job to fill my days, I would potter around the allotments most afternoons, and I started going to the meditation classes held in the treehouse twice a day, which definitely helped to keep me centred. I suffered with morning sickness pretty badly, and often felt so tired all I wanted to do was put my feet up with a good book. So, I took advantage of my liberty and lived life as easily as I could, resting when I needed to rest and being active when the energy arrived.

When I had my first appointment at the medical centre in town, David took me, but stayed in the waiting room while I went through. I was so nervous I felt my whole body trembling as I explained my history to my doctor. When I told her about my miscarriage, tears promptly arrived in my eyes, but my doctor put me at ease with her kind voice and sympathetic manner, telling me, 'Please try not to worry, Anastasia. You're in safe hands.'

She examined me, quietly talking me through everything she was doing, and when she had finished, she concluded she was very happy with my general health—I was so relieved! She told me they would request my notes from the hospital in Nottingham, and the next step would be for me to have a scan to confirm how far along I was. I swear, I walked out of her office glowing with joy.

During the days whilst we waited for the scan, David had a spring in his step every single day, as if he had taken up permanent residency on cloud-nine. And I came to realise a baby would be the only thing that could keep our marriage alive. As long as there was a child in our future, I was sure we would stay together and life would be wonderful. But if we were to lose our baby, I knew David would plunge into a state of despair, and I highly doubted that I'd be able to rescue him—we needed this baby as much as it would need us.

With Rose and Harry's baby due in less than six months' time, we had been discussing where we would go when they needed their second bedroom. Most of our ideas had involved leaving the commune altogether to start a new chapter, but not one had yet been crafted to deal with a baby joining our family.

When the day of the scan arrived, my pregnancy seemed to be going well as far as I could tell and we were in high spirits, praying for good news. I climbed on the back of the scooter, wondering how much longer I would be able to keep travelling that way, and I hugged David tightly all the way there, willing everything to be well inside me and begging fate to please be kind to us this time.

We waited in the maternity wing of the hospital for nearly an hour, anticipating my name being called at any moment. As the time passed, David squeezed my knee any time he saw a baby—whilst I kept thinking to myself that I so desperately wanted to keep him.

When we were taken through to a consultation room, I was asked to lie down, unbutton my jeans, and raise my jumper. The scanner was already on, and the nurse asked David (who looked rather disorientated, hovering somewhat self-consciously at the side of the room) to take a seat at my side.

She pulled the blind down to block out the sun, then picked up a tube and squeezed a clear gel over my skin. Apologising profusely for how cold the gel was (the extent of her apology baffling me a little, if I'm honest), she then pressed her device down quite firmly into my abdomen to start the examination, apologising again, this time for having to press so deeply.

I told her not to be daft, that I was fine, and then suddenly our attention was stolen by the image the scanner had found of our tiny baby and its beating heart. When she told us our baby appeared to be perfectly healthy, my world was complete and I allowed myself to revel in that moment without fear of the future.

Seeing our baby inside me gave me joy like I had never known. I remember looking at David and seeing him wipe a tear from his eye with the back of his hand; his face radiating relief.

We studied the fuzzy black and white image, whilst the nurse pointed out the baby's head and limbs; David squeezing my hand the whole time. Then after several breathtaking minutes, the nurse had all the measurements she needed, and upon making her calculations, she told us, very pleasantly, that I was just over eleven weeks pregnant.

I chatted with the nurse as the appointment came to an end, and as she congratulated us once more, I looked to David with a big grin on my face, only to see he was wearing a distinctly concerned look on his. He looked at me with a furrowed brow, and I suddenly realised that the question of Anthony lay behind his eyes.

We left the hospital with David walking briskly ahead of me, and I trotted just behind him across the car park to the scooter. He hadn't spoken since we had left the nurse, but as we put our helmets on, David looked at me straight in the eyes and said, 'Ana, I'm only going to ask you this once, and I need to know the truth. Is your baby definitely mine?'

It had been over three months since I had slept with Anthony, and I knew I'd had a period after our affair had ended. So, without any doubt in my mind, I replied, 'Yes. It's our baby, David. I promise.'

I waited whilst he silently processed everything, and then he kissed me, with a beautiful, heart-melting kiss and said, 'I love you, Ana…We're going to be parents, can you believe it?'

It confounded me how excited David allowed himself to be. As loveable as his energy was, given the pain we had gone through after the miscarriage, I hardly dared let myself imagine I would ever get to hold our baby in my arms—I thought it a little foolish of him just to assume everything would be alright.

When we got home we talked with renewed vigour about where we should live next; his enthusiasm making me yearn to believe that everything really could work out well for us. David suggested we move back to Nottingham, so we would have the security of our families around when dealing with a newborn. However, after living in Arcadia, there was nothing that appealed to me about returning to our home-town. For over a year, we had been living in a world without all the noise, pollution, and commotion of a big city, and the idea of going back to the same suburban life I had grown up with felt like a step in the wrong direction.

Of course, there had been the odd time when the police had shown up at Arcadia, and we had all had to pitch in and pay them to leave us in peace. But those occasions were reasonably few and far between, and aside from that we had lived in a chilled-out haven, cut off from society and the slavery of the rat race.

I could contemplate life in another city maybe, but Nottingham was completely out of the question for me. I hadn't spoken to my parents since they hadn't come to our wedding, and I had no desire to go back and have Mum rain all over another parade. My baby deserved better, and I was convinced there should be a more uplifting place to bring up our child—we just had to find it.

While Rose and Harry wanted to raise their child in Arcadia, that notion didn't sit comfortably with us, and we discussed our mutual feeling that we should settle down in a real house with a solid roof over our heads before our baby arrived.

We knew that without jobs we wouldn't be able to rent a place immediately, but we had enough money to cover our basic needs outside of Arcadia for about a month, so David suggested we would need to crash with some friends until we got ourselves sorted and said he knew people in London or Liverpool that we could look up.

He showed me the addresses he had written in a notebook, but as I had never been to either city, they meant very little to me. I thought London sounded more cosmopolitan than Liverpool and also deduced it would be a lot easier to get to than trekking all the way across to Liverpool on a scooter (to look up friends who might not even be there). So, with the nation's capital city seeming like our best option, we decided that we'd move out of Arcadia sooner rather than later and use our time to get settled well in advance of our due date.

I reminded David on a serious note that I'd need to take everything very easy and look after myself if I was going to keep our baby safe. And I recall him smiling and saying, 'Don't worry, babe. I'll look after you.'

We made plans to leave within two weeks, and I tried my best to keep a lid on my abundant hormones and maintain a peaceful composure. But unfortunately, we moved out of Arcadia in a much more abrupt fashion than we would have liked, and the reason for our departure came one night not that long after the scan.

I remember, that evening David and I were chilling in the cabin, after Rose and Harry had already gone to bed. The night air was crisp and cold, so we stayed inside listening to music. Lying back against cushions on the floor, we looked at the stars out of the windows which made up part of the ceiling—it was really special.

We were aware that many people were still partying the night away, and whenever there was a gap in between the tracks we played, we could hear the faint sound of music flowing out the main house. Then, suddenly, our peace was stung by the abrasive roar of motorbikes raging through the gates.

David jumped up immediately to look out the door, and I stood just behind him, attempting to see what on earth was going off. Through the trees, we saw a crowd of bikers race up the drive and then stride confidently into the main house.

As I stood, David gently moved me to the side and knocked on Harry and Rose's bedroom door. He opened it without waiting for an answer, and said into the darkness, 'Harry, get up. We've got trouble.'

Within seconds, Harry was zipping up his jeans and pulling a jumper over his head, while David told me and Rose to keep our wits about us. Then they left, with Rose and I standing together watching them from the window, trying to see across the dimly lit land.

We turned the music off and listened, waiting as the minutes went by. But just as Rose went to fetch a jumper, we heard the sound of a window shatter, and we flew out to stand on the doorstep, seeing a group of women run out the main house and scatter to their homes. We waited for our men, but then a gunshot pierced the air and a second quickly followed. With all the music stopped, the night was silent bar the shrieks that momentarily filled Arcadia as the women reacted, but no further sounds came from the manor.

I looked at Rose and although we were only lit up by the moonlight and a small oil-lamp, I could see her eyes filling up with tears. Putting my arm around her, I suggested she needed to keep calm for her baby's sake. And fortunately, only a few more minutes passed before the bikers started to leave. They climbed on their motorcycles, revving their engines until each of the bikes had a rider, and then departed in unison, dirt kicking up from under their wheels—as their final parting gift, one guy launched a rock and another window shattered.

Once the noise of the bikes had faded into the distance, we ran up to the house and, thankfully, saw David and Harry coming out before we got anywhere near the door. I asked what had happened, and David answered by putting his arm around me and turning us around to walk back to the cabin.

I asked if anyone was hurt and Harry shook his head, David telling us it had all just been a load of bravado with the bikers throwing their weight around to get what they wanted.

'And what did they want?' asked Rose, rather innocently I thought, as there was little our community had to offer that wasn't made in the lab or grown in the stables.

'Peace, love, and harmony,' David replied with a wry smile.

Rose's eyebrows knitted together inquisitively, failing to get the sarcasm, and Harry squeezed her lovingly, his arm locked around her waist as he told her, 'Drugs, baby. They wanted drugs.'

When we arrived back in the cabin, Rose bolted the door at the top and bottom (which was very out of character but understandable, I thought), and the four of us sat together as the boys recounted what had happened. They explained the gang had stormed in demanding to see the boss, and when Alfred had appeared, one of their guys had thumped him around the head and he had collapsed to the floor. The residents had quickly come to his aid, and when the gang had said they wanted to deal, Hamish had told them outright that wouldn't be happening.

After one of the bikers broke the lobby window with his bare fist, the women had been sent outside. Then, with the women gone, the bikers said again what they wanted, and once again the residents held their ground, insisting they were wasting their time.

It was at this stage, one of the bikers pulled out a gun and shot at the wall over Alfred's head. Apparently the bullet wasn't intended to come into contact with anyone, it was only meant to induce fear—but it did just what was intended, outside the house at least.

With our men refusing to back down, the biker pulled the trigger again, saying next time it wouldn't be the wall that he would aim for. With no guns on camp and no desire to see anybody get hurt, Alfred finally pulled himself up and said he would deal if the price was right.

When the bikers said they'd pay half, it looked like an all-out brawl was about to ensue, but then unexpectedly the frontman of the gang called his men to leave—there were far more residents than bikers, and although they had no guns, he'd apparently decided that was enough for one night. He announced they'd be back tomorrow to pick up the gear and then kicked over a plant on his way out, the pot smashing and leaving soil all over the floor. Calling to his men, he added, 'Come on guys, let's leave these hippy fucks to clean up their shithole.'

So, unfortunately that was how our time in Arcadia came to an end. David said we shouldn't hang around to see what happened next—he wanted to get me and our baby away from the tension, and I had no reason to disagree. We packed our few belongings up into bags the next morning and ventured back into the outside world.

Stopping at a service station to buy an A-Z of London, I had a pot of tea while David pored over the map. Watching the thick clouds pass slowly across the window, I thought it seemed an incredibly glum day to be travelling, and after the shock of the bikers' visit the night before, I was no longer feeling excited about our journey ahead—instead I felt we were running away from an unpleasant situation.

I wondered aloud if we should have stayed to help our neighbours, but David assured me that leaving was the best thing for us to do and said not to worry; getting our baby somewhere calm and keeping my blood pressure low was the most important thing. I knew he was right. I tried to reassure myself by thinking that if I hadn't been pregnant we would have stayed longer, but in this circumstance our baby had to come first.

After twenty minutes of quiet contemplation and David flicking between pages of the map, we were ready to hit the road. And as we left, I noticed it was beginning to rain.

CHAPTER SIXTEEN

At the end of our journey, we found ourselves outside a bright blue front door on the sixth floor of a block of flats, with concrete under our feet, and a bleak, grey sky surrounding us.

'Well, this is it,' David said with distinct apprehension in his voice. 'I guess there's no time like the present to find out if this has all been a massive waste of time?'

'Go for it,' I replied with a smile that I hoped would help to calm his nerves. 'Like we said, we can always find a guesthouse to stay at tonight, can't we?'

He knocked on the door as I looked out over the East End streets below. Then moments later, it opened on a chain and a hazel eye peered out.

'David!' came the reply as the door shut again, then reopened with full force. A man in his mid-twenties stepped out to greet us and threw his arms around my husband with a grin on his face.

'*Man!* What the hell are *you* doing here?!'

'Stu, I would like you to meet my wife, Ana; Ana, this is Stuart,' David announced.

He shook my hand and David tried briefly to sum up our situation, telling him we were looking for somewhere to stay, while I took in the punkish bloke who stood before us. He wore black, drainpipe jeans and bovver boots with worn-out laces; the sleeves had been ripped off his black T-shirt, and his head was shaved apart from at the centre where his dark hair had been sculpted into spikes. Stuart pulled the door shut behind him, and so we stayed out on the walkway as David continued to explain our surprise arrival.

'Ah, tough times, tough times,' Stuart empathised, his arms folded in front of his chest.

Then, when there was little else to say, David asked, 'So, can we come in?'

And Stuart replied, 'Yeah, you can come in for a cuppa tea if you like, but you can't stay here, brother. Sorry. We've got a houseful already.'

'Shit!' David exclaimed, then added, 'Sorry mate, this clearly isn't your problem, but I was really hoping we could crash with you for a while, just whilst we get ourselves settled and I find some work.'

Stuart laughed apologetically. 'Listen Dave, I understand, but that doesn't change the fact we don't have any room here. My bro and his Mrs have got the spare room, Barnsey's crashing on the sofa, and it's not even a big flat, you know?'

David exhaled the word, 'Fuck,' and looked at me with disenchantment to ask, 'So, what do you want to do now, babe?'

Honestly, I had no clue of anywhere that would be sensible to go, so I looked to Stu and suggested, 'That cup of tea sounds nice. Maybe we could just come in for half an hour while we come up with a new plan?'

The smile then reappeared on Stu's face and he said, 'Sure, beds I struggle with, but tea I can definitely do.'

He pushed the door open and we followed him into the small, smoky living room where a woman and two men sat sprawled out on sofas, watching a small television that stood on the carpet in the corner.

Stuart introduced us as we entered, and then pointed out his brother Alan, Alan's girlfriend Caroline, and Barnsey, who sat with his legs stretched out taking up an entire sofa.

'Oi, Barnsey, put your fucking feet down, will you?! Ana's got a bun in the oven for God's sake!' Stuart shook his head at his housemate and apologised to me, 'Sorry Ana, I don't know where his manners are. Please take a seat and I'll go and make us a brew.'

It appeared we had entered a punk household and, aside from Stuart, I detected general apathy from everyone there. Obediently, Barnsey swung his legs down and sat up so David and I could sit down, and we stayed there, with no one speaking until Stuart returned.

During the five minutes that Stuart spent in the kitchen, his housemates all carried on watching their game show. And feeling rather uncomfortable, I soon joined in with staring at the screen whilst we waited for Stuart to come back.

'So, how do you lot know each other?' Alan asked, when Stu finally reappeared. And as he placed the tray full of mugs down on the carpet in the centre of the room, he replied, as casual as anything, 'Oh, David and I were in the Young Offenders together.'

I must confess, I was shocked that we didn't seem to be able to shake the prison links no matter how much time went on—when I had asked David, back in Arcadia, how he knew Stu, he'd told me that they went back years and had neglected to pinpoint the exact place where they had first struck up conversation.

How they'd met didn't bother me, but I do wish I'd heard that out of David's mouth instead of Stuart's, especially when I was in front of a group of strangers.

We drank our tea quickly, and as soon as my cup was empty, I excused myself from the group, asking if I could use their bathroom. Stuart obligingly pointed me in the right direction, and once by myself, I found my heart racing a little with adrenaline over where we would go next. I tried to steady myself by taking some deep breaths and exhaling as fully as I could. I figured just taking a moment out for myself would help me to stay calm.

Alone in that small bathroom, I remember noticing their dusky pink suite was long overdue a good clean, and I believe it was that thought which grounded me. I considered that if there are four of you at home, watching TV on a weekday afternoon, you could at least spend ten minutes wiping the grime away from the bottom of the units. I imagined how my mum would have reacted walking into that room—*Jesus*, she'd have had their guts for garters!

There were three syringes lying on top of the toilet and the sight of them didn't surprise me at all; drugs were so common in my life, it was just another case of 'here we go again'—here's another group of people who use drugs as an escape route.

We were offered a second cup of tea, which I gratefully accepted before David had time to speak, and when Stuart left the room once again, I asked my husband where he thought we should go.

'I don't know,' came his reply. 'We can't afford to stay in a B&B long-term. We can't rent a place without having a job first, so I don't know; maybe we head up to Nottingham and go to my parents?'

'No way!' I laughed, finding humour in his immediate desperate response. 'There is no chance we're going to stay with your parents yet, we've not even been away one night!'

At that point, Caroline spoke for the first time since we had arrived and, with her eyes still fixed on the TV, she said rather dreamily, 'There's a flat downstairs that's been empty for a while...You could always stay there until you sort yourselves out.'

I asked, 'Do you know the people who want to let it out?' And when she took a moment to reply, I added, 'Do you think it would be cheap?'

'No, I don't think it's up for rent,' she replied, just as distantly. Then, after another pause, she looked at me and seemed to switch on; suddenly she became part of the conversation rather than just an observer of the TV. 'But that shouldn't matter, just go in then change the locks, and Bob's your uncle, you have a place to live.'

Stuart chimed in that the place had been vacant since the old woman who had lived there had passed away a few months back—and it appeared they all thought squatting was a very normal idea to suggest.

I looked at David and saw he wore an interested expression. Having adopted the classic Thinker's pose, his eyebrows knitted together and his hand supported his chin as he mulled over our situation. Then, after a few seconds, he asked, 'Could you help me change the locks, Stu? Have you got any tools?'

'Course, mate!' Stuart replied. 'No worries, I could help you to get sorted.'

The tones of voice they used made them sound as if David might have just asked for help building a piece of flat-packed furniture, and it was really bizarre to me how normal they made it sound.

'Do you want to nip downstairs to see the place?' Stu asked. And David agreed without hesitation.

When the pair of them stood up, David looked back down to me as I still sat on the sofa and said, 'We may as well take a look—right, babe?' He held out his hand for me to take.

Coming to my feet in bewilderment, I murmured 'OK,' and then followed them out the door.

Stood on the walkway outside his flat, Stuart paused in reflection and told us, 'Actually, just hang on a sec and I'll fetch my crowbar, so I can show you inside.'

So, we waited until he came back twenty seconds later, carrying it like he might just have picked up a tape measure. Then we followed him down two flights of stairs and along to the fourth flat.

The front door was bright green, not my taste in colour, and it needed a good scrub, but it was otherwise fine, and as I peered in through the window, trying to see through the old, frilly net curtains, I was pleasantly surprised. The flat wasn't full of an elderly woman's entire life possessions as I had imagined, but rather it looked empty.

After staring through the net curtains long enough, he asked what I thought, and I replied (with gobsmacked honesty), 'I guess it looks quite nice?'

'Come on, let's go in,' Stuart suggested. And before I knew it, he had jimmied the front door open, and we walked inside.

Stepping over a small pile of letters which lay behind the door, we found ourselves in the hallway with a lounge in front of us and the kitchen to the side. We walked around and quickly found a bedroom, bathroom, and no furniture whatsoever other than a huge wardrobe in the bedroom. In the kitchen, there was a gas oven that looked to be around twenty years old but in alright condition, and in the cupboards and drawers we found plates, a few saucepans and some old cutlery still in an orange plastic tray.

'My God, it's like the place comes with a complete squatter's essentials kit—you jammy bastard!' Stuart exclaimed with a grin, 'You really always do land on your feet, Dave.'

I looked around us wondering if I could feel OK ethically about occupying an empty flat. Then, catching David's eye, he smiled, looking somewhat excited and asked again what I thought.

'What do I think of squatting?' I replied earnestly.

'No, I mean, what do you think about staying here for a while, until we find a place of our own?'

'I think we'd be squatting,' I said—which may have sounded obvious but the illegality of what was being proposed didn't sit comfortably with me at all.

Still holding his crowbar in his hand, Stuart ventured, 'No, you don't want to think of it like that, Ana. This flat has been empty for a while now, and all it's doing is going damp from the lack of air circulation. The place needs to be lived in to keep it in good condition, so you'd actually be doing whoever owns the place a favour when you think about it. You could get the electricity going, get the place cleaned up, and if that's not better for it than just standing cold and empty, I don't know what is. I know I just bust the front door open, but we'll fix that for you and then the place will be secure again.'

I looked at David and asked with an eyebrow raised, 'Do *you* really think we would be doing the owner a favour by living here without their consent?'

'Well, we wouldn't be hurting anyone, would we? Right now, no one else seems to want to live here, so if we get some paint and spruce it up a bit, then yeah, I think it would be for the benefit of the flat. It could tide us over until we can rent somewhere properly.'

I nodded, taking in his point of view and considering it for everything it was. I've never been a fan of confrontation—always naturally preferring to go along with others than to cause a scene. So, knowing I was alone in my viewpoint, I swallowed my reservations and held them inside.

Thankfully, before I had thought of any words to say, David smiled at me, took my hand and said, 'Come on babe, we should go and find a B&B and get you some rest. It's been a long day.'

I remember breathing a huge sigh of relief that the discussion had come to an end, and I agreed, 'Yes please, finding a cheap hotel room and having a soak in a bathtub would be bliss.'

Walking back outside, David thanked Stuart for his hospitality, and as the time arrived for us to part ways, he asked, 'So, if I get Ana settled in a guesthouse somewhere for a few nights, can you definitely lend me the tools to get this place looking decent?'

Agreeing without qualm, Stu then enveloped him in a big, friendly hug and told him, 'It's no problem at all, brother—like I said before, it's really good to see you again. I'm happy to help however I can.'

Patting Stu on the back, David uttered the words, 'Cheers mate, I really appreciate it.' He glanced across at me with a smile and then added, 'Right, we better leave you to it. Thanks again, Stu. I'll see you in the morning.'

Within twenty minutes of being waved off, we had found a two-star guesthouse (which Stu had recommended) and checked in for four nights. And when I saw the room, I felt like I was in the Ritz in comparison to sleeping in the woods! The bed, made up with fresh, white linen, looked the epitome of comfort. There was a wardrobe and a small TV bracketed to the wall, and although we shared a bathroom, we were told that the other rooms on our floor were vacant, so the bathroom was only being used by us—it really did feel like we were in the lap of luxury!

Over the course of the following days, David got up early and left me in the guesthouse, telling me to take some time out and just relax. Then he would come home in the evenings when the daylight had given way to dusk, and we'd chill together in our room or play cards downstairs in the hotel lounge.

David didn't tell me much of what he had been doing each day—he said that he wanted to keep everything a surprise. And I couldn't help but feel that all his efforts, in whatever he was doing with that flat, were very sweet. The legality of it didn't bother him at all. When he left each morning, he wore a smile on his face, and I knew he felt he was doing something good for me and our baby—he was nesting in an old lady's flat, which no one else seemed to want.

ANA

When I asked him what we would do if we got a
visit from the police, David said we'd just gather up
our things and leave, no questions, but until that time
came we might as well make use of the empty space.
David reasoned that there were thousands of properties
standing empty around the country, going to waste,
and if you considered the number of people who were
homeless, the only crime involved was one against
humanity, and I struggled to argue the point.

During my three days in the guesthouse, I spent my
time reading books borrowed from the lounge; I took
long baths, watched quiz shows on daytime TV, and
when I felt the need for some fresh air, I went out and
wandered around the streets (which I must say were
rather drab). But I ended up rather enjoying my time
and feeling like I was on a kind of little mini-break.
Then, on our fourth night, David came home and told
me I could come to check out the flat in the morning
and see if I wanted to live there.

Our money was dwindling faster than we had
expected and I knew the only other option we had was
to head back to Nottingham and knock on his parents'
door, which didn't appeal to me at all. Don't get me
wrong, they were a nice couple, but I really wanted
for us to have more independence than I believed that
scenario would have offered.

The next morning, the air was fresh and the sky
pale blue, so when we pulled up outside the block of
flats, the appearance of the building was much more
appealing than it had been a few days before. This time
I noticed that some residents had flowers blooming
in window boxes and hanging baskets; I saw children

running around a grassy bank, and an elderly gentleman walking his dog who tipped his hat to us when we said hello. Two middle-aged women stood smiling and gossiping outside their front doors on the first floor, aprons tied around their waists, cigarettes in one hand and tea cups in the other. It was nice to see the beauty of the sunshine that morning had brought the residents out of their homes.

We went up the stairs (which did smell like urine, there was no getting away from that), stopped at the fifth floor and walked along to the flat. Standing in front of that familiar green door, David reached into his pocket and pulled out a key. He held it out for me to take and asked, 'My darling, beautiful wife, would you care to go inside?'

I took the key and teased, 'Well, I suppose I should at least take a look at what you've been doing these last few days!'

The energy between us was high, and David laughed as he replied, 'It would be rude not to, really!'

I turned the key and pushed the door open; the smell of emulsion and a splash of surprise hitting me as soon as I stepped in. *Boy, had my man been busy!*

The tired woodchip walls in the lounge and hallway were now a fresh, matt white, and the kitchen, bathroom and bedroom had all been painted in a cheerful pale yellow. The net curtains had been taken down in the lounge, giving a clear, magnificent view out over the city, and I was really impressed by how clean everything was! A double mattress lay on the floor in the bedroom, neatly made up with blankets and pillows, and a chest of drawers (which David explained had one broken drawer that he would need to fix) stood next to the wardrobe. In the lounge, the previously empty space was now filled with a dining table with three chairs, a two-seater sofa covered with an Aztec blanket and, my favourite item, a bunch of flowers in a pint glass which adorned the windowsill.

'So, do you like it?' David asked, once I had walked around the rooms.

'Yeah, I do,' I replied earnestly.

He grinned and then bounced over to the other side of the room, placed his finger on the light switch and said, 'And now for the pièce de résistance!'

'How did you do this?' I asked, astonished, as the light overhead came on.

'Easy, I rang the utility companies, explained I was the new tenant and got an account set up.'

'Really?' I asked, 'and that worked?'

'Evidently!' David replied with a laugh. 'So, will you stay here with me?'

Having no better alternative for that night at least, I replied that I would, although I stressed I really didn't want it to be a long-term thing.

When I asked where he'd got all the furniture, David told me he'd been down the rubbish tip and that I would be amazed at what people throw out. He said he'd been to charity shops and bought the blankets and soft furnishings for peanuts, but the paint he'd had to buy from a hardware shop as some things you do have to pay full price for.

David asked me if I would like a cup of tea, and when I asked, 'Do we have any?' he opened the cupboard above the kettle and showed me a stock of all the basic items a household needs. I must confess, I found everything he'd done incredibly thoughtful.

David had made that empty flat a home, and although it was far from a dream dwelling, I relaxed into the idea that we weren't hurting anyone or damaging the flat—and, undoubtingly, that we would move out immediately if we were asked to.

CHAPTER SEVENTEEN

ime passed quickly once we lived in the flat, and as the weeks went by, David struggled to find work. He applied for labouring jobs to no avail and did the odd job cash-in-hand, but it wasn't long before he was dealing to put food in our mouths and pay the bills.

David said straight away that he wouldn't grow plants at home, for the baby's sake, and so, for the first time, he started dealing cocaine. He was given stuff on credit from a guy Stu introduced him to, then he'd go and sell it at night and would make a profit he could keep after he had paid the dealer what he owed. The folk he dealt to were all in their twenties and liked to party, so David would work the night shift, sleep all morning and get up mid-afternoon.

Whilst I tried applying for jobs, it seemed no one wanted to employ a pregnant woman. So, my days were very quiet, and I focused on staying calm and keeping my baby safe. I read book after book, studying as much as I could. I joined the local library and spent hours pleasantly perusing stacks of books, deciding which ones to take home. I studied everything and anything that I thought might prove useful in the future, as well as the usual baby books, of course.

I read about basic accountancy principles, a psychology text book, I browsed medical journals, I copied out recipes from cookbooks, I dipped into travel guides, and I devoured a book on astrology… the list went on. I had always had a thirst for knowledge, and in those weeks, I had very little else to do.

As my pregnancy continued, I saw David less and less—our body clocks seeming to exist in different time zones. I would fall asleep by 10 p.m. then spend the night alone in our bed, whilst he would be out at work, hanging around parties, pubs and nightclubs, until the early hours of the morning. I missed him deeply.

Then, one morning when I was seven months pregnant, I woke up early with severe abdominal cramping and I knew I needed to get to the hospital. David was fast asleep next to me—he hadn't long been in—so, as we had a phone in the flat, I got out of bed and rang for an ambulance to come and get me.

Thankfully I wasn't bleeding, but the pain was intense and I was terrified that I was going into premature labour. I gently moved around the room, packing a bag with everything I might need, and, with a worried heart, I packed the tiny sleepsuits I had bought a few weeks before, unable to resist the cuteness of clothes so small. My mind became a constant stream of prayer, begging for my baby's safety.

When I had finished gathering my things, I eased myself onto the bed next to David and shook his shoulder lightly, repeating his name until he woke up. I told him I was going to the hospital, which made him leap out of bed in a blind panic while I continued to explain what was happening.

I was in a lot of pain and told him, 'David, I want you to come with me. I need you... I'm scared.'

Upon hearing those words, David seemed to get a grip on his anxiety, and he sat down next to me, kissed me on my forehead and told me not to worry. He said that everything would be fine—that we would get through this together.

An hour later, I was in the hospital, hooked up to all manner of machines and monitoring systems, with my nightdress scrunched up under my bust to accommodate the wires and straps they had wrapped around my bump. The doctors all looked concerned but easily located the baby's heartbeat, and when they said our baby was still responsive to their tests, both David and I cried with relief. I was put on a drip (I didn't know what for if I'm honest), but gradually the pain melted away, and the doctors continued to examine me as I drifted in and out of consciousness.

When I came around, David had gone, but the straps and monitors around my bump were still in place. The drip in my hand felt quite sore, and I saw a catheter bag attached to the side of my bed. Baffled by what had happened to me, I pressed the call bell, and when a nurse came over, she said I was going to be fine but they needed to keep me in hospital on strict bed rest until my baby was born. She told me David had gone home to rest, and I should just relax, let them look after me, and literally keep my feet up—so I tried my best to do just that.

I stayed in the hospital for over five weeks with the nurses monitoring my baby every few hours, and I can't thank the hospital staff enough for how well they treated me. They were so attentive and kind to me; they were like angels.

During those weeks, I read every book available to me, exchanging novels with other women on the ward, while David continued dealing to pay the bills. He would come to the hospital to visit me every other day, generally looking a mess. He said he missed having me at home, and I could see his loneliness and stress were triggering him to use drugs more frequently.

He had stopped trying to find a proper job as far as I could tell and he was now a full-time drug dealer, making money by selling coke more than anything else. The state he was in did seem to arouse concern amongst the nurses, but when I was asked one evening if I had been using drugs myself during my pregnancy the question took me by surprise. Initially unsure of how to reply, I decided honesty was the best policy and told the nurse I'd smoked cannabis and had a bit of cocaine very early on before I knew about my baby (one night in Arcadia when David had come home with a little), but I'd not touched anything since, and I had been living a healthy lifestyle. She accepted what I told her and thanked me for my honesty, and that seemed to be the end of the discussion.

At eight and a half months pregnant, I woke early one morning with pain in my abdomen, and when I pressed the call button a nurse rushed to my side.

A hive of activity rapidly developed around me, and the doctor advised me that they would need to induce me to get my baby out safely. I asked them to phone David, but a nurse returned a couple of minutes later to say there had been no answer and she would keep trying. They then took me off the ward into a labour suite, where they inserted a drip into my hand to feed a clear liquid into my veins.

As I watched the drugs flow, I wondered for all of thirty seconds what the effects would feel like, then my first contraction mowed me down like a steamroller and absolutely knocked me for six.

I had spent my pregnancy reading up on how the pain would build up gradually and how taking paracetamol in the early stages may ease the discomfort, but now labour was actually upon me, everything I'd ever read seemed irrelevant. I knew I had to be strong, that ultimately, I just needed to detach from the moment, trust my body and ride through the pain, but my God it was tough!

I breathed my way through the onslaught of intense cramps that hit me, and after fifteen minutes, my midwife, Lisa, told me she had to leave to check on her other patients. Honestly, the thought of being alone with that pain really scared me, but I told her I would be fine and said, of course, she should go—but really, underneath my words, I felt like crying, 'No, I'm not OK—where's my husband?!'

I was upset with David for not being at home that morning to answer the phone, but I didn't have time to really process those feelings for long, as I was only ever forty-five seconds away from the next round of the worst pain I had ever known...

Without a minute's break between contractions from the get-go, it didn't take more than sixty minutes before my sanity was on the verge of meltdown; my fingers grabbing at the cotton sheets, scrunching them into my palms, trying to take the intensity out on the inanimate object in front of me. Then each time a contraction passed, I would feel peace for a brief moment, before it started all over again.

I recall dropping to my knees at one stage and leaning forward against the bed, my head on my forearms, and praying for help. I wished with everything I'd got that David would just hurry up and arrive at my side.

Deciding the drip had been set too high for me, Lisa subsequently decreased the flow, which did ease the frequency of contractions. But after another two hours of hard-labour (and still no show from David), Lisa looked at me with her kind eyes and asked, 'Ana, are you sure you wouldn't like some pain relief?'

Now, I had intended for the birth to be natural, but having endured that drip and the worst pain of my life, I jumped at the offer, and replied, 'Yes, please.'

Seconds later, Lisa injected diamorphine into my thigh and then a sense of calmness floated through me, taking over my body and making me feel like I had been placed on top of a spongy, cotton-wool cloud. I remember lying down on the bed and feeling comfortable for the first time during the entire process.

Lisa's voice soothed me, and I rolled onto my side, my arms wrapped around my bump. Once I had caught my breath and she was satisfied the drugs had kicked in, she left me to get some rest and said she would check on me soon.

As the door closed behind her, I felt at peace and wonderfully free from pain. I thought about my baby who I would finally meet when this was all over, and I felt love warm me. Watching the seconds tick by on the clock on the wall, I kept thinking that labour was only a temporary situation and I would be out the other side of the tunnel soon.

Six hours later, I was still without David, and Lisa had refused to finish her shift when it officially ended. Although I told her she should go home to her family, she wouldn't hear of it and assured me she would stay with me until my baby was in my arms.

When she said it was finally time to push, she encouraged me to use every ounce of energy I had for every second of each contraction. And when I heard a cry, I cried myself; all the pain suddenly melting away.

'Congratulations, Ana, you have a beautiful baby boy!' Lisa beamed.

'He's a boy?' I asked in awe as I looked at him, with his head of dark hair and the most beautiful face I had ever seen.

Lisa nodded, glowing with delight, whilst another midwife cut the cord, and then they wrapped him up in a soft, white towel and Lisa placed him in my arms. He was here. My baby boy—everything that I had ever wanted—was real, healthy, and looking into my eyes.

At 4 p.m. that afternoon, David finally came blasting through the doors. He looked scruffy but very cute as he caught the wonder of the situation, seeing me holding our baby in my hospital bed.

He was more apologetic than I've ever known anyone before, and I felt instantly how saddened he was that he had missed the birth. He spoke with words coming out nineteen to the dozen as he approached me, saying how he'd crashed at Stuart's place after a long night at work, and then his words trailed off as he looked down at our son's face for the very first time.

'Have we got a boy or a girl?'

'He's a boy,' I smiled.

'He's absolutely beautiful,' David grinned. And when he kissed me, his kiss was so full of love, it rendered everything else in the world unimportant.

We were complete.

I asked if he would like to hold him and he obviously said yes! So, he leant in to take him and with a small initial cry from our baby, David uttered the words, 'Hello, my little man,' and cuddled him into his chest.

'He looks like me a little, don't you think?' David asked with euphoria oozing out of his every pore.

I smiled, 'Yes, he does.' And it was wonderful to see David recognise his own features in our baby—any doubts he may have held on to evaporated as he saw for definite that my boy was his. We named him Samuel, with the intention of calling him Sam, and there was no real reason behind the name other than we thought it suited him—which it does, beautifully.

They kept me in the hospital for a lot longer than I had expected to stay. I had seen other women have their babies and leave the next day, but I was kept in with no explanation of substance offered as to why.

After two days, the nurses told me Sam was looking a bit yellow, so they took him off me to put him under a lamp, and I was very much in agreement that they should do whatever was best.

I was feeding Sam myself, so after a couple of hours had passed I went searching for him. However, when I found him and asked the nurse about him needing to feed, she told me they had already given him a bottle. She said that I wasn't to worry and I should get back to bed and rest.

I felt like I had been dismissed, that I wasn't required to look after my son, and it sat very uneasily with me that they had taken that decision without consulting me. I swear, I never slept for even a minute until Sam was brought back to my side the following day.

We were kept in for six days in total and Sam was kept away from me in an incubator for a significant amount of time during that week. Whilst the hospital's behaviour both baffled and concerned me at the time, I was only told later in life by a kind doctor who read through my medical history, that the hospital had had concerns that Sam may have been experiencing withdrawal symptoms from exposure to drugs in my system. Whilst they fed him formula and we missed out on that skin-to-skin contact we should have been sharing, they carefully monitored Sam's condition and sought to determine whether I was a drug addict.

When their tests confirmed I was clean, we were allowed home, but we received a huge amount of attention in the days that followed—the health visitors watching us like hawks, knocking on our door early in the morning, trying to ensure Sam was safe.

You should remember that I was completely unaware at the time that they suspected I was using; the idea of taking drugs never entered my head, so it never dawned on me that the staff were concerned about my lifestyle.

I knew I was a good mum to my newborn; I was attentive to Sam's every whimper and I loved him with all of my heart and soul, so I never imagined that anyone would doubt my competence as a mother.

I ate healthy foods, I didn't drink, I didn't smoke, and I had no interest in anything other than my baby. Motherhood filled me with a deep happiness and I was thoroughly contented in my being.

When the midwives came, they would find me already up and dressed (albeit in very comfortable clothing with no make-up!) and Sam well fed and content. When they weighed him, he would always show healthy growth, so they found nothing negative to report on. I would make them tea and they'd stay until they had no further questions, and then I'd show them out, wishing them a nice day.

These impromptu, unannounced visits went on for a month until we were finally left in peace.

Despite the intense feelings of love that David and I treasured in miraculously having a baby, the weeks and months following Sam's birth were hard, as I know they are for a lot of new parents. Sam woke at all hours of the day and night, wanting to be fed, comforted, and changed, and we experienced sleep in short, sharp bursts seized at any opportunity.

Eating meals together seemed impossible as Sam would always cry when we ate (no matter what time I made dinner) and it seemed every cup of tea I had was stone cold by the time I got to drink it. Our only income was still earned from dealing, so David was venturing out most nights, and needing to sleep during the day. But he did often find it hard to get any decent rest at home, with me sometimes needing to ask if he could just help me with something or other, and with Sam crying to communicate his every need.

I can't fault David for helping with Sam when he was at home—he changed nappies and cuddled and rocked our baby in his arms, telling me I should put my feet up, or go and have a soak in the bath whenever I had the chance. And I was hugely appreciative of everything David did, but I could also see that he was looking drained from the many months that I had been dependent on him.

His complexion was pale from working nights, and the lines around his eyes showed real fatigue, which I didn't like to see. So, after a while, I did what I thought was the right thing to do and I offered to take a turn in being the one going out to deal for a while, enabling David to stay home with Sam.

When I aired my suggestion, David honestly looked like I had just lifted a tonne weight from his shoulders; he couldn't have accepted my offer any quicker if he'd tried. We both knew that I found dealing easier than he did, so David gave me his contacts and I took a turn in earning our keep. Donning my leather jacket, I went out every evening with a large amount of cocaine concealed in the zip pocket on my sleeve, and I would venture into the East-End nightlife.

Now, I'm not saying what I did was ideal, but it was the only way I believed I could immediately relieve David. I wanted to reciprocate the support he had given me throughout my pregnancy and afford him some freedom to breathe and enjoy our son. I wanted David to regain his energy and for us to somehow rekindle our relationship.

I was once told by a lady I love that I'm fiercely independent, and I guess that's true. The notion of being dependent on another person has never sat comfortably with me. So, whilst I understand class-A-drug-dealing wouldn't be everyone's go-to part-time postnatal job, it did feel like the only way I could make a tangible difference at the time.

CHAPTER EIGHTEEN

It was incredible really that we never received any backlash for living in that flat. We were accepted by our neighbours as the new occupants, and apart from the underlying fear that arose in me anytime there was a knock at the door, no negativity of that nature ever came our way.

During the first year or so of parenthood, we split the responsibility of dealing evenly between us, and we made enough to keep the utilities running and food in our mouths. But the expense of having a baby took us both a little by surprise, and the never-ending list of things Sam needed meant we never had any disposable cash. We lived from hand to mouth, each day presenting its own full agenda of tasks that had to be done, and we did everything it took to keep Sam well cared for and to make ends meet. Yet despite me working just as much as David, it shocked me that the tiredness I saw in him (that I guess hits every new parent) never seemed to diminish.

Whether it was morning, noon, or night, you could be sure David would be super tired. No matter how hard I worked to nurture our family, in every way a mother and a wife can, David always seemed to play the role of the victim, and for some reason, considered that he had it worse than me. When we did wake up together, he would normally complain about having had a bad night's sleep (even if I'd been the one who had tended to Sam during the night). And he frequently liked to count up how many hours of solid sleep he'd managed to get—the total always much less than he'd desired.

I suspect, looking back, that David was suffering from postpartum depression, because the man I lived with certainly wasn't the version of David that I had expected to see greet fatherhood. He would answer his tiredness with a joint, which might have been fine under different circumstances, but I was now in a place where taking recreational drugs held no interest for me—they were just a way of earning money. Often, we lived like ships that pass in the night, and even when we were in the flat together, I would go to bed early and he would rather stay up late watching TV. His affection for Sam was never in question, but we were on completely different wavelengths.

When Sam was about fourteen months old, there came a night when we were at home together watching TV and there was a knock on the front door. I recall looking at the clock, seeing it was past 10p.m., and how my heart-beat instantly elevated. David and I looked to each other, immediately concerned—as sometimes you just know instinctively when a knock isn't good.

Sam was asleep in the bedroom and I went to see who it was, simply because I was the more alert of the two of us. I opened the door with the chain on and saw three large men standing there wearing suits and expensive overcoats. I had dealt cocaine to them on numerous occasions and I knew them as heavies, for sure. I had no doubt that if you wanted someone knee-capping, you could pay them the right price and they would do it for you, no questions asked.

I knew the man in the middle was called Terry, and I recognised the men at his sides but I had never spoken with them to my recollection. I eased the door back, slid the chain off and greeted the gentlemen respectfully, asking what I could do for them.

Terry spoke for them all when he answered, 'We'd like to come in please, Ana.'

He led the way as they pushed past me, marching into our flat, and I can't tell you how vulnerable I felt with Sam asleep in the bedroom and those men in our lounge. David remained in his armchair whilst the men seemed to fill the room, looking generally mean and ill-tempered, and I stood with my back to the wall, waiting to hear what they wanted.

Before any words of significance were exchanged, Terry reached into his pocket, pulled out a flick-knife and threw it into the carpet between my feet. I had no idea what was going on; we had never let anyone down nor taken liberties with any deal; we didn't have debts—I had no clue why these men were in our home.

While David looked on from his armchair, wearing an expression much like a deer caught in headlights, I leant forward, pulled the knife out the carpet, closed it up and handed it back to Terry. I spoke calmly and told him that our son was in the next room—I asked him to please put the knife away, that it wasn't appropriate in a house where a child was sleeping.

Terry took the knife, agreed that was fair enough, and placed it back in his pocket. He said, in fact, he was a dad himself, so suggested that we take our discussion elsewhere. His eyes were narrowed and his face deadly serious as he told me I was to come with them.

I looked to David, waiting for him to do or say anything to help me out of the situation that was emerging. I had just had a knife thrown between my legs, and now they wanted me to go out at night with them, not even saying where?

Unfortunately, David did nothing to protect me. I guess he felt helpless in the face of three large men armed with knives, and most probably he'd decided that letting me go quietly was the safest option for Sam—at least that's the excuse I've given him since. I nodded in agreement and led them back out of the flat, grabbing my leather jacket off the hook in the hallway on the way out.

I did pause, just as I was walking out of the lounge to look at David, but there was so much fear in his eyes, he was no more use than a fucking ornament. I just shook my head at him, perplexed that he'd let three men take me away without question, and I said I'd see him later.

David nodded, without saying more than, 'OK, babe. See you in a bit.' And then I left with Terry and his entourage.

Once outside the flat with the front door closed, I asked again, 'Will you please tell me what's going on?'

But Terry just replied, 'We'll talk when I can be sure the walls don't have ears.'

They escorted me down to their car, where their driver was waiting, and with the back door held open for me, I was told to get in. When I asked where we were going, Terry said I was better off not knowing, so

I decided to stop trying to get any information and sat looking out the window, with Terry in the front and a heavy on either side of me in the back.

I tried my best to remember the route we took, noting land-marks as we drove across the city. Then after fifteen minutes or so, the car pulled down a side street that was only just wide enough for it to pass through and swung around the back of a building where gravelled wasteland and the bank of the River Thames lay beyond.

A few large industrial containers stood to the side of the area and I felt that this was exactly the kind of place you would bring someone to kill them. I honestly believed when we pulled up and they opened the door for me to get out that I was about to be murdered, there in the middle of nowhere, with no one around, whilst David sat at home in our flat with no clue as to where I had been taken.

I got out the car with as much composure as I could manage. Then Terry instructed me to follow him as he led the way towards a large building that looked like it might be some kind of factory.

His associates were on either side of me and the possibility of trying to run and escape didn't exist—if anything, running would have only made things worse, as, after all, they knew exactly where I lived and where my child slept.

Reaching the building, I followed Terry up a metal staircase to a fire escape door and was ushered into a cold, damp stairwell. We walked up two flights of dimly lit concrete steps, and after going through another heavy fire door, we arrived in what I can only describe as some kind of hardman's HQ hang-out.

There were easily more than a dozen men in that room, all very smartly dressed. Most of them sat playing cards around a long oval table in front of an open fireplace where large flames roared. I was told to wait by the door with my chaperones, while Terry spoke to a man who I presumed was his boss, and I watched as this older guy I had never seen before peered over his glasses at me. He then nodded to Terry, saying something I had no chance of overhearing.

In that room full of men, I was given very little attention. The majority continued to smoke and banter as if there was nothing unusual about me being there, and I still had no clue what was going on. But as Terry gave his men the signal they had been waiting for, they picked me up, walked me straight across the room and threw me on the fire.

I'll never know how I didn't suffer severe burns that night, but amazingly I didn't. My adrenaline must have kicked in and somehow I managed to scramble to my feet without so much as scorching my hair. I stood in front of the fire, relieved that at least no one seemed to want to throw me back on it, and completely stunned by the situation.

I patted myself down and tried to regain some composure, thanking God that I was wearing my leather jacket and jeans. But suddenly remembering my credit that was stashed in my zip pocket, I momentarily found myself more worried about the two hundred quid's worth of cocaine that I had inadvertently brought with me than anything else. My heart was racing so fast I couldn't comprehend what was happening, and I had no idea what I could do to save myself.

With a number of men laughing at me, Terry's boss called me over with an amused smile on his face and told Terry to pull up a chair for me.

'Now, Ana,' the man began. 'We've got a little job we need your assistance with, if you'd be so kind?'

I tried not to fidget or seem in any way put on edge by what they had just done to me. My mind was reeling in terror, but I knew I had to keep my composure and conduct myself like a businesswoman if he wanted to move on from the fire incident and now talk shop.

'What do you need?' I asked.

The boss then ordered Terry to fetch his briefcase, and seconds later, it was placed on the table in front of us. I watched as he rolled the numbers of a combination lock around until the catch released, and then he opened it up, revealing several cocaine bricks—which I would guess had a street value of over £100,000, easily.

I turned and looked him straight in the eye, still perplexed by what was going on and asked, 'I'm sorry, but what does this have to do with me?'

He explained they had bought it from a new supplier and were concerned about the quality, so he wanted a second opinion on what they'd been given. It seemed bizarre they would be doing this after they had already paid for it, but with no desire to go back on the fire, I knew that was none of my business. With my back straight, legs crossed, and my hands placed neatly on my lap, I replied, 'OK, but please can I clarify, did you really bring me here just to try your coke?'

'Yes,' the boss stated resolutely, while Terry looked on and the others got back to their card game. 'I believe you're the most clued-up dealer in town, with a discerning customer base, so I want you to try this and tell me if it's good.'

I cannot tell you how taken aback I was. But a bemused version of me agreed and I experienced a very strange feeling that wasn't quite relief, but some crazy mixed-up sensation that I couldn't trust.

He told Terry to make some lines, and it was strange seeing Terry play the role of a butler in this man's presence—I was dying to ask his name, but knew it wasn't my place. A few moments later, a line was made for me to take, and the boss watched me curiously as I inhaled it, awaiting my verdict like I was a sommelier who had been asked to critique a fine wine. I considered the texture of the powder, how it smelled and tasted, and how easily it disappeared up my nose; then I waited to see how I felt.

'Well?' the boss asked.

'It seems high quality gear to me,' I replied. Then, with my head still spinning out, I found myself adding, 'To know how good it really is though, you would need to chill on it for a while, take a few lines and see how it pans out over the course of the night; but yes, I think it seems decent.'

'OK. I get what you're saying,' the boss replied. 'Terry, make some more lines.'

And that was the start of my session with the heavies in their HQ, during which I was given a hell of a lot of cocaine. Despite my fear that I could be back on their fire any second, I carried on being as professional as I could in those very strange surroundings, and the more I took, the more I assessed it to be really clean stuff. I sat at the boss' side during the entire encounter, and after about four hours had passed, I told him I was certain he'd got a good deal. He then turned to me and said in what sounded like a genuinely grateful tone, 'Thanks for your time, Ana. Feel free to go home whenever you're ready.'

Now, I get that I had done what he had needed me to do, but his tone shocked me—I couldn't believe that I would be allowed to just get up and walk away. I didn't understand what all the violence had been about at the beginning if they didn't actually intend for me to come to any harm.

'OK, thank you,' I replied. 'If you're sure… I do need to get back to my family.'

'Of course. Don't worry about it,' he said and gestured to the staircase. 'Go ahead and go.'

I looked to the stairs thinking they looked a long way from where I sat, and suddenly I had a feeling that I wasn't going to make it out of the room alive. I felt stuck to my chair, as if my entire body was resisting the notion of moving. With no-one paying me the slightest bit of attention, I leaned a little closer to the boss and asked quietly in his ear, 'How can I trust that you're not going to shoot me on my way out?'

In response to my very sincere question, he gave a gentle laugh and said, 'Ana, you have my word. Go on home to David.'

I had no choice but to move, and as I eased myself out of my seat, the image of David sat in our living room came into my mind—my blood instantly boiled at the recollection. I put my jacket on and upon making eye contact with the boss one final time, I couldn't help myself but to probe, 'Can I just ask, if you know my husband, why didn't you have him come down here and do this for you?'

The boss laughed heartily this time and replied, 'David? What the bloody hell would I want David here for? He's such a mouse, he'd tell me anything he thought I wanted to hear! No, Ana, David is not someone we would call in for assistance. You, however, have quite a reputation and I knew you could be counted on to tell me the truth.'

I processed his words and decided now was definitely the time for me to leave, so I thanked the men for their hospitality and walked across the room. Although I had his word they wouldn't hurt me, I swear, I waited for the bullet to hit me from behind with every step I took. But it never came. I walked down the stairs, out the fire escape, and once I was out the door, I ran. I ran as fast as my wasted legs would carry me back down the side street and in search of the main road and a taxi.

By the time I arrived home it was gone 4 a.m. and I crept into the flat, trying to be as quiet as I could so as not to wake Sam. The only thing I had been able to think of all the way home was how the boss had laughed when I'd mentioned David's name and how he'd called *my husband* a 'mouse'. I was fuming.

I recalled how David had promised so many times during our relationship that he would keep me safe, and now those promises felt null and void. Where was my ally now? Where was my husband guarding his family? He was asleep in the armchair, with the TV set still on, half a joint in the ashtray next to him, and a can of beer by his feet. For the first time in our marriage, the mere sight of him disgusted me.

I walked to the bedroom and found Sam out of his cot and sleeping sideways across our double bed, as he commonly did in those days, managing to take up practically the whole thing by lying across the pillows, and my weary heart felt better in his presence. Without waking David nor Sam, I put my pyjamas on and climbed into bed, twizzling Sam around gently, so that I could lie next to him. I kissed his beautiful face while he slept and I wrapped my arms around him as I lay on my side, knowing he would always be the most important thing in my life.

Holding Sam, I felt sure I had done the right thing by getting Terry and his men out of our house and away from our home—my child was safe and that was all that mattered. These were the thoughts that I reassured myself with as my head hit the pillow, knowing that Sam would be waking up to start the day in just a couple of hours' time.

My life was so far from perfect, it felt like the floor was dropping out from under me. But with love for Sam in my heart, I knew I had to find a way to make things right; and 4.30a.m. was not the time to start brainstorming solutions.

CHAPTER NINETEEN

he next morning, I awoke to find David had climbed into bed on the other side of Sam at some stage while I had slept. I looked at his slumbering body and wondered where my beautiful husband had gone. He looked like the man I had married, but his character seemed to have changed beyond all recognition somewhere along the way.

I had no desire to wake him; I was still far too angry to want to hear any meek or mild excuse he might have for letting a group of men take me out of our home with no resistance.

I washed, dressed, and made breakfast for Sam before David woke up. And I was in the lounge putting my make-up on, with Sam playing building blocks at my feet, when David peered around the door in his dressing gown.

He asked if I was OK, and I looked at him with no idea where to begin. 'Well, I am alive, thankfully. But now really isn't the time to talk, David, not with Sam awake and within earshot.'

He nodded and I thought, there he is, there's my mouse with no fucking backbone, just a head that nods like a pathetic toy dog in the back of a car. I felt like screaming at him, but would never have done so around Sam, so I breathed deeply and stared back into my compact mirror to finish applying my mascara.

'Are you going out somewhere?' he asked, seeming a little taken aback by my brusque manner and early-morning efforts to make my face prettier than I felt inside.

'We're out of milk and bread, so I'm going to nip to the shop,' I replied—my clipped tone offering no invitation of discussion.

'Oh, OK. I'm going to make a cuppa, d'you want one?'

I shook my head. 'Didn't you just hear me say that we're out of milk?'

Suddenly, I couldn't stomach being in the same room as him a moment longer, so I stood up, kissed Sam on the top of the head and told him, 'Mummy's just got to go out for a while, darling. Daddy will look after you.'

I walked straight past David (who was now sheepishly filling the kettle, muttering something about not minding black tea), put on my coat, and picked up my handbag. As I zipped up my jacket, David appeared in the kitchen doorway and asked, 'Ana? Are you sure you're alright?'

I raised my eyebrows with a steely glare. 'Do I look like I'm alright?'

He then literally looked me up and down and said, 'Yeah, you do, I think…It's hard to tell really…'

I shook my head and gave him another disappointed stare. With no words that I wanted vocalise in Sam's presence, I opened the front door, walked through it, and pulled it shut behind me.

I went to the corner shop and got there far too quickly to comprehend the situation I now found myself in, so I walked straight past the Happy Shopper, not caring which way I walked. I felt that continuing my brisk pace was helping—I needed some fresh air and some space to breathe if I was to work out what the hell I was going to do.

I tried to pinpoint when David had lost his nerve, and I decided it had coincided with when he had started selling coke. It seemed we had been on a slippery slope ever since we'd arrived in that squat, and rather than him using it as a stepping stone to a better life like he had intended, he'd just wallowed in fatigue and what was perhaps depression ever since.

The main thought consuming me was that it was time for a massive change. I didn't feel safe in my home, in my marriage, or in my line of work, so something had to give.

The route I took that morning was far from picturesque, I just walked in a straight line all the way down the main road of the bleak, run-down area we lived in. I side-stepped mothers with pushchairs, walked past elderly folk chatting outside the post office, and bypassed bored-looking youths queuing at bus stops, generally finding normal life quite a tonic for the utter head-fuck I was experiencing.

Approaching a newsagent's, I decided to go in, and a couple of minutes later I emerged with a local newspaper, a writing pad, some envelopes, a book of stamps, and a heap of resolve. I headed to a nearby café, which was basic but homely (David and I had been in there many times before), and a nice waitress, who was old enough to be my mum, took my order and invited me to take a seat.

Making myself at home at a table by the window, I laid the newspaper out in front of me and placed my new stationary at my side. I found the classifieds section just as my coffee arrived, and with everything around me that I needed, I focused. I desperately needed a proper job.

I stayed out that entire morning, circling adverts in the paper and writing up my résumé half a dozen times in my best handwriting. Then I made phone call after phone call in the nearest telephone box to companies advertising for clerical staff, slotting ten pence pieces into the machine to keep the credit running, whilst I wrote addresses onto envelopes, leaning on the little ledge inside the booth.

After I had placed six job applications in the post, I walked back to our corner shop, bought milk and bread, and went home.

Back in the flat, I avoided any conversation of substance with David until Sam was settled for his afternoon nap. And when I was sure he was soundly asleep, I walked back into the lounge, where David sat in front of the TV.

He looked up at me and I sat down on the chair opposite him, wondering how to begin.

'Are you going to tell me what happened?' he asked.

'Well, they took me to their clubhouse somewhere near the docklands, and then they threw me on top of an open fire.'

'Jesus, Ana!' he exclaimed; his eyes wide with disbelief.

'Yep, they threw me on their fire and then after I'd pulled myself out, they asked me to try some coke they'd bought and asked me if it was any good.'

His hands briefly massaged his brow in bewilderment as he commented, 'That doesn't make any sense...'

Then that was it. I completely lost my cool and replied, 'I'll tell you what doesn't make any fucking sense, David, is that you would let a group of men come into your home and walk out with your wife!'

He seemed to struggle with my train of thought. 'Jesus! I didn't know they were going to throw you on a fire, did I?'

His response didn't surprise me, but it irritated me beyond belief. 'Terry threw a knife in between my feet, David! It was pretty obvious that something ominous might happen, don't you think?!'

He didn't reply, but rather just looked at me with anxious, confused eyes—yet although words escaped him, I had a torrent of them waiting to be unleashed.

'So, when trouble came knocking on our door, what did you do, David? FUCK ALL! That's what. You did FUCK ALL but sit here on your backside while you let me handle them!'

'Well, you've always been better than me with that kind of thing,' he retorted. 'Plus, I couldn't run after you with Sam asleep in the bedroom, could I?'

'You could have done something, David! You could have done a hell of a lot more than let me be the one that pulled the knife out of our carpet!'

I saw red. I saw nothing but a mouse in front of me and I let him have it with everything I'd got—all whilst talking in a semi-hushed tone of voice, so that I wouldn't wake Sam.

I told him he was useless to me, that he moped around at home all day and night, and that he was more than fine with letting me be the one to do everything to keep our family secure. It was awful.

He called me a load of horrible names, and maybe I was all those things, I don't know. But when I told him Terry's boss had referred to him as a mouse, he was up and out of his chair, livid at how I dared tell him such bullshit.

I told him to lower his voice. Then when I heard a whimper from Sam, I left David and went through to the bedroom where I found Sam was still sleeping, his arms raised to the sides of his head, his hands lightly curled by his ears.

Even though Sam slept, I walked into the room and sat on the edge of the bed to look at him. I searched my soul and senses for what would be the best thing I could do. Then David came in the bedroom, not content with having me walk out on our argument, and started up immediately where we had left off.

His voice was loud and I told him to hush, that we should go back into the lounge. But as I stood up David did something which was so out of character and so unacceptable, our relationship ended right then and there. I watched in disbelief as he threw his beer bottle across the room. It shattered against the wall.

Amazingly not one piece of glass landed near Sam, but the noise, of course, startled him and he cried, shrieking that his slumber had been disturbed by such a violent sound. I picked Sam up, held him close to my chest, and told David that he needed to leave. I asked him very quietly and very calmly to go and never come back.

He immediately tried to apologise, but I wasn't interested. In smashing that bottle he had crossed a line that I knew instantly I could never forgive, so I implored him to leave and told him Sam and I didn't need him in our lives anymore. I pulled a hold-all bag out of the wardrobe, placed it on the bed and told him to pack up his things. His anger dissipating, David welled up as the world around us crumbled.

I took Sam into the lounge and stood holding him in my arms, his head resting on my shoulder. Swaying from side to side, I felt numb and unable to fully process the true depth of what was happening.

A few minutes later, David appeared in the doorway and announced, 'I'll go and stay with Stuart.' His voice was much lower than before. 'Maybe we can talk again tomorrow? What do you think?'

But, for me, things between us had already been stretched too far. I shook my head. 'No thank you, David. Thinking about this for eternity can't change what's happened, let alone twenty-four hours.'

With no further words, my husband walked out the front door, and as tears streamed down my face, I began to mourn our relationship and the dreams of family life we had once shared.

Thank god, a break in the clouds arrived when, within a week of David's departure, I was offered a full-time job as an office clerk. So, I found a childminder and rapidly carved out a new life for me and my son.

Once I had been in permanent employment for three months, I decided the time had come to stop squatting and to find somewhere to rent, legally. It seemed fate for once was kind, as things slotted into place fairly easily and I found a small one-bedroomed flat that I could afford.

I paid the deposit and we moved in quickly. With no interest in neither drugs nor men, I aimed high for a new, clean start and a shot at a normal family life with my son—even if our family unit now only had the two of us in it. I gave Sam the bedroom and I slept on the sofa most nights, thinking Sam shouldn't grow up always sharing a room with his mum. I painted his room blue, stuck glow-in-the-dark stars on the ceiling, and glued a border with toy trains on it around the middle of the walls, making it into the child's bedroom he should have had from the start.

We ate healthily and I paid the bills, but having stopped dealing, I was living on a shoestring and there was certainly no spare cash left over at the end of the month. We did, however, have a legal roof over our head and some stability in life, and that felt like a wonderful change. I lived in fear of the rent going up or the electricity bills climbing higher, but I did it, I made ends meet and provided for us.

Many months went past like this and each day rolled into the next as I saw to the continual tasks of combining motherhood with a full-time job—always counting down the days until my pay packet arrived.

Then came one day when I was at work and I got a call from our receptionist saying my husband was waiting for me at the front desk. Feeling rather overwhelmed, I walked out to the lobby and saw a fresh-faced David stand up to greet me.

He started talking, but I said to wait until we were alone, and ushered him out the building. It was over a year since he had smashed that bottle in our bedroom, and I have to say, he looked good—he looked *really* good.

'What are you doing here?' I asked, taking in the newly improved David, from his smart clothes to his shiny, leather shoes. His eyes were bright, he didn't look stoned, and his complexion suggested he hadn't been dealing all night. When he reached for my hands, I let him hold them, and he looked into my eyes as he told me, 'Ana, I'm so sorry for everything that happened between us.'

I nodded and my heart was racing as he continued, 'I'm here because I miss Sam. And I wondered, regardless of the problems that we've had, if there's any chance you'd let me see him again, regularly? I want to be a part of his life—a big part.'

I asked where he was living and if he was working. So, he explained he had stopped crashing on sofas a long while back, and that he'd met someone new. He said he was living with her, in her apartment, and he had a steady job on a construction site, which her brother had apparently helped him to get.

Despite the anger I had felt towards David, and the fact that our relationship was over, to hear of him being in love with another woman was like a bullet that ripped into my chest. The revelation speared my heart, and I was so gutted that I started to feel sick.

I fell silent. I wasn't sure what to say, so he asked again if I would consider letting him see Sam, now that he was back on the straight and narrow.

Wanting to be decent and fair, I did what I thought was the right thing and I let the words 'Yes, I suppose that would be fine' tumble out of my mouth.

That night, when my day was finally over and Sam was asleep, I poured myself a large gin and tonic, having decided I needed something to help me get through the evening. My world felt to be dropping away from beneath my feet, and as I took that first sip, I wondered what his new girlfriend had about her that I didn't and how she'd been able to successfully raise David's spirit.

Tears started streaming down my face and I doubled over as if the pain I felt in my heart was physically real and sucking the life out of my core. I guess I hadn't expected him to stay in a state of depression forever, but to see him looking like he was back to being the David I had first fallen in love with, and to think of him sharing his life with another woman, when we were actually still married, was too much for me to bear.

I sat on the lounge windowsill clutching my drink, looking out from my third-storey flat, down to the street below and the people walking by. And then I thought, I know what will help me: a joint. A joint would ease the pain and help me to get my head straight. I needed to gain some perspective and remember that this was a man who I did not want to be married to—a man who I believed had failed me and my child.

Despite being off drugs for a long time, I had a matchbox full of weed somewhere in my belongings, I knew I did. So, I started rifling through the drawers and cupboards like a woman possessed until I found it in a shoebox full of old bits and bobs I had never wanted to throw away. I emptied out a cigarette and made a joint from the little paraphernalia I still had, then I opened the window wide and sat alongside it, my legs stretched out the length of the sill.

With time, I regained some composure, drank my gin and smoked cigarette after cigarette next to the open window, before I decided I had done enough thinking for one day, and settled down on the sofa to sleep. Too tired to change my clothes, I pulled a blanket over me, and sleep came easily that night.

The days and weeks that followed were tough; I would be lying to suggest they were anything else.

First, David came around to our flat after work one evening to play with Sam. Then, the next time, he came on a Saturday to take Sam to the park, and true to his word he brought him home on time and without issue.

Sam loved being around his dad, and I thought it was right that the two of them should be allowed to know and love each other. As a result, I tried my best to be accepting and to put my personal issues with David to the side.

The following week, David asked if he could have Sam to stop overnight at his place and also asked if I would like to meet his girlfriend, Marie, so I would know who he was staying with.

Well, the suggestion seemed to slap me around the face, and the thought of seeing this woman who had won my husband's heart was far too much for me to entertain. So, I politely declined the offer and told him that I trusted him to look after Sam—meeting Marie wouldn't be necessary.

When the first sleepover had gone well, David was quite quick to ask if he could have joint custody, and believing that it was in Sam's best interest, I agreed.

During the nights that Sam stopped at David's, I had absolutely no idea what to do with myself—the loneliness was biting. But as my bills were rising and my salary wasn't, I decided to use those evenings to get out the flat and do what people had once told me I did well: I started dealing again.

It was easy to get back in with suppliers, and before I knew it, I had a crowd of people who only bought from me. I may have been a drug dealer but I was professional in my approach, and I decided early on it made no business sense whatsoever to deal poor quality gear— your customers wouldn't come back and moreover they would spread the word around that your deals were rubbish. So, I always avoided the cheaper stuff and I would never cut what I bought to make it go further.

Money troubles eased, and with no one waiting for me at home, I would often stay at a party when I was invited to. I'd indulge in the odd line here and there, and I would try to forget the marriage I'd lost—and how Marie had now taken my place, no doubt sharing a bed with both my husband and my son, as I stayed up late into the night looking for distractions.

Now, I know the choice I made by starting to deal again was my downfall, and you could so easily judge me here and think 'Ana, what the hell were you doing?!' And maybe if you had been there to shake some sense into me at the time I could have heard your concerns, and maybe I could have figured out a different path to take. But at the time, I was stuck in survival mode. The pain that I felt inside consumed me, and when Sam was with David (and Marie), our flat felt so empty. The space I occupied didn't feel like home without my son. I was just contained in four walls, feeling imprisoned with no-one to love.

I knew it was completely fair and just that David should have access to Sam, and it was understandable that David would have a new girlfriend after a year of us being apart. But the problem was that, deep down, I was still in love with the man that I had married. And seeing that another woman had been able to help him to turn his life around was incredibly hard to bear.

I missed our marriage, and I felt so alone without Sam. Thoughts of the three of them having fun and cuddles together, when I sat at home by myself tormented me unlike anything I had known before. So, I used the only way I knew to get out the house, to escape the solitude, and to distract myself from the emotional pain that I struggled to process.

I've never found it easy to ask anyone for help. And at the time I felt trapped, stuck in a state of inertia—all I could do was continue in my powerlessness.

I had always struggled with issues of self-worth, like I was unimportant in the big picture, and although I knew you shouldn't compare yourself to others, I couldn't help but feel inadequate in my being.

Marie had arrived in my husband's life, and lifted him up in a way that I hadn't been able to do for years. And in my eyes, at the time, it was like I had been replaced in my own family with a woman who David thought was 'better' than me.

I felt unlovable, without value, and insignificant. The pain was incredibly hard to withstand.

Alcohol helped me to numb my emotions, to make it through the lonely evenings whilst I counted the hours until I would be with Sam again. And I considered that the money I received from dealing did help me provide better for Sam. But the reason that I dealt wasn't solely based on money—my underlying motives went far deeper than that. I had so many suppressed emotions buried inside me, and being alone with myself was the worst company I could endure.

CHAPTER TWENTY

n the months and years that followed, I did my stint in running the rat race: forever the hamster on the wheel. I woke up to an alarm clock, Monday to Friday, and got Sam ready each day when he would rather have stayed in his pyjamas watching cartoons. I took him to the childminder's house so I could be at work for 9 a.m., and I held down the stable job I needed to support us—when I really just wanted to stay at home with Sam, but I realise this was the norm for many other families too. I looked forward to the weekends immensely, yearning for our quality time together, and the emptiness of those weekends when Sam was away never subsided.

When Sam and I were together, we revelled in each other's company, and there was nothing I loved more than when we played with his cuddly toys together. His favourite was a big monkey he named Moon, and Sam would giggle delightfully when I'd work Moon's head and arms to make him come to life. The personality we created together for Moon was mischievous, and we'd cuddle up together on the sofa, talking to Moon and asking him questions to which he would always nod or shake his head. I'll never forget the way my boy's face lit up during those times, and I think any parent would agree that your child's laugh is the most wonderful sound in the world.

At work, I fitted into office life without a problem. There were about thirty of us working for that company, and I did make a couple of friends, but mostly the staff were older than me and quite quiet in their work. The colleague I got on best with was a sweet Irish woman called Roisin, who was a fair bit younger than me—probably about twenty at the time. She was a clerical assistant and her desk was across the office from mine, so we didn't chat much during the day, but when we were stood at the photocopier together, she would tell me about her love life and we'd share a few laughs. Occasionally, we'd go and get a jacket potato together at lunchtime, but as I would always rush off to collect Sam as soon as the clock struck 5 p.m., we never went out together or socialised outside of work.

Whenever Sam was at David's, I continued to deal. And as time went by, things got a little strange. A crowd of regular customers asked me if I could get them some acid, and I agreed I would see what I could do.

After making a few enquiries, I ended up in the dodgiest bar I had ever set foot in, and sure enough, this was the place to buy LSD. There was almost an industrial feel to the interior of the bar, with its steel flooring, grey walls, and exposed ventilation pipes; the furniture and bar stools were old and shabby, with tears in the leather and threads hanging from the edges. A bar ran down the side of the room where a serious-looking bartender stood drying glasses, and the air was so smoky it seemed like they hadn't opened a window for years.

When I walked in, I felt the whole bar turn to look at me, as if to say, 'You've never been in here before.'

I persevered, and before long, the bartender knew my name and the regulars stopped looking at me as if I might be a copper. I bought from a guy who called himself Big Den, who normally sat at the bar and dealt very openly, provided he knew everyone in the place on first-name terms.

People seemed to be taking all kinds of drugs in that place—I certainly think there was crack floating around—in fact, you name it and you could probably get it there. The majority were high on acid, I believe, and you'd see some folks in a crazy blind panic, darting around, trying to figure out what dimension they were in. There was quite a lot of violence there too, and it wasn't unusual at all for a brawl to break out. Then, one night, I was stood at the bar waiting to be served and I had my arms resting on the counter as I tried to get the barman's attention. I was quite relaxed, just minding my own business as usual, waiting for Big Den to finish a deal, and as I waited, I became aware that the woman stood to my side was staring at me.

She had an oddly menacing expression on her face; her eyes were like huge dark circles and her hair had been back-combed to look somewhat like a bird's nest. She appeared traumatised and yet vacant at the same time. So, I asked if she was OK, and, no word of a lie, she smashed her glass of beer against the bar and then stabbed the jagged piece that remained in her hand straight down into my arm.

I screamed in utter shock with absolutely no idea why she would do that. She was definitely high and spinning out on a bad trip, but why she had felt the need to stab me I don't know—I think perhaps that place just bred violence. Blood poured out of me, and the bartender literally jumped over the bar to wrap a cloth tightly around my arm.

It turned out to be an arterial bleed, so I lost blood quickly, and as I went light-headed, the bar descended into chaos. A couple of women started screaming at the sight of all the blood and then folks started running for the door, while I sat down and tried to maintain my composure. The only thoughts in my mind were of Sam and how I couldn't lose too much blood, I had to be OK... for him.

The bartender stayed with me and told me to raise my arm up, whilst lowering my head between my knees. And someone must have phoned the emergency services as the paramedics arrived quickly, stitching me up in the back of their ambulance. The police, however, were never summoned and no one ever tried to identify the woman who had stabbed me.

There weren't any doormen or anyone else to deal with the attack; it was just one of those things. When the ambulance left, I took a taxi home, accepting that sometimes bad things happen and no one ever had ever told me life would be easy.

A month or two later, I saw that woman again in the bar and she apologised to me, saying she hadn't meant to strike out; it had been one hell of a bad trip. I told her that what she had done wasn't cool and that I'd lost the ability to bend my right thumb properly as my nerve had been damaged. I said I thought I deserved some gesture of compensation, but like everyone else in that bar she had no money, so it amounted to nothing. When I look back now it seems it was just another of life's oddities—someone simply stabbing me in the arm when I had least expected it. But if you play with fire you'll get burnt, and truly, I should never have been going there in the first place.

I'm sure you can therefore imagine my disgust when some time after the attack, I arrived at that bar one night to pick up, only to see an infant in a pushchair parked alone in the corner of the bar. As a woman who has always tried to be the best mother I could, it sickened me to think someone would bring their child into a place like that. The pushchair was facing the wall, but I could see the legs of the sleeping child dangling off the seat. Then, in one of the worst moments of my life, I recognised those legs and I ran over to find my four-year-old boy asleep in a pushchair that was far too small for him.

I gasped with my hands over my mouth, speechless and shocked to my core. Then, when I looked up from Sam and cast my eye around, I saw David stood at the back of the bar having a drink with Big Den. He had a beer in one hand, a cigarette in the other and he was laughing, so engrossed in his conversation, he didn't notice me as I stood on the other side of the bar staring at him with dead eyes.

I don't think I've ever felt so repulsed by another person's actions in my whole life, so without saying even one word to David, I took hold of the pushchair and wheeled Sam to the door. With the door handle in my grip, a punter I knew jumped up from his seat and offered to hold it open while I pushed Sam through, and at that moment David finally spotted me and yelled my name.

I didn't stop, I just wanted to get Sam away from there as quickly as I could. But then David was at my side apologising on the street, and I couldn't have been less interested in hearing anything he had to say.

As he tried to string together his excuses, I cut him dead, making it abundantly clear that arguing his case, now, or at any point in the future, would be futile.

I haven't seen David since.

CHAPTER TWENTY-ONE

When Sam stopped staying over at David's, my opportunity to deal disappeared and we scraped by on what I earned from my job while I tried to think up a better life plan.

I applied for many positions offering a higher wage, but unemployment was high and there were plenty of other applicants out there after the same vacancies. I was a thirty-year old, single mum, with significant childcare commitments, and it became obvious, in the eyes of a prospective employer, I was never the most desirable candidate.

In the months that led up to Sam starting school, the cost of parenthood seemed to soar, and as my wages never left any disposable cash at the end of the month, I became stuck for a way to pay for Sam's new school uniform. So, after Roisin floated an open offer to babysit for me any time I needed, I took her up on it twice a week, paying her £15 a night for her time—and I started to deal again, just to make ends meet.

Having been out of the system for so long through squatting and living in Arcadia, the idea of completing government paperwork to claim benefits filled me with dread, and providing a list of my recent addresses and occupations so someone could analyse my situation, was something I couldn't bring myself to do.

During that year, I worked like a dog to provide for us; we were our own little unit and I did everything I could to keep Sam in a safe, loving, and stable environment.

I was no longer heartbroken over David, nor jealous over Marie taking 'my place'—finding him in that bar with Sam was unfathomable to me, let alone unforgivable. The man that I had married didn't exist anymore and Marie was welcome to him. Any trust I'd had in him had vanished, and I honestly felt that the only way he would ever be able to take Sam off me again would be over my dead body.

Then, a few weeks after Sam had started school, I arrived at work one morning at nine o'clock on the dot and breezed into the office, ready to greet my colleagues with a round of chirpy hellos, only to find it bizarrely deserted. I hung my coat on the back of my chair and seeing that there were indeed other coats dotted about, I was a little baffled as to where everyone could be.

I then heard, 'Ana, can you join us in here, please?' and I turned to see my boss peering around a meeting room door.

I walked in to see the entire company staff gathered around the conference table, and with no chairs left, I went to join the late arrivals at the back. Once my boss had confirmed that all the staff were present, we listened to the director explain they were in severe financial difficulty and the company was being dissolved.

They said they had no money left to pay us beyond the end of the week and that there was no need to stay to work the remaining days—we should all gather up our personal belongings and go home. There was obviously a fair amount of contempt within the room as people were left high and dry. However, no matter how much complaining anyone did, the situation didn't change. The company was bankrupt and that was that. I was immediately unemployed.

Devastated, scared, and filled with nervous adrenaline, I went home and scoured the newspapers for job adverts, but a gut wrenching reflex reaction which I felt deep down, told me the only pragmatic choice I had to keep food in our mouths was to deal. That was the only way I knew how to keep money coming in while I looked for another job, so that's what I did.

Spending my days as a stay-at-home mum, I applied for jobs whilst Sam was at school. Then, Roisin would come over to babysit after I had put Sam to bed.

My days started early with Sam and finished late, so to combat my tiredness I started having a line of coke every evening before I left the house—just to pick me up from my general fatigue and to raise my energy level enough to start work for the evening. I've heard cocaine described as 'marching powder' and that's exactly how I used it, just as a boost to get me out the house and into my working world.

Roisin was rather innocent when it came to drugs and I'm confident she had no idea I was using, as I always held myself well when I was high. In fact, I wouldn't even have admitted to myself that I was high at the time—I believed I was just more alert than I would have been without it.

As the months went by (and I had no luck with finding a real job), the scene started to change and my clients started mixing with people taking much harder stuff. I'd go to a house party to deal and suddenly be surrounded by people smoking crack or injecting heroin, and it was a real bolt out of the blue the way the change occurred.

You should know that aside from that dabble in the acid market, I only ever dealt hash and cocaine and I never sold heroin or crack. I never wanted to get involved with that stuff, but to my surprise, I found myself subjected to those circumstances and it was in those times that I made the biggest mistake of my life: I tried crack cocaine.

You know I've taken a fair amount of coke in my time, and even when I wasn't using myself, I felt at ease around others who wanted to get high. So, I guess there was an element in me that was simply intrigued by what crack must actually be like to experience. When I asked questions, I was told crack was a version of coke that was mixed with water and baking soda, and that the high was experienced in shorter, more intense spells. Foolishly, I tried it. I didn't have to be home to relieve Roisin for several hours and I was told the high wouldn't last long. So, unfortunately, as curiosity is known for killing the cat, the temptation was too great for me to resist, and I figured I was strong enough to make sure I never did it more than once—I couldn't allow myself to—I would just find out what it was like and that would be it…

I felt like I had been struggling in survival-mode, forever experiencing constant cognitive dissonance in knowing that I shouldn't be dealing or using drugs, and yet I had no idea how to rescue myself from my own life. I was desperately lost, and the idea of getting high like I had never known had an appeal—however exploring that avenue was the most irresponsible and regrettable choice I could have ever made.

The feelings I experienced immediately after smoking crack were intensely powerful. It changed the energy of everything around me and life seemed extraordinary just for a few short, sharp minutes. I felt like I had temporarily caught a glimpse of the wonder of our world, and I realised my problems were microscopic in comparison to the beauty of our existence.

I was a child of the Universe, connected to love, and then as the euphoria quickly passed, I came tumbling back down to earth, into an edgy state of nervousness. All I could do was try to suppress any thoughts of having another hit.

I left that place as soon as I thought I was fit enough and remember getting home to Roisin and feeling so ashamed of myself. I tried to cover my comedown by saying I didn't feel well, then I paid her rather abruptly and apologised that I needed to get to bed quickly and lie down.

Just over a week passed before I found myself taking it again, unable to resist the temptation of the inner comfort that I knew would come. This strange scenario didn't go on for more than a handful of weeks, but you should know that no matter what I had taken the night before, I was up at 7 a.m. to look after Sam. I started every morning by getting up to make tea and toast for the pair of us, then we would sit and have a cuddle after breakfast and watch a cartoon before getting washed and dressed.

When I think now about how taking hard drugs physically changes your appearance, I must have looked like trash when I dropped Sam off at school—thin, pale, and tired. I always washed, brushed my hair, and put on clean clothes, so I wasn't dirty or at all unkempt, but I know my lifestyle was written all over my face.

At the time, I considered that all the other mums looked a little like they thought the school run was some kind of fashion show—and then there was me with my second-hand clothing and dark circles around my eyes. I saw the way the other parents and the teachers looked at me, but I didn't know how to be anyone else.

I did try to stop; I didn't want to be a junkie. However, I found I couldn't shake that lifestyle. I was trapped. I was living in poverty with no time to detox. I just had to keep on going, surviving from one day to the next, with the most important person in the world depending on me to provide for him.

Despite the state I was getting myself into, I still always conducted myself professionally in my trade; I would never dream of selling bad stuff and I was very 'ethical' in deals. I remember a guy coming to me once wanting to trade his wedding ring for a bag of coke and I looked at him and refused point blank to take it.

I thought it was so sad that a person would be willing to trade something of such sentimental value for a quick fix. Knowing the woman he was married to, I told him to drop the idea. I said his wife had done nothing wrong and I gave him a bag of coke to go home with. A lot of people may call me stupid for doing what I did, and maybe he went straight around the corner to another dealer and traded his ring for a second bag, I don't know, but I personally couldn't take a wedding ring from someone in exchange for a temporary high.

So, clearly, things weren't going very well for me, but Sam was doing brilliantly at school and he was perfectly fit and healthy, just as a five-year-old boy should be. And truly, that was the only thing that was important to me—I had to keep Sam safe and well.

Then came a night when I was sleeping on the sofa after an evening's work, and I woke to the sound of Sam coughing and crying out for me. I dashed into his room and found him stood next to his bed being sick all over the floor. After I had nursed him and cleaned up without turning on too many lights, I climbed into bed with my boy, stroking his hair and told him he wouldn't be going to school in the morning. I switched off our alarm and rested so peacefully that night, in a proper bed (rather than on the sofa) with my arms wrapped around Sam like he was the most wonderful teddy bear. I kissed the top of his head several times and then, gradually, we drifted off to sleep.

The next morning, I woke up in a moment where I couldn't quite work out what was going on, nor process everything around me quickly enough to understand what my eyes could see. The space next to me was empty, except for Moon lying where Sam had slept, and daylight seemed much brighter than it should have been. I called out for Sam and hearing no reply, I got up and frantically rushed around shouting his name. He was gone.

I checked my watch and seeing it was ten past nine, I ran to the door and found his coat, shoes, and school bag all gone. I flew out of the flat quicker than I had ever moved in my life and I ran across the streets to Sam's school like a woman possessed—hair not brushed, last night's make-up still smudged under my eyes, and a coat over my leggings and t-shirt that I had slept in.

With the school day already underway, I ran straight to Sam's classroom, and looking through the window of the door, I saw Sam sitting behind his desk, looking pale and tired, with a pencil in his hand. Thanking God that I'd found him, I flung open the door, and I cringed inwardly as I apologised to his teacher and explained how Sam was poorly and how he shouldn't be at school. After telling Sam to come with me, I walked out with my boy, apologising to the teacher once again, and I took Sam home to give him a bath and the day off that he needed.

The next day, Sam bounced back to full strength. He hadn't been sick again, so I took him to school, dropping him at the classroom—whilst taking the usual disapproving looks from the women who sat on the PTA. I apologised profusely to his teacher for what happened the day before, and feeling incredibly uneasy and distressed by my own behaviour, I returned home, washed the dishes, and then collapsed on the sofa for some much-needed rest.

Half an hour or so later, as I dozed between dimensions, I was snapped back down to Earth by the sound of the telephone ringing. So I pulled myself up to take the call.

When I said 'Hello?' the voice on the other end explained she was a child protection officer and that they had found the need to remove Sam from my care. She told me if I went to my letterbox, I would find a letter which had been hand-delivered to explain what would happen next.

I dropped the phone and ran to the door, where sure enough there was a letter lying on the doormat. I fell to my knees; my entire body shaking as I ripped it open. My mind then exploded as I read the words which confirmed that Sam had been taken by Social Services.

As I held that letter, the tears that streamed from my eyes weren't enough to let out my turmoil, and a truly primal scream escaped from my core. I was broken, not just heartbroken, but entirely broken.

Every atom of my existence shattered in those moments. My child had been abducted, taken from me by the State, and there was nothing I could do about it.

CHAPTER TWENTY-TWO

In the days that followed, I lived in a state of perpetual panic. I visited the Social Services offices, I made phone call after phone call, but they wouldn't tell me where Sam was, no matter who I asked. All I knew was that he had been placed in a children's home and the social workers said it was in Sam's best interest for me not to know his exact location

My God, the weeks that followed were hard. I was like a dog in the street smelling the air and trying to work out where he was. When night fell, with nothing in my life, I turned to drugs to try to find some relief from my devastation and I lost it big time. I was a shell of a woman with nothing on the inside.

Don't get me wrong, I absolutely understood the reasons why Sam had been taken from me, but understanding why I was an unfit parent didn't make the situation any easier to deal with. I didn't think in my heart that I had ever been a bad mother to Sam, I had been everything I could have been, and looking after Sam had been my number-one priority since I'd discovered I was pregnant.

I couldn't deny that my job wasn't suited to motherhood. But I didn't know any other way to put food on the table at the time.

The life I lived seemed unrecognisable to me, and I was so ashamed of myself. The idea of contacting my siblings in Nottingham felt like a task I was completely unable to undertake. I'd got myself into this mess, and I knew I needed to get myself out of it. The idea of being hugged by Louisa or Jimmy did appeal, and sometimes I seriously considered picking up the phone, but I really didn't want my siblings to know what I had become. I didn't feel worthy of their love or attention, all I saw was that I would be a burden to them if I got in touch.

I so desperately needed to get out of the drug scene. I needed to stop dealing and find another way to pay the bills, and I knew that only then, once I had turned my life around, would Social Services consider giving Sam back to me.

Reflecting that I needed to start a new, clean chapter in life, I would like you to take a moment to imagine what a state I must have looked at this stage. The option of walking into an office and finding a normal job as quickly as I needed to just wasn't there for me. I was so obviously a broken woman, no regular employer would have touched me with a barge pole, and therefore my alternatives to dealing were extremely limited.

I phoned Social Services every day without fail, not because I thought it would make any difference to Sam being in care, but because I wanted to check on him all the time and make sure he was OK.

Each day, I would be told he was in good care and not to worry, to concentrate on getting myself clean. But with no tangible opportunity for change appearing, the hours in between those phone calls turned into a blur and I struggled to find anything positive about being awake. I felt as if I had been placed in hell and that's the only way I can describe that period to you.

In an attempt to find work, I ventured out one day to a bar I had once picked up from, which was within walking distance of my flat. The bar looked nothing from the street, and in fact, you wouldn't have even known it was a bar unless you had heard through word of mouth, but once you walked in through an inconspicuous doorway, you found yourself inside a reasonably large pub, which had been fitted out as a western saloon. There was a long, wooden bar at the back of the room with a row of stools lined up in front, and a dozen or so tables were dotted around. The pub was well kitted out with a pool table and a darts board, and it was busy with men from all walks of life. But what made this bar unique was that their menu didn't list spirits, instead it offered a variety of services you could purchase from the girls who worked upstairs.

You should know immediately that I never worked as a prostitute; I never sold my body for money, but I did desperately need to find a new way to earn money. I had heard that the bar employed women as waitresses, who didn't perform sexual services but just worked in the bar talking to men, getting them to stay and spend money. And for all the drinks a customer bought, their waitress would be given a commission. Figuring that this would be a step up from dealing, I went in and applied for what was essentially a hostess position.

The manager met with me that afternoon and, after a ten-minute chat, he said he would be willing to give me a trial. He told me that there was no basic salary and the only way to earn money was through selling lots of drinks—unless I wanted to go upstairs, which I assured him I didn't. So, I started working there, and it was OK, in as far as you could imagine working in a brothel to be. There was a fair amount of bitchiness, but many of the girls were sweet and most had suffered some kind of misfortune. Certainly, it was nobody's dream job.

The bar would open at lunchtime and stay open all through the night until about 5 a.m., so I worked some strange shifts, and whilst I did manage to stop dealing, I'm sorry to say that I didn't manage to stop using. Drugs were everywhere in that place, so taking coke remained something I would do quite frequently; the manager even gave us the stuff as a perk of the job. I guess it helped put us in the right mindset, made us a bit freer with ourselves, more talkative and confident—which no doubt paid dividends for their drink sales. And my own level of mental health was so frail, I simply didn't have the strength to abstain and refuse my boss when he'd tell me to take a line.

I would arrive at work through the side door (so no customer would see me go in) and I'd go straight up to the staff dressing room to get ready. There would usually be a few other girls in there too, and I'd take a seat in front of the long dressing table and mirror which ran the length of the room. I'd touch up my make-up, so it was immaculate, I'd make sure my hair was nicely styled, and then I'd choose a cocktail dress off the rack provided by the bar, which I'd wear with my own high heels.

My own clothes would stay in the changing room in a bag with my name on until I finished my shift. Then I'd be free to change out of my costume and return to being Ana, the unfit mother, again for a few hours until I was back at work the next day.

Please know, whilst I worked there, I did continue to search for a clerical position, sending my C.V. out to prospective employers every week, but my applications were never pursued. I felt I had no choice but to continue working at the brothel.

The clients who came in to see us were diverse to say the least. Most came in alone and it was the norm to take a drink in the bar first. Some would take their wedding rings off (their tan lines betraying them), but some would leave them on and not give a hoot. There would be a couple of hostesses on each shift and we'd play the clients between us, acting our roles, flirting and chatting as if their conversation was the most entertaining thing we had heard all day.

Sometimes the men were charming; a few were really good looking, and I wondered why those men chose to pay for sex when they could find it for free in a dozen other bars... Maybe it was the element of discretion or 'no strings attached' that drew them in.

The managers seemed fair enough, but my God, you didn't want to get on the wrong side of them. Our bosses were certainly capable of smiling and cracking a joke with the punters, but at the end of the day, they were drug-dealing pimps; they certainly weren't employers operating by any ethical code. The longer I worked there, the more I saw how it worked: if a girl crossed them she'd be out on her ear as soon as they looked at her, and no one went seeking a dispute with them, ever.

So, I minded my own business, trying to conduct myself professionally, and I never joined in with any of the bitching or arguments that went off. I metaphorically kept my head down, while I literally kept my chin up with a false smile on my face at all times. I went there for one thing: to get the money I needed to live another day and pay for my next phone call to Social Services.

Then one night, after I had been working there for about a month, I had been chatting to a customer when I started to sense trouble. He had been casually looking at the menu during our conversation, and after two drinks, I tried to uncover if he really did want to go upstairs that night or not.

I asked if I could make a reservation for him and started describing once more the girls who were working, but I thought he seemed to be only half listening. When I took a natural pause, he lowered his menu and asked, 'How much would it be for the full works with you, then?'

I smiled and politely told him, 'I'm sorry, but I'm not for sale. I only work in the bar, not the bedrooms.'

It would be fair to say he badgered me, he certainly was tenacious. But I obviously had no desire to have sex with him and, seeing as that wasn't my job, I excused myself from his company and said for him to let me know if he decided he did want to visit one of the girls upstairs.

Needing a couple of minutes' break, I nipped to the back room where customers weren't allowed and lit a cigarette. A nice girl called Lily (although I doubt that was her real name) was having a ciggie in there too and I was telling her about my pain-in-the-arse customer, who wouldn't take no for an answer, when surprisingly, that same customer appeared in the doorway.

Our conversation interrupted, Lily excused herself and pushed past him to get back out into the bar, and as I attempted to do the same, he drew himself up tall and looked down at me. Blocking my exit, he told me that I shouldn't go around prick-teasing customers if I had no intention of seeing it through and ventured some bullshit about it being false advertising.

I apologised, 'Look, I'm very sorry that you've misunderstood my position, but I really do need to get back to work.'

However, when I attempted to walk past him, he pushed me hard and I fell down into an old bath tub—which for some reason had always stood at the side of the room, not even connected to any water. As I pulled myself up in outrage, I asked, 'What the hell do you think you're doing? You know, we've got security who'll throw you out if you don't leave me alone!'

As I stepped out that bath, I tried to calm myself and added, 'If you've got a problem with the house rules, take it up with the management—they don't employ me for prostitution.'

That seemed to do the trick and he turned saying, 'That's exactly what I'll do…' Then he left me alone, my breathing heavy and my heart beating too fast inside my chest.

I steadied myself for a few moments, reflecting on how it certainly wasn't good to have a customer complain about you. But I knew I was in the right, so I tried to dig deep and pluck up the courage to go back out with confidence and a smile for my boss.

Once out the doorway, I came face-to-face with my manager, Neil, who asked, 'Ana, can I have a word?'

So, I retreated back into the staffroom and said, 'I take it my customer has just been to see you?'

But instead of him answering me, I felt the full force of Neil's right hook come out of nowhere and belt me around the jaw.

I doubled over, clutching my face, struggling to think what I could say that would help him understand what a jerk that guy had been—I really didn't see that I'd done anything wrong. I wasn't employed to be a sex worker.

'Neil,' I began, as I looked up to try to start some kind of rational conversation. But instead of letting me speak, he punched me again, hitting the bottom of my chin so my head flailed backwards and I went flying across the room. My face was on fire, and never before had the term gob-smacked been so appropriate for how I felt.

The next word I tried was 'Please,' and as I attempted to pull myself back to my feet, I saw a look of disgust on Neil's face and he seemed to ask me quite genuinely, 'Who the FUCK do you think you are?'

My words failed me. I have no idea if I said anything at that point or not, but what I do recall is another punch in the mouth and then another around the side of my head.

He was using me like a punch bag, and when my imbalanced body gave way to gravity, I ended up in a heap on the floor by the side of the bath. Lying on the cold, tiled floor, I tried to protect my head from his kicks, but all I knew was pain. He was relentless, and as I dipped in and out of consciousness, I saw Lily open the door and heard as she exclaimed, 'Jesus, Neil! You'll fucking kill her!'

I watched through blurred vision as she literally pulled him away from me and told him he was needed back in the bar. And I believe it was Lily who at some point carried me out to the street.

I don't remember getting in the taxi which she hailed down for us, and I don't really remember the drive to the hospital, except for vague memories of Lily holding my wrist to check my pulse. I don't remember arriving at Accident and Emergency, nor her talking to the doctors for me as I couldn't talk for myself. And I don't really remember the days and weeks that followed—there were just a series of moments when I would open my eyes, see wires and tubes all around me, feel like death might be near, then I'd close my eyes again.

In that attack, my jaw, my nose, and several of my ribs had been broken, my face had been beaten to a pulp and I was unable to talk, or even communicate, for I don't know how long. During that time, without me realising, I lost my flat, and all my possessions were taken by bailiffs to cover my unpaid rent—but apparently I was lucky to be alive.

When I had recovered enough to regain control of my speech, a social worker arrived to see me and took me, in a wheelchair, to a private consultation room. She asked if I wanted to press charges against whoever did this to me, but as an ex-dealer and a drug addict working in a brothel, I knew there was no point. She was a nice woman, I don't remember her name, and I did try to talk to her about Sam, but it was so hard. That primal scream was still inside me and I could do little more than sob when I said his name. When she asked about drugs, I was honest and urged her to believe that

I wanted to change. I needed to get Sam back and to love him the way he deserved to be loved. I *had* to find a way to offer him a stable, wholesome life.

The next time that social worker came to visit me, she told me that we needed to make plans for where I would go when I was discharged. She asked if I had any ideas and I drew a blank on how to reply. I did think of contacting Louisa and Jimmy, but as they both had children, my gut instinct told me once again that I didn't want to risk being a negative disruption to their lives.

I guess I must have looked vulnerable, as she only let a few seconds of silence pass before she spoke again, suggesting she could refer me to a safe house she knew of, for women who had lost their way, if that would help. She said it could only be a temporary measure but asked if I wanted to apply.

With no thought necessary, I answered, 'Yes please.'

CHAPTER TWENTY-THREE

When the doctors felt that I had recovered from the attack, I was sent to the safe house, where I stayed for several weeks, sleeping in a dormitory with a dozen other women. There were no ladies in that establishment, just women who found themselves somehow adrift in the dregs of society, washed up and useless to the mainstream flow of the modern world. Most had been working in prostitution, some had been forced into it, and I think just about everyone was trying to escape drug dependency.

I lived with women who would do literally *anything* for a hit, women who suffered from mental illness, who had given up on dreams and had completely lost their desire to live and the ability to cope. It was such a depressing place.

I couldn't really believe I had ended up there. All I had ever wanted was a chance to live a normal life with my son, but with no money, I'd been in survival mode for so long that I couldn't see the wood for the trees.

I did genuinely appreciate the roof over my head while I was in that house, and the fact that I had no bills meant I didn't have to worry about paying for anything. So, I used the time there to focus on staying clean, and whenever I would meet with one of the staff, I would talk constantly about how I wanted to get Sam back.

I remember one of the counsellors saying to me, 'You're different, Ana, do you know that? You're not like the regulars we have come through our doors. I see a real future for you—but you'll have to work hard to get there.'

I thanked that woman for her kind words and I knew in my heart I was different. I had my own very special reason to get out of there and to live again: I had Sam. And in Sam I knew true love. He needed me to get well, to turn my life around, and I knew I had to do whatever it took to earn back my rightful place at his side.

Three months had passed since Sam had been taken from me, and the staff assured me they wanted to help reunite me with my child. They even accompanied me to court when Sam's case came up before a judge, and they championed me, stating that they believed I would be an excellent mother once I had found some stability in life. I listened to their kind words which told the judge of how I was improving and the strong desire I had to care for Sam myself. But obviously, the judge ruled that Sam should remain in care indefinitely and I knew his verdict made sense—I had no house, no job, and a history of drug abuse—he was never going to say anything else.

The road ahead of me was long, but, in Sam, there was always a light at the end of the tunnel and that's what kept me going through those very dark days.

As the safe house could only be a temporary stop for any woman needing its protection, the staff had started looking for alternative accommodation for me from the second I had arrived. With my notes from the hospital and through their own evaluation of my situation, I was told one day that they had matched me with a drug rehabilitation centre in Cornwall and asked if I would be happy to apply to go there. It was described as a large farm in a remote area, which had been recently turned into a rehab centre. I was told that placements there were few and far between, but they genuinely believed I stood a chance of getting in.

I thanked them for taking the time to help me, discussed the issue of my proximity to Sam and how that could affect my court case, and once satisfied that my going there would be beneficial to my plea for custody, I accepted with real enthusiasm. The idea of living at a farmhouse in one of the most beautiful parts of the country appealed to me very much.

After a few days of waiting to hear back on my application, the safe house manager came to find me and asked me to step into her office, saying she had some news. I remember sitting down at her desk which was stacked high with paperwork, and looking at the woman who already knew my destiny. The second her lips broke into a smile, my energy lifted, and when she spoke it was like a flame had just been relit inside my core, raising me up from the depths of despair and filling me with hope.

She beamed as she told me, 'Ana, your application to join the programme at Sunrise House has been approved. Congratulations!'

I jumped up and hugged her, I was so thrilled—I don't think that woman got many hugs from residents (it wasn't really the done thing there) but with a surge of immense gratitude running through me, it was the only reaction I knew.

A week later, I was escorted to the station and put on a train to Cornwall, with the management agreeing that under the circumstances they would trust me to travel alone. They told me that if I could arrive in one piece (without making any stops to get drugs along the way) it would be a real testament to my desire to change—and I was also warned that if I didn't reach Cornwall when I was expected, my placement would be instantly rejected. Honestly though, I think you'll find it easy to believe that there was not one little bit of me that would have wanted to score on route.

I was told I'd be collected from the train station in Cornwall and was kindly provided with a bag containing a few items of donated clothing and sanitary products. Hearing the advice the staff gave me as I left, I took their words as pure kindness, urging me to succeed.

I was given a novel for the journey, which I did read a little of, but rather than digesting the words, I found myself simply holding the book open, while staring out the window, watching how the city turned into the countryside and how the landscape changed with each mile that I travelled. I looked at the fields, the sky, the wisps of clouds, and the crows flying alongside my carriage…and then the ocean came into view as the train ran down the coast. I felt like I was finally starting to breathe in a new life.

I was met at the train station by a large, fortyish man holding a piece of paper with my name on it. He looked, I thought, to be about the same size as a grizzly bear—

his face was just as furry—and his long, brown-but-slightly-greying hair was tied in an unruly ponytail at the nape of his neck. He introduced himself as Simon, and gave my hand a firm, hearty shake; I felt very physically small in his company, but his tone of voice was gentle and I immediately warmed to him.

We walked across the car park making nice, polite chitchat about my journey, and when we arrived at his bright orange Mini, I couldn't help but smile at his choice of car—he looked like a giant climbing inside! Anyway, we started our journey, and Simon described how the Sunrise Project was a very special initiative that he was proud to be a part of.

We chatted easily and he told me that they were a unique establishment in a very special setting—he suggested that if I couldn't get clean at Sunrise House, I wouldn't be able to get clean anywhere. And when he then momentarily took his eyes off the road to look at me, we both smiled as our eyes met and I knew there was no toxicity lurking behind his expression; he was virtuous. I had encountered a human being who looked at me as an equal despite my troubled past, and I remember thinking he shone.

Simon told me they had a very simple mission statement, which was that Sunrise residents would learn how to exist without drugs and create new, healthy, and fulfilling lives for themselves. When I heard his words, they were like music to my ears. I felt sure there had to be a better life awaiting me in my future. Feeling filled to the brim with courage and determination, I believed at my core that I would walk out of Sunrise House as a woman who was worthy of motherhood.

The drive to the house was beautiful; it was late afternoon and the sun was beginning to descend, so the thin clouds which stretched across the sky, were tinted with gold. When the ocean came into view, I suddenly felt like I had come home, memories of standing on Skegness pier and the feeling of being at one with the sea came flooding back—the power and majesty of the ocean had me in awe.

You can imagine my delight when Simon continued to drive along coastal roads and after twenty minutes, we pulled up in front of a traditional farmhouse surrounded by rolling fields with an ocean view a moment's walk away. I climbed out of the car and saw a few people milling around, all busy in their own tasks, and I was really impressed by how well maintained the centre and its land appeared.

When Simon took me inside the farmhouse, I immediately felt its positive energy. The walls were a cheerful yellow, the rooms were clean and tidy, and there were a lot of homely touches that made it feel more like a shared house than a centre for drug addicts.

The kitchen was large and well equipped, and Simon introduced me to a lady chopping vegetables, explaining that she worked as a part time cook, and a man kneading dough, who said he was a resident—both seemed very pleasant. The atmosphere was encouraging, and Simon told me all residents were asked to make their own breakfast and lunch, plus you could also help prepare the evening meal if you wanted to. His energy was so inspiring I couldn't wait to pitch in.

We then walked through to the lounge, where there were sofas and several armchairs, a small television, a few pot plants, and a large bookcase full of old books. I smiled saying I thought it looked like a nice place to relax; everything around me seemed very comfortable. I liked the house very much, and the more I saw of it, the better it got.

Simon showed me a room filled with instruments where he said music therapy sessions were held, and housemates were encouraged to come together to sing songs from all over the world. But when he asked, 'Can you play any instruments, Ana?' an involuntary cynical laugh escaped me as a thought of my mum popped into my head.

I told him, 'When I was young, I once asked my mum if I could learn to play the violin and she gave me a clip round the ear!' But Simon's face remained straight, and I realised it actually wasn't funny at all.

Whilst his eyes momentarily acknowledged my childhood pain, he asked, 'Do you like to sing?'

To which I replied, 'I can't sing, but I do like to—especially with Sam.'

He smiled sympathetically and told me, 'We can *all* sing. Not many of us are lucky enough to sound like professionals, but we can all do it. The aim of our music sessions is just to enjoy them, to allow yourself the freedom to feel the rhythm without feeling self-conscious about how you sound. Music is a gift that can naturally lift our energy, so when we're looking for alternative ways to pass time instead of taking drugs, music can offer a very wonderful, natural high if you let it flow through you.'

I commented that I thought that sounded lovely, and then Simon led me down a corridor with small consultation rooms on either side, which he explained were used for counselling on the occasions when you wanted to be assured of some privacy—I thought even those looked welcoming. There were pictures of the sunrise on almost every wall and at least one plant in each room; it was all so light, with the ocean air flowing in through open windows. I reflected that the opportunity to confide in a counsellor would do me a lot of good. I had buried so many secrets inside me for so long, the chance to really talk to someone who wouldn't judge me and to release the emotional burdens I carried seemed like a very comforting offer.

The tour ended with Simon showing me the recreation room, where patio doors opened out on to the garden, and he interrupted a group of three men having a cup of tea and a cigarette on the doorstep to introduce me, telling me that they were all residents in the programme.

They nodded in recognition of my existence, and then Simon teased them with a broad smile, 'Isn't there anything more productive you could all be doing with your time?'

'I'm pretty sure learning to talk about your problems is an important step in recovery, isn't it, Si?' one man retorted with a chuckle.

'Well, yes, it is,' Simon replied, bowing his head with playful respect. 'Please do carry on with your good work… Ana and I will continue on our way.'

Simon then led me across the room, pointing out all the facilities (such as table tennis, a pool table, and a small gym-cum-exercise room), but I found my attention waning slightly, as I couldn't resist gazing out

at the countryside. The views were simply stunning—
it felt as if just looking at the greenery out there was
good for my soul. As the light of the day was dimming,
with the sun low in the sky, Simon suggested we should
leave our exploration of the land until the morning and
I agreed that was fine with me.

He said he would show me to my room, so I could
rest a while before dinner, and when we arrived at my
bedroom, I immediately fell in love with my space. Sure,
the room itself was nicely adequate with a single bed, a
small wardrobe, and a bedside table, but what I loved
was the view I had out the window. Past an expanse
of greenery, I could see the ocean, and above it the sky
glowed with a mix of pink, red, and golden colours, as
the sun was starting to disappear behind the waves.

'Wow! You should have called this place 'Sunset
House'!' I exclaimed.

But Simon replied with a serious yet loving tone, 'No,
we couldn't have done that. This is a place where you're
invited to begin a new chapter; where the darkness
ends and you can embrace the new day—somewhere
that helps you let light come into your life.'

My smile was heartfelt as I looked into Simon's
eyes, my gaze alone communicating how his words
resonated. Having lived with so much darkness in my
life for so long, connecting with the light was something
I yearned for deeply.

With his head tilted to one side, Simon looked almost
vulnerable momentarily as he added, 'I hope that proves
to be true…I feel it is.'

We paused for a moment, looking out at the
sunset together, before he snapped out of his brief

contemplation and said he'd leave me to unpack my things. Then, as he held the door handle, he turned back and welcomed me to the house once again. He told me, 'It's a real pleasure to meet you, Ana. I hope you'll find happiness here.'

I thanked him and watched him leave, thinking he was possibly the kindest and most inspiring person I had ever met.

I remember sitting down on the end of my bed watching the sun finally vanish and the darkness expand. Looking out into the evening sky, I spoke aloud to the Universe and said I was so grateful for this opportunity. I prayed for the help I needed to get Sam back, and I promised I'd do everything in my power to turn my life around and be the best version of myself I could be.

After resting a while, I decided I had too much adrenaline flowing through me to lie down any longer. So I ventured downstairs in search of some people to chat to. I walked around the house, not quite sure what to do with myself at first.

In the lounge, I saw a few folks watching TV, who didn't seem to notice me hovering in the doorway. Then I continued to the recreation room where I found a couple playing table tennis, but they were too engrossed in their game to acknowledge me either. So, I decided to get a drink, and whilst on my way to the kitchen, I passed a young man standing in the lobby who was putting his coat on with a letter in his hand. As I walked towards him, a female staff member approached from the other direction and asked, 'Are you alright, Lenny?'

'Yes, thanks,' he replied. 'I just need to nip out to post this letter.'

Both the lady and I knew instantly that the letter was a decoy, and I couldn't help but overhear as she told him, 'You don't need to go out for that, Lenny. Just put it with the post in the staffroom and we'll take care of it for you.'

As I passed the pair of them to go to the kitchen, I saw Lenny's face drop and his disappointment was immediately evident, bless him. I really felt for him.

He turned around to go back upstairs to his room, the letter still in his hand, and I knew, just as the staff member did, that he had no intention of finding a post-box. In the middle of nowhere, I couldn't imagine where he thought he'd be able to buy drugs, but I suppose, where there's a will, there's a way.

I drifted about for the rest of that hour not finding any residents who'd make enough eye contact with me to strike up conversation. But I was fine with that and happy just to wander around and take in my new home.

When 8 p.m. arrived, fifteen out of the sixteen people who lived there gathered in the dining room, all sitting down at the huge table, and noticing an empty chair, Simon looked around the group, then asked openly, 'Where's Lenny?'

The woman I had seen in the lobby told him he was in his room, and Simon said he'd check on him after dinner, before focusing the group and leading a short prayer to give thanks for our food. It was then, as we all started serving ourselves from the variety of dishes on the table, that a loud thud came from outside.

We all turned to look, and, through the window, we witnessed a kerfuffle in the hedge, followed by a figure scrambling up and scurrying down the driveway.

Immediately, Simon dropped his cutlery and sprinted out the house.

With respect for Lenny's privacy, the dinner continued with polite conversation that didn't question his behaviour, but as I ate I couldn't help but puzzle over why Lenny had felt the need to jump out of the window. We weren't in prison—we were all free to walk out the door anytime we wanted.

Later on that evening, I visited the bookshelves in the lounge looking for something to take to my room. I chose a book about the Human Potential Movement and Spiritual Awakening, which looked incredibly interesting and I read it from cover to cover in just that one night.

That book explained to me how serendipity will deliver the right information into your life at just the right time to help you to move forward, and on that night in Cornwall, the Universe gave me the exact words that I needed to read. I had never heard of the Human Potential Movement before, but when I read, I felt so uplifted by the philopsophies. It was mind-blowing.

I read how natural it is to feel restless in our lives because we've collectively lost touch with our Spiritual nature, and it gave me a vision of the Bigger Picture of Life and a sense of belonging to the Universe like I had never felt before. It explained how we're all slaves to our past hurts and egoic dramas, until we learn to rise above them by stabilising our own energy and divine connection. It spoke about uncovering the true meaning of life through Love and actualising our self through realising our talents and potentialities—I devoured that book as if it were food for my soul.

Before I went to sleep that night, I stood at my bedroom window and gazed out at the stars. A rush of warmth running through me, making all the tiny hairs on my arms stand on end, I felt a deep sense of encouragement and motivation flowing through me. I felt suddenly just as important as the next person, I wasn't a failure, I was a still a child of the Universe, trying to find my way home.

As I stared at the sky, I knew deep within me that no matter how many drugs I took, they would never heal me. Narcotics had never offered me anything except temporary relief from my turmoil and escapism from the sense of emptiness that dwelled inside me. Now the time had arrived for me to address that void, to tackle my fears, my self-doubt, and emotions which I had forever tried to suppress.

It was time to get in touch with my true self, to shine a light inside me and work to remove shadows of anxiety, fear, and hurt. I no longer felt alone, sinking into never-ending quicksand—at Sunrise House, the opportunity to find my feet and to pull myself up from the depths of despair was finally at hand.

CHAPTER TWENTY-FOUR

I had trouble sleeping at Sunrise initially. It was so dark when all the lights had been turned out—even in Arcadia the night hadn't seemed so black. I found the dark absolutely terrifying at times; the absence of light combined with the depths of my inner turmoil sometimes overwhelming me, I would switch my bedside lamp on in the middle of the night to escape my panic. With the light on, I would then rest easier, but it took a long while before I felt safe enough in my mind to consistently sleep with it off.

I had arrived with an empty shell of a life which I needed to rebuild, but becoming part of the Sunrise community was the start of my transformation. It enabled the Me who I was, to become the Me who I am today—it was my salvation.

With the mission of getting custody of Sam held firmly in my mind, I accepted that I had to draw a line in the sand, get a grip on my sanity, and give myself permission to move forward into a state of strength and well-being. I knew Sam had wounds that I needed to heal, but with Simon's support, I was able to admit that I had wounds too—and I needed to heal internally before the social workers would trust me with my son.

I'd had enough of living my nightmare and I needed to find a way to be able to live healthily in the future. But the longer I stayed, the more I realised how strong my psychological dependence on drugs and alcohol had been during my lowest periods.

Some days, I'd hit rock bottom and just want to cry—about Sam, about having no family around me, no husband—and I'd endure many tormented moments when I'd imagine David living happily and sleeping with Marie in his arms.

Everything in my past seemed so dark, I felt jaded. At times, I would fall to pieces, feeling like the Universe had dropped from beneath me, but Simon always assured me I was doing well. So, I kept going, just focusing on each set of twenty-four hours that arrived and continuing to walk this new path under Simon's guidance, one step at a time. He told me there would be three stages to recovery, which were early abstinence, maintained abstinence, and then advanced recovery—and only once I'd reached the advanced recovery stage would the courts consider returning Sam into my care.

Simon promised me he was committed to helping me get my son back, but said I would have to work hard to fill the void that lingered inside me in order to find a sense of inner peace—and the only way to address that emptiness was to open up and trust him with everything I had ever endured.

In the privacy of our 1-2-1 counselling sessions, I confided in Simon, explaining my upbringing and the events of my life which had led me to this place. And he quickly deduced that I had much suppressed anger inside me, which had arrived through a state of feeling powerless to stop the various forms of abuse I had suffered. I hadn't felt able to control my own life, and feeling unloved by my mother had impacted every area of my existence. I'd tried to find solace in alcohol and drugs from my teenage years onwards. But of course, they'd never healed me, they'd just offered a temporary escape route which had never led anywhere. All they'd ever done was numb the pain I'd forever carried with me, and I cried many, many times with Simon when explaining the darkness I'd journeyed through.

Simon invited me to talk openly about my mother, and encouraged me in releasing the anger I harboured deep down over how she had failed me. I resented her for never nurturing me, for never hugging me, nor telling me that she loved me. Feeling unloved by my mum had instilled a sense of worthlessness in me; I had done everything my mum had ever told me to do, yet my actions had never warranted her praise or affection. Growing up I had felt worse than invisible. Only the role I had played in our family home had been of importance, whilst any personal qualities or elements of uniqueness had been ignored.

But with Simon's help, old wounds were aired, trauma processed, and wisps of the light at the end of my tunnel finally began to reach out to me. Simon gave me his energy in abundance, and when he assured me that I had many good qualities, beginning to list a host of personal positive attributes that he saw in me, I became overwhelmed with emotion and tears poured from my eyes. His words, empathy, and encouragement were so soothing, I felt endorsed as a human being for the first time in my life.

He said I had been clinging to the idea of my worthlessness, and that it was time to let go of it, for once and for all. With his guidance, I was able to release my suppressed anger and hurt in a positive manner, and the blockages which had kept me locked in distress finally began to melt.

Simon helped me to see how I was important not just as Sam's mum, but in my own right. And gradually I began to accept myself as being significant, valuable, and loveable, with a lot to offer the world.

The staff at Sunrise encouraged me to structure my days with activities and build a routine in which I nurtured myself and contributed actively to our community. I gave the programme everything I'd got.

At first, I had to tear myself from my bed to go to the yoga and meditation class at dawn, but after a while of persevering with the early start, I found it came to be one of the most enjoyable elements of my routine. I found I loved the experience of waking up and stretching my body out with gentle exercise, while appreciating the beauty of daybreak through the windows.

Truly learning how to meditate and finding the ability to tame my mind (so that it stopped constantly whirring at nineteen to the dozen) was a life-skill I shall always be grateful for. Through silencing my inner voice and focusing on love, I was able to locate peace and soak in energy from the atmosphere around me. And this ability filled me with light, grounded me, and placed me at a vibrational level where the sadness of my past was no longer dominant.

After a while, I no longer felt any reluctance from my body in getting up while it was still dark. My body clock was gradually moulding to the demands of my routine and I was benefiting from it immensely—not only physically and mentally, but spiritually too. I began to feel inspired by life and confident that I could make a success of myself. I no longer saw myself as failure personified. I was Ana, a human being who was just as worthy of love and happiness as everyone else.

There were allotments on the land from which we harvested a lot of food; we had hens, a dog named Daphne, a donkey named Bruce, and we were encouraged to care for them all. Working the land gave us all a chance to get back to basics with Mother Nature, and being outside in such fresh air made me realise how much time I had been spending cooped up indoors since I'd left Arcadia. I'd become totally cut off from nature and immersed the concrete jungle under-world whenever I'd left my flat.

As the only resident who was a parent, I felt different from my housemates and I knew they felt it too. There was nothing nasty about the way anyone treated me, we were all just on different pages, and I was fine with that. I wouldn't say I had any friends there, but everyone was respectful to each other (at least most of the time). And if anyone ever acted out of line, the staff would step in and address inappropriate behaviour with their unending professionalism.

Looking after the animals and getting in touch with the Earth was an important part of the therapy offered, and I volunteered immediately to help look after the dog and the donkey as much as I could. I found great comfort in the way the animals asked nothing of you other than having a good heart and kind intentions.

They didn't care about my past, they had no interest in judging me, or labelling me as a drug addict or a bad mother. They just looked at you, saw your soul through your eyes and instantly knew if that was enough for them to accept you. In caring for those animals by grooming them, giving them their food, and exercising them, I got to know their personalities, their likes and dislikes; and in bonding with Daphne and Bruce, I made two wonderful friends.

It was possible to earn day trips away from the house for good progress and, after six weeks, Simon told me I had earned my first day out. Now, I know it was the norm for residents to delight in the opportunity of a few hours of freedom, however, I felt that unless they were going to let me go to see Sam, there was nowhere I wanted to go.

I was simply consumed all day, every day, with doing everything I could to complete the programme. I needed to get Sam back as quickly as I could. I missed my boy with every second that passed; I missed seeing his smile and hearing his little voice; I missed the feel of his skin and the smell of his hair. I continually replayed scenes in my mind where I'd watch Sam giggling at Moon the monkey doing somersaults on the bed, or I'd see him handing me pictures that he had drawn especially for me. I missed the tenderness of his embrace, the way he would throw his arms around my neck when I tucked him in at night, and how we'd always insist, 'I love you more', 'No, I love *you* more.'

I could well up so easily during that time, as my mind would constantly be unpredictably reeling through moments of happiness with Sam. Just the thought of missing hearing him shout 'Mummy!' a hundred times a day, could cause my bottom lip to tremble; his voice echoed constantly in my mind.

After several months, my routine consisted of getting up, doing yoga and meditation, feeding the animals, mucking out the stable, tending to the plants in the allotments, preparing some lunch, attending counselling or a music session, getting back outside to take the dog for a walk, then yoga and meditation again at sunset. And every evening after dinner, I read, mostly in my room and occasionally on the sofa in the lounge.

When it rained too hard for me to get outside during the day, I would help more in the kitchen, maybe bake bread or read more. But every day, the one task I would always undertake as my highest priority was to visit Simon in his office and ask if he'd heard anything from Social Services about my request to visit Sam. Simon did assure me that the second he received any news he would come and find me, but that never stopped my eagerness to ask.

Finally, after I'd been in rehab for five months, Simon came outside looking for me one morning; he was shouting my name, and as soon as I heard him I knew there was only one reason he could be calling me with such vigour. I ran out of the stable like lightning—I don't think I'd ever run faster—and when I saw Simon was carrying a letter, my heart went straight to my mouth.

'It's about Sam,' he beamed, as soon as we were close enough to speak without shouting. Then I was right in front of him, and he handed me the letter, smiling tenderly, with tears causing his eyes to momentarily glisten. 'It's an appointment for you to visit him.'

I threw my arms around Simon and hugged him so tightly; my own tears falling quickly onto the sleeve of his bottle-green sweatshirt. Trying to catch my breath, I thanked him profusely for everything he was doing for me. I was overwhelmed with gratitude. Getting Sam back meant more to me than life itself, and to be acknowledged as worthy of seeing him again meant I was definitely on the right track.

The letter told us how Sam had been placed in a residential care home in Surrey, and the child protection team had decided as I was making good progress with my rehab, I could visit Sam the following week. Well, as you can imagine I was like a dog with two tails, I couldn't stop grinning, and yet I felt so emotional it was almost impossible to stop crying.

After dinner that night, I took myself to my room but found it hard to concentrate on any book I opened. It was even harder to sleep as I found my excitement turned to fear. I worried over what kind of reception I would get from Sam and whether he'd be angry with me or resent me for our awful situation.

I tried to meditate, but felt my situation was too intense to clear my mind. I don't know why everything always seems worse at night—maybe it's because you're alone with your thoughts; or maybe it's something to do with the feelings of vulnerability that can come all too easily when you're alone in the dark. Anyway, I can tell you, the nights that led up to our visit were hard and very long.

Simon arranged my travel for me and said I would need to take three trains to the area where Sam lived; I'd stay in a local mental health care home the night before our visit, and I'd travel home after I had seen Sam. Now, the idea of staying in a care home I didn't know didn't thrill me, but I would have slept outdoors in the Arctic if it had been a route to Sam.

When the time came for me to go to the train station the following week, Simon took me in his Mini and gave me some money to pay for taxis—which I'm pretty sure was his own cash. I've never liked to take hand-outs from anyone, but at times when life has chewed you up and spat you out, you just have to be grateful that there are generous people in the world who will help you if they can. So, I took the money and hoped one day I would be in a situation where I could offer the same kind of support to someone myself. With everything that Simon did for me, never asking for anything in return other than my commitment to the programme, he proved to me that genuine kindness really does exist.

When I arrived in Surrey, I found a queue of black cabs waiting outside the train station, and as I approached the first car, the driver leant out of his window and called out, 'Where are you off to, love?'

He promptly agreed to take me to the address I gave, and I climbed in the back. Then as we pulled out of the taxi rank, he asked, 'So, are you visiting a family member at the home, this evening?'

And for some reason, instead of smiling the question away, I replied truthfully and said, 'Oh no, I just need somewhere to stay for the night while I'm in town and Social Services recommended I stay there.'

Well, you should have heard the 'Oh…' that came out of his mouth as his reply—it was so full of awkwardness that all I could do was offer a brief smile into his rearview mirror before he locked his eyes back on the road. He didn't say another word to me until it was time to ask for his fare. He had branded me with the label "Mental Health Problems" and had become immediately on edge in my presence. Within five seconds, I had gone from being viewed as a normal person who was perhaps visiting a sick relative, to being someone who he was too uncomfortable with to even talk to. It seemed he couldn't get me out the car fast enough.

I stayed in that home overnight, grateful for the roof over my head and the bed which had been made to a military standard. When morning arrived, a staff member called me a taxi and I was out of there as soon as the clock struck nine.

I guess most taxi drivers pass their shifts by chatting to their passengers, and under normal circumstances, I would have been more than happy to natter a journey away. However, that morning, when the driver asked me, 'Do you work for Social Services?' I didn't know how to reply and simply made the noise 'Mmm…' from the backseat of the car.

The driver then commented, 'I bet they're tight with their pay—you lot deserve medals for what you do.'

To which I replied, 'Thanks', and then resumed my position of staring out the window, watching the neighbourhoods roll past and the cars weave around each other on the roads that led to Sam.

Ten minutes later, the driver pulled up and I stepped out to look upon the place my son called home: a red brick building with a sign that read 'Brookfield House'. It seemed in fairly good order from what I could see, and the noise of the children was audible from the doorstep—their day evidently in full swing inside. With my pulse racing, I rang the bell and waited.

It didn't take long for the door to open, but in those few seconds, I was consumed by how fast my heart was pounding, and I could feel tears start to prick my eyes.

A man, probably in his early fifties, wearing corduroy trousers and a white shirt rolled up neatly to the elbow, answered the door. 'May I help you?'

'Hi, yes please,' I replied. 'I'm Samuel's mum, Ana—I'm here to visit?'

The man stepped back for me to come in, then shook my hand and introduced himself as Tim. We spoke for several minutes in the lobby, Tim filling me in on how well Sam had settled into life in their home.

He told me to try not to worry, assuring me Sam was in good hands, and he went on to talk animatedly about what a bright child I had. Leading the way to a space they called the 'Family Room', Tim invited me to take a seat whilst he went to fetch Sam.

I swear, I felt like running through the house screaming Sam's name to find him. I imagined myself flinging every door open and looking in every room to try and get to him as quickly as I could. But because I was expected to stay in that room and behave myself, I waited patiently for a stranger to bring me my child.

When I heard the sound of Tim's voice calling, 'Sam, will you wait for me, please?', combined with the sound of young footsteps (which clearly had no intention of waiting), I jumped out my seat and dashed to the door. As I pulled it open, my beautiful boy pushed it from the other side and practically fell into the room and straight into my arms.

'Mummy! Mummy!' he beamed as I scooped him up.

'Oh my little darling,' I replied, whilst covering him in kisses. With his arms around my neck, he squeezed me tightly, and when he put his head on my chest, my eyes closed momentarily as I breathed him in.

It was over eight months since I had seen Sam, and after all that heartbreak and agony, the feeling of having him back in my arms was the most wonderful thing in the world.

From the second I held him and nuzzled my face against his, I knew it was going to be near impossible to leave him. I wanted to run out the door with him and take him far away from all the mess we'd been enduring. I wanted to rescue him from the bad situation I had created through my terrible choices and start a new life together, being the good mum I knew I could be. And of course, whilst I understood why I wasn't allowed Sam with me, those reasons weren't easy to accept—I loved my boy more than anything in the world.

Sam sat on my knee whilst Tim talked, and we held hands and kissed each other constantly with loving little pecks, wearing big daft grins on our faces. Then, when the formalities with Tim were over, he told us we had two hours to do as we pleased and that Sam was expected back in time for lunch.

It felt so bizarre to have someone tell me what I could and couldn't do with my son, but I soon let that sensation wash away, simply revelling in the experience of feeling Sam's body next to mine. The huge, gaping hole in my core had vanished.

We walked out of the house, hand in hand, euphoric smiles on our faces, delighting in the experience of being together. I took Sam to a café for a lemonade and a jam doughnut, where Sam told me about his life and the people who looked after him. He said he missed me with all his heart, then while licking sugar off his sticky fingers, he asked me, 'Mummy, when can we live together again?'

I told him, 'We'll be together again as soon as we can, my darling. I've been poorly, but every day I'm getting better, and I promise you I'm doing everything I can to make sure we can live together again soon.'

I assured him he was my world; there was nothing more important to me than him. And I was in absolute awe of how my little cherub accepted me and everything I told him.

Thank God, Sam didn't show any resentment towards me, nor did he have any tantrums or shout at me as I had feared he might—my little boy only showed me love, and that amazed me.

CHAPTER TWENTY-FIVE

As those moments that we revel in tend to be over in the blink of an eye, I was back at Sunrise House before I knew it, asking Simon every day when I could see Sam again and at what stage he thought realistically I would get him back. A few weeks later, my heart lit up when I was given another chance to visit. Then, following that, a report was issued which confirmed the staff agreed everything had gone well. Consequently, Simon called me into his office one morning to discuss an idea he'd had.

As you know, Simon was passionate about helping me regain custody and he had been fighting my corner since the moment we'd met, championing me as he continued debate after debate with the child protection officers. Well, the idea Simon suggested was that we campaign to have Sam come and live with me at Sunrise House, assuming they could secure a place for Sam at a local primary school. That way I could be allowed to prove myself within the safety of our home and under his supervision.

Never before had a child been allowed to reside in the centre, and I'd forgive you for thinking thoughts like, 'That's no place for a child to be!' But when Simon suggested his idea, I got goose-bumps. I thought it sounded wonderful. I had no issue whatsoever about Sam living there with me—Sunrise had such good energy, and it offered me the uplifting support I needed, for which I will be eternally grateful.

When Simon raised his proposal with my case workers, they were against it initially. But after they'd visited the home a few times and experienced the energy of the community for themselves, they appreciated how there was nothing threatening or alarming about our centre, nor the residents who lived there.

After many weeks of phone calls, endless meetings, and reams of paperwork showing proof of excellent progress, it was finally agreed that Sam could come to live with me. And when the day of Sam's home-coming arrived, Simon and I drove to Newquay Train Station to meet him and his care-worker who had escorted him across the country.

Oh my goodness, the relief I felt was overwhelming when I saw Sam running towards me with his little Thomas the Tank Engine rucksack on his back. His chaperone was calling, 'Sam! Sam! Don't run, please! Walk with me!' but he paid that woman no mind whatsoever as we sprinted toward each other as fast as we could. I picked him up and swirled him around, tears pouring down my face.

I remember Sam asking me why I was crying and I replied because I was very, very happy. But remembering it now, I can tell you those tears were also filled with liberation; our nightmare finally seemed to be coming to an end.

We drove back to Sunrise House and the whole way there I was so scared I hardly spoke; I panicked that it was too good to be true and half expected the police to wave us down saying they had made a mistake and actually I couldn't keep him. I was terrified they would take Sam off me again, and it took a long while before those nerves disappeared completely.

I'm pleased to tell you that Sam settled in very well at Sunrise. Life there was wholesome and nurturing, and much like me, Sam loved looking after the animals. He'd often start his day by nipping out to the chicken coop to find eggs for breakfast; we took delightful walks, picking berries from bushes as we ambled across the land; we read together; we played Sam's favourite card game most evenings; and although we slept next to each other in twin beds, every night Sam would crawl into my bed during the early hours for a cuddle—and honestly, those cuddles were the best gift that life could have possibly given me.

After a week together, Sam started school. Every day, Simon continuing to support us by driving us to the local primary school, then repeating the journey in the afternoon with me to pick him up. And with my hand on my heart, I can tell you that I will always see Simon as an angel that I was so very blessed to have encountered. With Simon's backing, and Sam once again at my side, the emptiness I had endured was healed, and I felt as if my own wings were finally beginning to open. I had found peace of mind, and I knew deep inside me that everything was going to be OK—the sun was rising, just as Simon had assured me it would, and the darkness was now behind me.

During the eighteen months I spent at Sunrise House, I saw a lot of people come and go. Most completed the programme within six months, but I was the only one with a child in tow, so my situation was treated very sensitively and a huge amount of time was invested in ensuring I was fit to care for my son.

When Sam first moved in, he was accepted by everyone apart from one man named Nigel, and it was obvious to me that Nigel believed (without knowing me or Sam at all) that my son shouldn't have been living there. He huffed and puffed whenever Sam was in the vicinity and if Sam was watching cartoons after school in the lounge, Nigel would walk over and change the channel without a word—he generally made Sam and I feel unwelcome in our own home. Rather than squaring up to this guy myself, I eventually went to Simon to air my concerns, and when I told him he went bananas! He called Nigel all manner of names, swearing like a trooper, and stormed out the office on the warpath.

When Simon found Nigel in the lounge, he summoned him into a meeting room, and I'm sure the whole house heard the way his voice boomed out of the room. I had never heard Simon raise his voice before, but learning that a grown man was making a six-year-old boy feel uncomfortable seemed to have touched a nerve; it was something that he just wouldn't tolerate. When they came out, Simon walked straight to the lounge and put a children's programme on the TV, and Nigel left us to it—he never bothered us again.

Life in the Sunrise community continued well for us; we were at peace with our surroundings and I took each day as it came, knowing that with each hour that passed, we were an hour closer to moving out and setting up life as our own little family.

Then, a couple of months after Sam had come to live with me, I was walking out of the stable one morning after taking Sam to school, when I noticed a newcomer standing outside the house talking with Simon. With a well-used rucksack on his back, the man looked a couple of years younger than me; he was tall, slim, with broad shoulders and had dark brown hair that wasn't long enough to tie back, but rather fell in no particular style around his rather handsome, unshaven face.

When I approached the house, they both looked in my direction, so I smiled and said hello, and the pair replied the same before continuing their conversation. Pushing the front door open, I was certain the guy was looking at me—I thought I could feel his eyes—so I turned to look back, and sure enough, he was.

While Simon continued telling him about the land, the guy was certainly listening, but his attention seemed drawn to me. And I suddenly did something I hadn't done in years: I blushed.

Later that morning, when I was out in the stable brushing the donkey, I saw the new guy walking over to me, and as he got closer, I found myself blushing again. I cringed a little at how windswept I must have looked. But when he reached me he smiled, introduced himself as Aaron, and asked if he could give me a hand.

I happily agreed and passed him a brush; a smile quickly appearing on my face. We chatted easily as he got to know Bruce, and I have to say it was incredibly nice, as a young woman, to be paid attention by an attractive man of a similar age. I was thirty-one years old at the time and my life had been so intense for so long, it seemed like an age had passed since I had felt the energy of sexual desire race through me. When I looked at Aaron I suddenly felt young again—he came as a real surprise.

Aaron's presence gave me butterflies, and when he flirted with me, I couldn't believe I blushed as much as I did. I had thought blushing was something I'd done as a young girl and even then, not much; it was so unexpected to have a man affect me like that. I told Aaron about Sam immediately and learning I had a child didn't change the way he spoke to me at all.

As time went on, Aaron didn't really make friends with any other residents, but it wasn't because he was unpopular, he was just on a different wavelength to everyone else it seemed—just like me. The way he spoke and acted with me was comforting as well as flirtatious, and the thrill of imagining where our friendship could go gave me the first taste of romance and sensual energy that I'd had in a long time. We very quickly started spending all our free time together.

I discovered that Aaron was a nurse and he'd worked in a hospital until he'd been dismissed for drug abuse. He told me that morphine was his vice that he needed to work through, and as I certainly wasn't in any position to judge; I found it easy to accept him for who he was and the person he wanted to be. When I remembered how it had felt when I'd been given diamorphine during labour, I could understand why he'd been attracted to that high.

When Sam was at school, Aaron and I would often work the allotment together, and when we took breaks, we'd relax in each other's company, looking out at nature and appreciating the beauty of everything that surrounded us. He told me he was interested in spirituality, and we talked at length, deeply, every night after I'd put Sam to bed. We would stay up late, staring at the stars from deck chairs on the patio, and we'd contemplate why we exist and what our purpose here could be.

Aaron told me of how he had seen ghosts as a young boy and experienced poltergeist activity in a flat when he'd first moved out of home. And in return, I told him all about my studies of the Tarot and Numerology and how every reading I had ever done had blown me away with resonance. I confessed that I hadn't read cards for a long time—my deck having been taken by the bailiffs when I'd lost my flat. But even before then, since I'd lost my office job and tried crack, I'd been too scared to draw my own cards—I'd lost my connection and felt that my life had gone too dark for me to want to see any confirmation from the other side that I was screwed.

However, with Aaron around, I began to think I might like to open myself up to reading cards once again. And if I'd had a deck with me at Sunrise, I believe I would have had the confidence to take the cards in my hands and use them to talk with the Universe.

So, it came to be, that I fell in love, hook, line, and sinker. Aaron not only physically won my attention easily, he also connected with me mentally, and finding a romantic relationship with Aaron gave me an extra level of unanticipated security that definitely helped me to complete the program.

Thankfully, there were no rules against residents becoming romantically involved at Sunrise. I had never been aware of any of my other housemates dating, but there was nothing to say you couldn't—as long as the relationship didn't inhibit your recovery.

After Aaron had been at Sunrise a month or so (and we'd spent every moment we could together, revelling in each other's company), our relationship naturally evolved to the next level. I'd just returned from dropping Sam at school one morning and had nipped upstairs to fetch something, when I saw Aaron on the landing stepping into his bedroom. Seeing me, he stopped in his tracks, and with no one around, we stood for a few moments talking about nothing in particular. While we spoke, I found myself watching his mouth and thinking how I'd love to know what it felt like to have his lips touch mine.

If you could have seen my aura at that time, I'm sure it would have been glowing with sexual energy. As Aaron stood directly in front of me, well within my personal space, you can be sure that he felt the electricity that was racing through me.

After a few moments, Aaron asked me if I would like to come into his room, so I agreed, and before the door was even shut, we were kissing. I stood with my back against the wall as the intensity of our kissing increased, and when he ran his hands lightly up my body, his touch re-awakened within me a heightened sense of being alive that I had forgotten I could feel. It had been years since I'd made love with anyone; I'd been celibate since David and I had split up, and an eternity seemed to have passed since I'd felt passion rise up in me and bubble out. So, with no thought necessary, we gave ourselves to each other that morning—it was the natural progression from our kiss, and it was beautiful.

We'd already been enjoying each other's energy for weeks in the conversations and smiles we'd exchanged; we'd got more and more tactile with each other as time had gone on, and it felt appropriate that this would lead to us sharing our bodies with each other. *And oh my word, what a body he had!*

Sex with Aaron wasn't just sex, it was passion, love, and a connection to my spirituality all in one. He connected my mind and beliefs with my body and grounded me into the moment with the act of lovemaking. I melted in his arms, and when we became one, he completed me in a way that I hadn't previously conceived possible.

After years of feeling that I had to face the world alone, Aaron came along and swept me off my feet beyond my wildest dreams. He opened himself up to Sam too, and Sam quickly adored the man I'd allowed myself to fall in love with.

Once several months had passed, I no longer talked about when Sam and I would move out—rather, we talked about how the *three* of us would move out when we completed the program.

Not having any children of his own, Aaron told me that he was sure, without a shred of doubt, that he wanted to be a part of what I had with Sam, and that he'd like to build on that family and have children of our own, if we could. Our excitement, inspiration, and anticipation of the future came as the final rock set in the foundations I had been laying at Sunrise House.

I was finally ready to move on.

CHAPTER TWENTY-SIX

Moving out of Sunrise House was an intensely emotional experience. We'd already taken Sam to school that morning, and I remember standing outside the farmhouse, Aaron holding the keys to his car, and me holding the key to our new flat (which Simon had helped us to acquire). As Simon stood with us, he smiled at me lovingly; his eyes glistening with tenderness.

I thanked Simon from the bottom of my heart for everything he had done for me and Sam, and when I hugged him, he held me close and told me, 'You go out there and be happy, please Ana. You deserve it so much. I'm so proud of you.'

My breath catching in my throat, I softly replied, 'Thank you. You can't imagine how much that means to me—how much you mean to me.'

When I pulled back from our embrace, I looked up to see a tear run down his cheek, which he rapidly wiped away with a laugh.

Seeing him cry, of course, caused my own tears to spill over, but it was with big smiles on our faces that we shed tears. I was overwhelmed with gratitude and love, yet saddened at the same time to be leaving Simon—the man who had shown me the most support and the greatest friendship I had ever known. During my time at Sunrise, Simon had been my family, my ally, my confidant, my angel. And he very much resembled the energy of a doting father as he stood on that driveway, ready to wave us off.

When Aaron shook Simon's hand, Simon pulled him into a bear-hug and patted him heartily on the back. Then, after the two of them had exchanged earnest sentiments, I told Simon, 'I sincerely hope we can keep in touch.'

'You better believe it!' Simon replied, before he added with a wink, 'Just let me know when you're settled and I'll let the pair of you cook me dinner one night!'

'It'll be our pleasure,' Aaron affirmed. 'You're welcome any time, brother.'

After I'd had another huge hug with Simon, my amour and I got in the car and drove off, metaphorically into the sunset—but literally to a small apartment block in a neighbouring village, ten minutes' walk from Sam's school.

With Simon's support, we had both found jobs before we moved out: I was to work during school hours as an assistant for a small accountancy firm, and Aaron had secured a full-time position in the local hospital. Our names were put on the rent book, and, at last, I experienced a time in life when enough money landed in the bank each month to cover our bills, put food in our mouths, and clothes on our backs. It was so wonderful to live a 'normal' life.

We acquired our furniture from charity shops and other 'pre-loved' items from adverts in the post office window. We had a hanging basket outside the front door and a small balcony overlooking gardens at the back, where Aaron and I would often sit and play cards after Sam had gone to bed.

All three of us were happy, and Sam finally got to experience childhood as it should be. He had his own bedroom (where Moon the monkey took up his rightful place of sitting on Sam's pillow every day), we did his schoolwork together at the kitchen table, and his friends regularly came over to play. When I dropped Sam off at school there were never any stares of disapproval shot my way when I walked across the playground. It was very much the fresh start that we all needed. No one knew us in our apartment block, so we could arrive as a new family with no one judging us and slot straight into the community. We made friends easily, and it was utterly uplifting to be trusted to live without having anyone watching us, or monitoring how we behaved.

I was deeply in love with Aaron. He was kind, sweet, sexy, and his sense of humour matched mine to a tee. The spiritual connection that we shared was profound, and the life we built together grounded me and enabled me to start living as a free woman, doing exactly as I wanted with my time. I had a family who I loved beyond words, and I felt stronger than I had ever felt in my life.

A few months after we'd moved in together, Aaron made a very kind-hearted gesture, which I found very touching. He returned from a shopping trip, looking pleased as punch and was holding something behind his back.

He asked me to take a seat on the balcony, open my hands, and close my eyes. So I did as he asked, with a smile lighting up my face.

Feeling a delicate weight touch my palms, I opened my eyes to look upon a paper gift bag holding a small, beautifully wrapped, oblong box. Without taking off the wrapping, I immediately felt that it was a deck of tarot cards, and I looked up inquisitively to ask, 'Is this what I think it is?'

He smiled, sensing I already knew and suggested, 'Why don't you open it and find out?'

Sure enough, the wrapping paper peeled away to reveal the most beautiful deck of Rider-Waite tarot cards. The sight of them and the thoughtfulness of his gesture really moved me. Aaron knew that I believed in a superstition that you should never buy your own cards, that they had to be given to you when the Universe felt you were ready. And when I jumped up to hug him, he told me gently that he hoped I was now ready to read again—and his timing was right, I was.

I felt centred like I had never before. I knew love. And through combining all the skills I'd learned at Sunrise House with the spiritual aspects of life that I'd discovered, I was energised on a soul level. I'd been set free from the trauma of my past, and it felt wonderful.

I kept to my routine of beginning and ending my days with meditation and yoga, finding them both wonderfully empowering activities which boosted my energy and washed any stresses away. I felt peaceful, and I practiced with the tarot regularly, drawing at least one card out the pack for daily guidance each morning before work.

As time went by and my passion for the tarot continued to deepen, I started reading for friends and subsequently, friends of friends, more and more. If the weather permitted, I would do my readings outside on the balcony, finding the uninterrupted view of the trees and greenery in the communal gardens helping me to earth my energy. And when I looked up into the sky whilst meditating on the pack, asking the Universe to guide me to the cards I needed to pick, I would frequently see the most beautiful energy twinkling in the atmosphere. I soon realised how much I had missed the feeling of security that the cards brought me, and every reading I did was encouraging.

With my newly developed sense of inner security, at thirty-two years old, I sensed the time had come for me to try to get back in touch with my siblings. So, one afternoon, I conquered my anxieties and phoned the landline number I still had for Louisa—which I hadn't dialled in the nine years since leaving Nottingham.

My heart was pounding as I heard the line ring out. Yet although my adrenaline was racing, I wasn't scared. I just wanted to hear Louisa again—to find out if she was well—and I hoped with every ounce of my being that she still lived in that house.

After three rings, a voice I knew and loved so deeply answered, "Hello?"

With tears immediately welling in my eyes, I replied, "Hello Sister, it's me."

I swear, as Louisa spoke, it was like her words enveloped me in the most amazing hug—like we were in the double bed we had shared growing up and just her presence alone soothed my entire being.

"OH MY GOD ANA!! Where the hell have you been! I've been so worried about you!!! OH MY GOD!!!" As she spoke, I could hear a smile arrive on her face, and I could sense the love within her that she still held for me. It was breath-taking.

We stayed on the phone for over two hours and I'm sure we could have chatted for *much* longer if I hadn't had to go and fetch Sam from school. Louisa told me how she had wanted to contact me for years—that she'd never wanted to lose touch—and I apologised profusely for my disappearance, which she accepted in an instant. She assured me that the past was in the past and she was really just so grateful that I had called.

I explained how I'd been caught in a downward spiral—that I'd made terrible decisions—but that my life was settled now and I was back on track. But before I went much further, Louisa took control of the conversation, and told me that our dad had passed away eighteen months ago after suffering a heart-attack.

Although I felt incredible guilt and sadness at the thought of never being able to speak to him again, when Louisa assured me that his death had been for the best, and that it had freed him from his ill health and depression, it made sense to me that he was no longer with us. The Universe had given him his liberty in death, which he'd always struggled to find in this dimension.

Louisa told me that our mum had sold the family home after dad passed over. Apparently, she hadn't wanted to stay in that big, cold house all by herself, so she'd moved to a smaller property with central heating on the outskirts of Nottingham.

I asked if she saw Mum regularly, and she replied, 'I haven't seen her since she needed help to move house… But you know how Mum can be… It's never easy.' Then after a heartfelt pause, she changed our direction swiftly with, 'Anyway! Tell me all about you! Where are you living now?'

So I told her all about Sam, about Aaron, and our new life in Cornwall. And when she found out she was an auntie, Louisa cried openly down the phone, telling me how she couldn't wait to meet her nephew.

In turn, she said that she had news of her own, and that she'd had another baby, Steven, who was now five years old. When I heard she'd had a son, I cried too, with both joy and sadness at having been absent from my sister's life for so long—we had missed so much of each other's lives.

Louisa told me all about Daisy, her daughter, who was now coming up thirteen—but going on thirty in her attitude, by all accounts! And Louisa assured me that she and her husband, William (or Bill for short), were still happily married and enjoying family life together.

She told me that Jimmy and Yvette were still living in Nottingham, and that Chloe (Yvette's daughter) was now eighteen and had recently moved out of home to live with two of her friends. She said Jimmy and Yvette had had a child of their own seven years ago, a daughter they had named, Suzanna. And when she told me that the 'anna' part of her name was attributed to me, tears fell down my face so quickly, I had to excuse myself to fetch a box of tissues to take back to the phone! It was mind-blowing.

To hear that Jimmy and Yvette thought so highly of me that they would include my name in their daughter's, well, that's something I'd have never even dreamed of. With this, all my insecurities about how I was viewed in the eyes of my family finally melted away.

I learned that my younger brother, Paddy, who was now twenty-seven, had met an American woman who he'd fallen madly in love with several years ago, and that he'd emigrated to the United States to live with her—which I thought sounded super romantic and exciting. I was delighted for him for having undertaken such a huge adventure! And I was even more delighted when she told me that his wife was heavily pregnant!

She told me that Finn, our youngest brother at twenty-six, was still in Nottingham, and that although he'd had a string of girlfriends, he seemed to have no intention of settling down just yet—but he was happy enough in his bachelor life. She said that Finn regularly came round to her house for Sunday dinner, and suggested if Sam, Aaron, and I would like to come up to visit one weekend, it would be wonderful if we could join them. Through even more tears, I replied, 'Oh Louisa, that would be magical… I'd love to. Thank you.'

Louisa laughed in a loving, nurturing way, that no other woman in the world could have ever laughed with me, when she told me, 'Oh jeez, don't be daft, you don't need to thank me! That's what big sisters are for! Come up as soon as you can and give me one of your great big hugs!'

So, I did. The following month, Aaron, Sam, and I drove for five hours up to Leicester, and when she answered her door, we fell into each other's arms.

'Oh ANA!' Louisa exclaimed as she nuzzled her face against my hair, 'My God, how I've missed you.' As we held each other, I knew we'd never lose touch again.

Her husband, Bill, was very welcoming, and he and Aaron quickly slotted into each other's company, chatting together with ease, which was heart-warming to witness.

We introduced each other to our children, which was simply wonderful. Daisy was stunningly beautiful, polite, and charming, with long, blonde curls cascading down her back. And Steven was absolutely adorable, with the cheekiest smile I've ever seen!

Only five minutes after our arrival, Steven asked his cousin, 'Sam, would you like to come and see my climbing frame in the garden?' And Louisa and I watched as our sons ran outside to play together.

With a lump in my throat, I grabbed hold of my sister's hand, and with one look into my eyes, she conveyed the meaning of a thousand words. The love we had for each other hadn't gone anywhere; it hadn't changed or altered in any way over the years. We were the same two young girls who had once shared an attic bedroom, yearning for freedom and love, and here we were, in our independence, with love flowing out of us and spilling out on to everyone around us. We'd done it. We'd survived life, and being together allowed a physical manifestation of our love to play out, so that we could each tangibly feel just how much the other meant to us.

As the afternoon went on, our brother Finn arrived, bearing a bunch of flowers for me, bless him, and a Matchbox toy car for Sam. And after we'd hugged, kissed, and I'd cried a little more, Finn strode out into the garden to find Sam, calling, "Sam! Come here and give your uncle a hug!"

Sam, being a little shy, held back for a second, before Finn literally chased him around the garden, with Sam suddenly in fits of giggles. Then, upon catching him, Finn picked him up and raised him high up into the air.

'My God, you're a good-looking little blighter, aren't you?!' he said with a laugh. And Sam went bright red, before Finn pulled him close and squeezed him, saying, 'It's really good to meet you, little buddy.'

As the hours flew past, Louisa and I drank tea like it was going out of fashion, and before long the men swapped their tea for beers. All of us sitting out in Louisa's garden, we caught up on our lives and revelled in each other's company. I can't tell you how uplifting it was to be there. It was one of the most wonderful days of my life.

When six o' clock arrived, the back gate opened and to my delight my big brother arrived, wearing a huge grin on his face; Yvette just behind him, holding the hand of their little Suzanna—a gorgeous girl, with dark brown hair and big brown eyes. Well, I was out of my chair faster than lightening, and I ran to Jimmy as if we were teenagers. Holding me tightly, my tears poured on to his jacket, taking me straight back to the day he'd got out of the Young Offenders'. We didn't need words, really. When we looked into each other's eyes and smiled, the love between us was immense.

I had my family back, and a new niece and nephew to boot… I was in heaven.

After Yvette embraced me warmly and told me how good it was to see me, I crouched down to Suzanna's level (not wanting to be too full on, as I know young children can often be timid) and said, 'Well, Suzanna, it's an absolute pleasure to meet you. I'm your auntie Ana… Do you think we could have a little hug?'

To which Suzanna nodded, and with the green light given, I scooped her up in my arms, kissed her cheek tenderly, and told her that I loved her very much—meaning it with every fibre within me.

'She looks like you, don't you think?' Jimmy asked as he watched us together.

To which I replied, 'Oh gosh, I was never as pretty as this little munchkin! She's gorgeous!'

Then Jimmy put his arm around my shoulder, in the way that only a big brother can, and commented with a smile, 'Don't put yourself down. You were always a stunner… Now, introduce me to my nephew and this new man of yours—I want to see if he's good enough for you!'

Laughing, we made our way back into the garden, and I called out for Sam and Aaron to come join us.

It was simply wonderful.

We stayed overnight; Aaron and I sleeping on a blow up bed in the lounge, whilst Sam slept top to tail with little Steven. And once the kids had all gone to bed, our conversation took a more serious tone as we talked at length about our parents and our upbringing. I explained that I didn't feel that I could contact Mum myself, but I did say that my siblings were welcome to tell her that we were in touch, if they ever felt the time was right. I told them I couldn't contact Mum directly—I wouldn't have known what to say to her. But I did think that if someone else brought me up in conversation with her, then we could judge from her reaction if there would be any point in us speaking again.

When we left Louisa's house on the Sunday afternoon, we were all in high spirits. Sam couldn't stop talking about his cousins and how cool he thought his Uncle Finn was. Whilst I rabbited constantly too, relaying to Aaron the conversations he'd missed when we'd been in different rooms. The time we'd spent with our family had been so incredibly uplifting, it was joyous.

When we got home that evening, I put Sam to bed and then went into the lounge, only to see that Aaron had taken two glasses and a bottle of red wine out on to the balcony. Sitting in his chair and looking so devilishly handsome, he asked me with a definite twinkle in his eyes, 'Would you like to come and join me?'

With a grin rapidly appearing on my face, I agreed, 'Yes, please. I'd love to!'

I took a seat as he poured me a glass of wine, and then he raised his own glass to me and said, 'Cheers, my darling. It's really nice to see you so happy.'

I smiled as we chinked glasses. 'It's been a lovely weekend, hasn't it?'

He sipped his wine, then grinned, 'Yeah, it's been great. I really enjoyed meeting your family…'

'You did?' I asked—keen to learn more about how he'd felt around my siblings.

And he nodded his head earnestly. 'Yeah, I really liked them. They're a nice bunch.'

I looked out at the gardens beneath us, taking a moment to relax into my chair. And as I looked back to Aaron, he continued, 'It got me thinking when I was listening to you talk about *your* family so much on the way home. I realised that I don't want you to see me as being an outsider in your life. *I* want to be your family.'

I held his eyes as he spoke, and before I had chance to reply, he reached into his pocket, pulled out a ring box and placed it on the table in front of me. I watched as he opened the box, revealing a beautiful gold ring with three diamonds.

He told me, 'This was my grandmother's engagement ring. My mum gave it to me after Gran passed away... She said that she wanted me to have it ready for when I met the woman who I wanted to spend the rest of my life with... I've had this ring for twelve years now, and never before have I ever wanted to offer it to anyone. But with you Ana, I know, I am deeply in love with you. You've taught me what love really is... Sweetheart, will you marry me and let me be your family?'

I leant forward and kissed him. Placing my arms around his neck, I pulled myself on to his lap and kissed him again whilst wearing a huge, beaming smile. Then through our kisses, I whispered, 'Yes, Aaron Thompson. Yes, please. I'd love to marry you.'

We stopped kissing just long enough for him to slide his grandmother's ring onto my finger, and then, as we kissed again, our passion elevated and Aaron commented, 'Maybe this is a little more than the neighbours need to see?'

We laughed like teenagers, before he looked more seriously into my eyes and asked, 'Ana, can I take you to bed?'

To which I replied, 'My darling, you can take me anywhere you want to.'

CHAPTER TWENTY-SEVEN

efore Aaron and I could marry, I had to get divorced from David. So, not beating around the bush, I hired a solicitor who assisted me with contacting him. Twelve months later, I was free of my past and at liberty to step forward into my future.

Aaron and I decided we wanted a very simple ceremony, and when our wedding day came, we tied the knot at the registry office and then celebrated with dinner and champagne at a restaurant at the beach.

It was such a beautiful day.

My siblings and their children all came, and Aaron's parents and sister came too. When I saw our family all mingling together in the evening, with the kids running around on the beach, I truly felt that I was home.

My mum and I had never got back in touch, so she didn't come to the wedding. It seemed she never changed and I was always an outcast in her eyes.

Louisa did tell me at one stage that she had been to visit Mum and she'd told her that she'd seen me. She said that she'd explained that I had a son, that I was in love, and living happily in Cornwall not far from the sea. But when my mother had only replied by scoffing, 'Well, that must be nice!' Louisa deemed that it would be futile for me to try to contact her—there was no relationship to salvage.

As my protective big sister, she counselled me, 'Ana, know that you don't need to see her again. You don't need to put yourself through that. If you go, she'll only make you feel uncomfortable and then give you a list of things she needs fixing around the house! Don't worry, just focus on loving everyone else that's in your life and don't feel guilty about it.'

So, I never did contact my mum, and I tried to make my peace with her from a distance. Although, I do carry guilt over our estranged relationship, I think I'm old enough now to realise that a relationship is a two-way street, and if she had wanted to see me, she could have said so to Louisa. But she never did. And I accept that—as hard as it is to do.

Shortly after our wedding, Aaron and I started trying for a baby. He had always been open with me, saying that he'd love for us to have a child of our own, but until we were married, I hadn't felt truly stable enough to actively contemplate bringing a new life into the world. However, presented with the reality of what felt like the perfect family life, the idea of being a mum all over again definitely did play on my mind, and I found I yearned to expand our family as the months ticked by—feelings of broodiness sweeping over me anytime I walked past a parent with a pram.

Aaron obviously knew about my fertility issues and how Sam had been a miracle as far as I was concerned, so he didn't pin all his hopes on having a baby. But I did believe in my heart that we were in a healthy situation, worthy of supporting a new life.

From here, the months ticked by, and Aaron, Sam, and I lived happily, enjoying our family life, visiting my brothers and sister whenever we had some spare cash to cover the petrol. And, every now and again, one of our siblings would arrive with their family in tow to stay with us for the weekend. It was delightful. I felt as if we were really making a go of our lives, and the roots that Aaron and I had put down were stable and sustained by a love that nourished us both.

As time passed and no baby came our way, I hit my thirty-fourth birthday, and I started to feel a bit restless and uninspired by my job at the accountants. So, I decided to start a part-time course in Social Pedagogy, which teaches the theory and practice of holistic education—a discipline that straddles both social work and education. I felt that changing my career would allow me to contribute more actively to society, and I believed if I could care for other people's children, helping them through tough times, I could hopefully give something back to the system that had given me so much.

I signed up for a two year course, and this allowed me to feel focused in my life. Not only was I going to have a family I loved, I was also going to have a career that I could love too, which would hopefully be of real service to others. So, I studied hard when Sam was in bed and Aaron was working nights, and honestly, I loved the experience of being a *proper* student for the first time in my life.

Now, I should also mention that during that period, credit was being thrown at the nation in the form of cards, loans, and finance agreements. And Aaron suggested we take out a loan, get a new car (which we needed) and take a family holiday abroad as a treat for ourselves. I had never once been out of England, and when he suggested we take a plane and find some sunshine somewhere, I thought it sounded wonderful.

Sam was ten years old at the time, with lots of friends who had visited Spain and France, and we knew he had always been envious of the stories they'd come back to school with after the summer holidays. So, the idea of all of us taking a 'break from the norm' felt like an opportunity for a real adventure.

I agreed we could use a new car—the old banger Aaron drove was definitely ready for the scrapheap— but we didn't have the savings to finance these ideas ourselves, so why not take out a loan?

You know the concept of debt has never sat comfortably with me, but after a lifetime of feeling like I had very little to offer my son apart from love, the idea of taking him on a family holiday abroad felt like an experience worth getting into debt for. Our minds made up, we visited the bank one Saturday morning, applied for £10,000 and were subsequently approved.

In the weeks that followed, I was in my element exploring travel ideas, poring over glossy brochures offering holiday packages—which all seemed far too expensive once you got to July or August! And after we had spent many lovely evenings dreaming of where we'd go, we made our decision and opted for the Greek island of Corfu. Biting the bullet, we signed a holiday form to take Sam out of school for two weeks, and a few months later, at thirty-five years old, I went on an aeroplane for the very first time.

I remember getting onboard and feeling like an exuberant child. My goodness, I was so excited. I felt like I was sitting on a plane that was about to take me to heaven—it was a such a wonderful experience.

Attractive air stewardesses with flawless make-up, big smiles, and pink scarves tied around their necks served us buck's fizz in small plastic cups as soon as we were settled in our seats. They offered everyone hard-boiled sweets out of wicker baskets just before take-off, and when the drinks trolley came around, they gave me the smallest bags of peanuts I've ever seen—which I ate one nut at a time just to make the experience last! There was a film playing on small TV screens dotted around the cabin that you could buy headphones to listen to, so we bought a set for Sam. Then Aaron and I spent the flight nattering, laughing, and gazing out the window at the magnificent views beneath us.

When we stepped off the plane at Corfu Airport, the heat of the day hit us instantly. The island looked lush and green; I was in awe of its natural beauty as soon as I laid eyes on it. The sky was the most beautiful shade of blue that I had ever seen.

A bus took us to the terminal and we entered a pleasantly air-conditioned building, where the tiled floor was so shiny I initially thought it was wet—I couldn't help but smile when I thought how impressed my mum would have been to see a place so spotless!

We showed our passports to a police officer, then waited at the side of a rickety carousel, which creaked loudly as it lumbered along. And after being reunited with our suitcases, we walked out to find our travel rep and shuttle-bus bearing the holiday company's logo.

We sat on the bus for an hour or so, as it trundled around the rugged landscape to the various hotels, dropping the other holidaymakers off, before finally, when the bus was nearly empty, it was our turn to start our holiday. I was so pleased with our accommodation. We'd chosen a self-catering apartment in a complex of two-storey buildings with creepers growing up the whitewashed walls, and the cobbled pathways meandering between the apartment blocks were edged with the prettiest flowers.

Arriving there made me think that even the glorious photos in the holiday brochure hadn't done it justice— it was breathtaking. There was a large swimming pool just yards from our apartment and a sea view from the pool area to boot. It was a perfect holiday, and we spent it sightseeing, relaxing, and laughing.

We found comedy in the fact that no matter how early we got up, all the sunbeds were already reserved with the towels of people who didn't want to use them until much later on. So we ventured out each day, pottering contentedly around Corfu, exploring white sandy beaches with turquoise waters, and then we would often return to the complex for a dip in the pool, late afternoon. But regardless of what we were doing each day, we absolutely delighted in our time away.

We sat through cabaret acts in the evenings, drinking cocktails while Sam played with kids from other families; we took lunch at beachside tavernas where we ate an abundance of olives and feta cheese—feeling sorry for the overworked donkeys whenever they walked past. We looked for crabs in rock pools and played dominoes out on our terrace, basking in the beauty of the dramatic sunsets we witnessed each night when the sky and the water turned golden as the sun disappeared beneath the sea.

No matter if I was watching Aaron and Sam playing in the pool while I read my book, or if we'd hired a pedalo and pedalled out further than we were allowed, I was in a state of pure bliss. During those two weeks away, everything was momentarily perfect, and if I could choose to live any two weeks over and over again, those would be the weeks I would choose. We talked about how amazing it would be if we could stay there forever, and once we had passed the halfway mark of the holiday, the days suddenly went by too fast. Before we knew it, the time had come to pack up our suitcases, and none of us wanted to go home.

When we arrived back in England, Aaron busied himself with finding our new car, and once he'd chosen the one he wanted, I went with him to the used car dealer to buy it. We handed over a cheque for several thousand pounds and bought what turned out to be an incredibly reliable, family car. Then, the most amazing thing happened the month after we'd returned from our holiday: I missed my period.

As you can imagine, after years of unprotected sex with Aaron, finding out that we had conceived a baby delighted us. We were absolutely over the moon

Of course, I worried that the pregnancy would be complicated, but I allowed myself to be happy with the knowledge I had a baby growing inside me—and if my baby needed me to take things slow, that's what I'd do.

When we told Sam, he was thrilled; the idea of having a sibling sat well with him—although he did tell us that he would prefer a boy to a girl! As you can imagine, I was eager to have all the tests going to make sure my baby and my body were healthy. So, after four months of pregnancy, I went up to the hospital one afternoon for some blood tests and an appointment with the gynaecologist. Aaron had to work, but I was quite used to nipping for check-ups by myself, so this really hadn't fazed me.

The weather that day was grim, and I had taken two buses to the hospital, sheltering under my umbrella as I'd trotted briskly across the streets. Once I'd had my blood taken, seen the gynaecologist, I was subsequently asked to wait for my results in a seating area with a stack of old magazines.

I sat there watching the thick storm clouds rage past the window, silently flipping through magazine articles for what felt like forever, until I started to notice that women who had come in after me were leaving before me. After an hour and a half, I checked with the receptionist to ask if there might be a problem and was told the doctor was working on my file and he would be with me as soon as he could.

As time went on, I continued to sit there, watching the various comings and goings. And I went to stand up at one point as my consultant appeared at the end of the corridor, but instead of approaching me, he avoided eye contact and went quickly into the reception area to shuffle a few papers and get whatever he needed. After leaving the office, he walked past me with nothing more said than, 'I'll be with you as soon as possible, Mrs Thompson.' So, I smiled politely and settled back down into my seat.

I stayed in that waiting room all afternoon, and after four hours with no meaningful words said to me, I knew something must be very wrong.

When my doctor finally arrived in the waiting area, his expression was weary but kind, and his body language carried an overtone which conveyed he found his job difficult in that precise moment. We went into his office and he invited me to take a seat at his desk. With my coat folded in my lap and my handbag at my feet, I looked into his eyes and watched him search for the right words to say. I knew in my heart that he was saddened by my situation, and then he finally spoke.

'Mrs Thompson, I must sincerely apologise for keeping you waiting all afternoon. Your tests showed some deeply concerning results, therefore I wanted to check everything thoroughly and make sure that I knew the facts before I spoke to you about your condition.'

I didn't need to speak, it wasn't necessary for me to respond; I just looked into his eyes and silently asked him to continue.

'May I call you Anastasia?'

I nodded.

'Anastasia, I am so sorry to tell you this, but I'm afraid your blood tests showed seropositive for HIV.'

As my mind struggled to comprehend his words, my soul flew out of me and, I swear, I shot up to view the moment from the corner of the room. In consciousness, I was completely separate from my flesh and bones, and through an out-of-body experience, I watched myself sit there as the doctor continued.

'Our tests suggest you have a life expectancy in the region of eighteen months.'

It was too hard to traverse that pinnacle shift within the constraints of my body, so, temporarily, I had to leave it. My mind had literally exploded and I was forced to make the shift from being a very happy woman with a lot to live for, to a person who suddenly saw death on the horizon.

After I'd come back down to Earth and we'd talked through what they could do to help me and what the next steps would be, the doctor personally booked me a taxi, and I went home to tell Aaron, absolutely terrified that he would have the virus too.

CHAPTER TWENTY-EIGHT

I t's truly a very strange sensation being told that you're going to die. Obviously, we all know that we will die, and normally we have no idea whether that will be tomorrow or decades down the line. But when I suddenly knew just how finite my time here was, I knew it wasn't enough.

I wasn't ready to go. I wanted to raise Sam, to have another baby and a beautiful life. My body had turned against me, and I quickly began to feel very detached from it.

Amazingly, Aaron hadn't contracted HIV from me; he had been miraculously immune to it, so thank God we didn't have to try to prepare for us both to be hit with AIDS. But obviously my news devastated him, and we decided not to tell Sam the gravity of my condition immediately. There was no way I could tell my son that the doctors suspected I only had eighteen months left. The only way I could possibly think to describe my condition to him was to say that I had become sick, and I was going to get sicker, and the doctors didn't know how to make me better. I felt that was enough, without adding the intensity of a timescale for my death for him to try and process.

I was in and out of hospital every week, and two weeks after having being diagnosed with AIDS, I lost my baby. The doctors had warned us that our child would have most likely been infected with HIV, so it was suggested to me that maybe his or her own passing was a blessing in disguise. But there was nothing positive that I could find in any element of our situation, and they were very dark days to endure. Whilst grieving our baby, we could only see my own death ahead.

I found it impossible to think of any good that could possibly come from what we were going through. Imagining Sam growing up without a mum was absolutely heart-breaking, and the guilt I carried over that was more intense than I can put into words.

I got very ill very quickly and began to spend more time in hospital than I spent at home. I saw specialists regularly to have more and more tests, and I was prescribed all sorts of medicines to treat the various things that started to go wrong with my body. However, when it seemed the clouds couldn't get any darker, a ray of light appeared.

In the 1990s big things happened with the research into AIDS. My doctors told me of a new treatment that was becoming available for testing, and remarkably, I was invited to take part in their medical trials.

The doctors explained they were conducting what they called a double-blind test, where the project team would give some patients the real drug and some a placebo, and neither the patient nor their doctor would know who had been given which. The researchers would then analyse their results and judge if the treatment was a success.

Thank God, destiny, and that team of medical researchers, I was given the real drug. And that miracle medicine is the reason that I'm still here today.

While those pills would never cure me, they would enable me to live with AIDS (albeit as a heavy burden forever crushing my shoulders) and would allow the meeting I had booked with death to drift away. So once again, I could settle back into the more natural state of not knowing when I would die.

I had stopped doing tarot readings ever since I had found out I was carrying the HIV virus—once I'd been told I only had up to eighteen months left to live, I found I had no desire whatsoever to try to ask what the future held. I just wanted to hang on to my present for as long as I possibly could—I didn't want the future to come. But towards the end of my thirties, armed with my new medication, I became very strong (both physically and mentally) in coping with AIDS and I started reading the cards once again.

When I reviewed my life, I realised how much I had forever been scrambling through, constantly living in survival mode up until I'd moved in with Aaron. I knew I had made a number of terrible decisions that had led me to my turmoil, but as I assessed my journey, I knew that I had to be more than just the woman who'd drawn the short straw or won the unlucky lottery.

My Numerology birth chart had told me that during the last two chapters of my life, I would be called to be of service to others, and even though I had previously doubted that I would live long enough to reach that stage, when this pinnacle shift happened within me, it suddenly made so much sense.

Feeling centred in myself, I would meditate every day in gratitude for the life I still had and the love of my family. And gradually my perspective sharpened to a point where I knew that I had to become a real Giver in life, if I wanted my life to soar.

I felt I had a debt to repay to society for all the support I had received at Sunrise House. And feeling strong in myself, I decided the time had come to pay forward the kindness that Simon had given me and help as many other people as I could.

Having attended just about every support group I'd ever heard of during my early years of suffering with AIDS, I decided it was time for me to go back to those groups—but this time around, my only intention was to give support and help others. When I started actively volunteering in these networks, I suddenly found more friends than I had ever known before. It was wonderful.

I met a lot of people who didn't have anyone to care for them at home. And knowing the full force of the social stigma that AIDS brings, I understood how easy it would be to lose yourself mentally if you didn't have love in your life.

I've found HIV and AIDS to be greatly misunderstood by many, and the unfortunate souls who have to live with AIDS seem to be treated unfairly by a significant portion of society—or at least they have been during my generation.

I've seen healthcare professionals reach for face masks in my presence; I've seen care workers wear boiler suits and rubber gloves to attend to AIDS patients. And I felt very passionate about trying to do something to address this kind of ignorance.

I have found that in addition to suffering AIDS, it is very common to also suffer from judgments made by others in parallel. I believe these are often made through a lack of awareness in the mainstream, and this was an area where I saw that I might be able to help.

Would it shock you to learn that I contracted HIV through a blood transfusion after being beaten up at the brothel? I wouldn't blame you for having already assumed I must have got it through drug abuse. But getting AIDS can happen to anyone; HIV is not picky about who it consumes and it definitely doesn't limit itself to drug addicts and homosexuals.

I've heard it said that the best way to cope with trauma or tragedy is to always look for the silver lining to your cloud, and that when fate delivers us a blow, there is normally a constructive outcome that can occur as the result. Whilst I had felt that having AIDS was the biggest cloud I could have encountered, I decided that if I could help raise awareness of HIV and possibly prevent others from contracting the virus, whilst at the same time compassionately supporting others, then this would be my silver lining. I would make sure something positive came about as the result of all the negativity I had endured.

So, with a loving family behind me, I decided to go very public with my condition. Working closely with my support groups, I started campaigning hard to help spread AIDS awareness; I felt I had a mission to try to stop the unfair social labelling of people with HIV/ AIDS. I wanted to do everything I could to shift the general opinion away from it being something taboo, to it simply being a very harsh infection that some people are unfortunate enough to have, whilst also educating people about how HIV is transmitted.

I gave talks in village halls, colleges, community centres, libraries—in fact, I would talk publicly anywhere I could. I worked repeatedly with two gay gentlemen and when we addressed a crowd, we'd often start by announcing that one of us had AIDS and we'd ask the audience if they could guess who that was—they would always choose one of my colleagues. When I then stepped forward announcing it was me who had the infection, there would be audible gasps and you could see people's foreheads furrow as they acknowledged their misconceptions about HIV.

I wasn't able to work in the traditional sense of the word, nor did I have the physical energy to pursue a career in the field of Social Pedagogy as I had once envisaged I would. But in my volunteering efforts, I did feel that I had a full-time job, and I spent most of my time (whilst Sam was at school) visiting other people living with AIDS in neighbouring communities. I would go around to their houses and clean for them, I'd take them shopping, and care for them in any way that would be of service—being there for them in their isolation, never judging, never thinking I knew what they needed, just supporting them however they individually found beneficial.

There was one lady I became very close with, called Jacqui, who was a single mum, and I helped her by liaising with Social Services to organise care for her teenage daughter for when she passed away. I remember going to her house one day and finding her in such a state, it was awful. She was running a temperature of forty-one degrees and looked like death warmed up. When I asked her, 'Jacqui, did your care assistant come this morning?'

She told me, 'Yes, but she left... I don't know when... We argued... I don't know why... I'm so cold... Is it time to get ready for work?' She was absolutely delirious. She hadn't had a job for over two years, and regardless of anything Jacqui might have said to cause offence to her care worker, she was so obviously unwell it amazed me how anyone could have left her as she was—without so much as even calling a doctor. The care assistant had essentially left her there to die by not phoning an ambulance, or maybe not even noticing that she was in such a state.

After calling 999, Jacqui was admitted to hospital and the doctors started treating her for an infection that she had succumbed to. So I worked with Social Services to ensure her daughter was placed with a local foster family, who could care for her in Jacqui's absence.

When I got back home that night, I was still absolutely furious about how Jacqui had been treated by her 'care' assistant, and I phoned up that agency to give them a piece of my mind. With the branch manager on the line, I told him, 'You should be ashamed of the conduct of your staff. You took Jacqui's money, pretending to give a damn and then deserted her when the going got tough!'

I was certainly more hot-headed than I like to be, but when faced with negligence, my throat chakra opened easily and I felt that I was justified in speaking my truth exactly as I saw it.

I genuinely cared about every person that I helped, and I regularly took on other people's battles, fighting their corner for them when they lacked the physical or emotional strength to do it for themselves. In return for all my efforts, I found the Universe rewarded me with an abundance of deep connections.

Whilst my illness was crippling, the friendships I gained gave me wings and a dozen reasons to smile every day. In my voluntary work, I found having AIDS myself put me in a position where I could empathise with everything my friends were going through—we were in the same boat, and as hard as that boat was to live in, we navigated the waters and made it through our experiences together.

As time's gone on, a lot of the people I've been close to and cared for have passed away. I've seen death arrive many times, take its victim, and leave a gaping hole which the bereaved must try to cope with. I've learned to recognise the signs when my friends have started to slip away from this dimension, and in line with my spiritual beliefs, I've tried to comfort them and assure them not to fear passing over, asking them to have faith that death is not the end—it's just a transformation of energy and a gateway to the next stage of existence.

I've held the hands of so many that I've cared about during their final hours, and I've been asked to speak at twenty-six funerals during the last fifteen years. Whenever this honour has been bestowed upon me, I've spoken from my heart, talking about what made that person special and how they touched my life. These days, I find I'm easily able to see beauty in every soul I encounter, and I feel blessed any time I'm asked to share my sentiments with others. Even when I'm grieving the loss of a friend, I find the Universe gives me strength to talk with conviction, and I feel as if I'm now able to act as a vessel through which love can share its message with the world.

When my illness has made me physically weak, love has kept me mentally and spiritually strong, and I've refused to be beaten by my body into living a life of fear or withdrawal from society. My body may be consumed with heaviness, but in my soul, I feel the light, and it's a beautiful sensation.

CHAPTER TWENTY-NINE

When I was forty-three and had been living with AIDS (and the host of other physical problems that had arrived) for eight years, Sam completed his course at college and applied successfully to the University of Bristol to study Social Work. With a real drive about him, he was eager to stand on his own two feet—he was certainly never timid nor lacking in self-belief. He took a student loan to pay his fees and sorted his accommodation in the halls of residence very independently. My boy had become a man, and he was a man I was overwhelmingly proud to be associated with.

When Sam moved away to Bristol, I missed his presence in our home; the flat was so quiet without him—music no longer blaring from his room. I missed seeing his smile and hearing his laugh, but more than anything, I felt happiness for my son, and I was really pleased for him that he had flown the nest. The best way to explain how I felt was that I yearned for Sam to have a taste of freedom. I wanted him to have fun, to focus on living life to the full, and to enjoy the opportunities that destiny had waiting in store.

Some people doubt if eighteen-year-olds are in fact adults, and say that adulthood doesn't arrive until you're in your twenties, but at eighteen, my son was more of a man and a gentleman than any male I'd ever met before. He was strong-willed, in touch with his emotions, and wise beyond his years. He's always grasped things quickly, then gone on to develop ideas with his logic and clarity—and from an early age, his inquisitive spirit and natural perspective on Big-Picture thinking have amazed me.

After Sam left for university, he never returned to live in the family home and chose to remain in Bristol after he completed his degree. And I understood his decision without question. He had a good group of friends there, and he'd also met a stunning young lady, called Melissa, who he'd fallen happily and healthily in love with.

Unfortunately, as the years continued to tick by at home, it seemed that Aaron's mental well-being deteriorated in parallel with my health—he needed me to be strong, which I still was in my mind and spirit, but physically I was lacking. This affected Aaron in a way that I never really expected. I started seeing changes in his behaviour when we were at home together in the evenings, and we just didn't really mentally connect any longer, yet I couldn't put my finger on why.

Being a nurse, Aaron knew how to care for me on a professional level, and when I was really ill, he took control of all my meds to make sure I took what I needed. But often, he would go out after he'd sorted my personal care and leave me just like I was his patient, rather than his wife or soul mate. Let me be clear, I didn't resent him going out—Jesus, I knew the situation was tough for him and he needed to get out the house at times to keep sane. But when he'd return home, I'd struggle to talk to him normally. We didn't see eye to eye on much, we argued quite a lot, and we would regularly agree to differ in our opinions. I still loved him without doubt, but I missed our relationship, and I felt saddened that our circumstances had chipped away at its foundations and weakened it so.

Things finally came to a head one day when I awoke in the morning to find Aaron slumped in an armchair, still in his work clothes, his face dropped on one side. I struggled to get any words out of him and those he did manage were slurred—I was convinced he'd had a stroke. I phoned an ambulance and we went to hospital, then, thankfully, as the day wore on, Aaron came round and he was absolutely fine. The doctors had spoken to him privately about his condition and when he reported back to me, he told me they had said his heart was good, there were no signs of a stroke, and they discharged him that evening.

When we got home from an incredibly frightening day, I told Aaron to rest up and I set about making dinner. It was only when I came to take my pills that I realised exactly what the nightmare had been about— my stock was significantly depleted. Aaron had taken my medication.

As soon as I realised this, it explained everything to me—the distance between us, the differences in our mental wavelength, and the reason he went out so much. He'd turned to using again as an escape route, and he'd felt unable to come clean to me as our whole relationship was based on having built a drug-free, wholesome life together.

When I asked him about my missing pills, he denied it completely. I tried to approach the situation sensitively, telling him, 'Darling, I can understand why self-medicating might seem like a crutch... I get it, I really do. You don't need to hide this from me. We can get through this together.'

But he couldn't admit that he'd relapsed and told me, 'Ana, you're imagining things. I haven't taken anything.' And he walked out the room with nothing more said than, 'Really, this is crazy... Just drop it, please.'

It was so saddening, but from that day on, I took strict control of my medication. I counted my tablets and unbeknownst to Aaron, I kept written records of the exact quantity of drugs that should have been in the cupboard. Unsurprisingly, the distance between us continued to grow.

When I saw my drugs disappearing at a much faster rate than I was taking them, I had all the proof I needed to confirm I wasn't disillusioned in any way. Regrettably, Aaron denied the situation for a long time, and as a consequence, I began to love him less.

I remember the pair of us going to a funeral one day, where I'd been asked to say a few words for a dear friend, and as we walked behind the coffin, Aaron put his arm around me, appearing to be supporting me through a tough time. I recall shrugging him off, unable to bear the weight of him around me in that moment. He looked supportive, but all I felt was drained.

As time went on, Aaron kept taking my meds (sometimes to the point where I'd have none left), so I bought a safe and started locking up my pills, sleeping with the key inside my pillow. It was a terribly upsetting situation to be in, but our strained relationship carried on like this for over a year. I see with hindsight that we stayed together far longer than we should have done—Aaron couldn't cope with the body that I had, and I couldn't cope with his mindset.

Then, five years ago, there was one very significant weekend when Sam and Melissa (now his wife) came to stay with us, having announced they had some very special news they wanted to share in person. They arrived buzzing with a beautiful energy, and as soon as they'd taken their coats off, Sam announced, 'Mum, Aaron, Melissa's pregnant! You're going to be grandparents!! Can you believe it?!'

As any overjoyed parent might do, I welled up with elation for them—it was amazing to watch the success Sam was making of his life. Melissa is such a sweet-natured woman, very successful in her career, and a hundred-percent doting and committed to her husband. So, to see them have the honour of a child bestowed upon them felt perfect. They were, *and still are,* an adorable, level-headed, kind, intelligent, and well-balanced couple—I remember thinking, 'Yes! This is how family life should be!'

During the weekend they stayed with us, despite the amazing news we were being invited to share, Aaron still seemed distant and it appeared that even this wonderful new chapter of life (a new generation no less) couldn't draw him back in. I'm sure that he didn't get high whilst they were visiting, but he certainly wasn't engaging fully in our family celebration. He frequently wandered off to check his phone and he was really rather aloof throughout their whole visit.

His behaviour irritated me to boiling point; I just couldn't fathom him. I thought this should have been news which pulled us together—even if just for two days whilst Sam was home—but it didn't, it just set him further apart.

After waving Sam and Melissa off from the door and watching their car disappear around the corner, I went back into Aaron who was sitting on the balcony smoking a cigarette, and I had him for it. I was absolutely raging. I asked him, 'Aaron! What the hell is going on inside your head?! You've been on another planet all weekend! Is it too much to ask that you delight in Sam's news with me? Melissa's pregnant for God's sake and you sit there with a face like a wet weekend? What the hell?!'

For the first time, Aaron found the courage to face up to a problem he couldn't bear any longer. Holding a cigarette close to his lips, he told me, 'Ana, there's someone else. I've met someone else.'

I believe my reply was, 'Oh.' And I turned around to go inside, shocked to my core by the revelation. After making a cup of tea, I sat down in the lounge to have a cigarette myself and process what I'd heard.

I think I smoked a few cigarettes, one straight after the other, whilst I added everything up. It made perfect sense that he had someone else. We hadn't been on each other's wavelength for a long time; I was so ill and detached from him, I had no interest in sex, nor recreational drugs—which he evidently still did.

After a while, Aaron came to sit with me and we spoke, Aaron excusing himself for what he'd done and explaining his reasons. He told me, 'She's a nurse at the hospital; she's a good woman… And being with her and having her support helps me to have the energy to be there for you… I know you need me, and I'm not going to leave you, Ana. But honestly, I'm a man, and I need something on the side for my own sexual needs.'

The words that came out of his mouth left me speechless, and I ended up saying, 'Do you know what Aaron? That's fine… I don't care… You're welcome to each other.'

There was so little left between us. He was someone I'd once loved sharing life with, but now he was a person I didn't recognise, who was having sex with someone else. My spiritual state of well-being had tumbled so far from being centred that I was beyond flat. The hurt that I felt in my heart numbed my mind, and I failed to see anything positive about this revelation. I just felt alone, and lonely, even though Aaron was sitting right next to me.

We lived like this for a little while, with me knowing about his new romance and kidding myself that I didn't care. But then the time came when I finally found my inner strength and decided it wasn't healthy for either of us to continue sharing a home any longer.

The realisation came one night when I was in bed struggling to sleep. Aaron had been working a late shift and I'd watched the red digits on my bedside clock change since midnight. By 2 a.m., I knew that Aaron had decided to sleep in her bed that night. And in those dark hours, I realised that no matter how poorly I was to become, I would always be better off single than in a loveless relationship.

My hurt had morphed into clarity, and I realised that his new relationship was the catalyst that had been necessary to force us apart. Aaron was struggling with life, and in turn, I had lost my footing too. I felt like I'd been swimming against the current for so long in trying to hold on to some semblance of a relationship that we used to enjoy—which simply didn't exist anymore.

Feeling certain that there would be a positive release from my turmoil—our turmoil—by letting him go, I packed up Aaron's things before he came home the next day and had them ready and waiting for him when he walked through the door.

He pitied me, I think that's the reason he'd stayed with me. He had felt too bad about leaving me to actually leave, so I did it for the pair of us—freeing him from the burden of a very ill wife and setting myself free myself from a relationship that hadn't nurtured me mentally for a long time.

As a sideline to all this, the loan that we'd taken out donkeys' years before (to pay for our holiday to Greece and the car) still hung like a slack noose around my neck, and it still does even to this day. Unable to work and reduced down to life on Aaron's income, we had never been able to keep up with the repayments the bank asked for, so we'd arranged to make token payments for years. And all the while, the bank had been adding more interest.

We'd experienced the bizarre phenomenon whereby even though we were making payments (small though they were), the debt never got any smaller, instead it just grew bigger and bigger and bigger.

By the time Aaron and I split, the debt had doubled in size from the amount we had originally borrowed. Then, when Aaron was no longer in my life, he disappeared, and I was left with the bank writing to me every few weeks, demanding money.

As a single woman, I've survived on benefits for the last four and a half years and I've made goodness knows how many phone calls to the bank, where I've explained my situation, detailing what I can and can't afford to give them each month—having lived through bailiffs taking all of my things in London, the threat of them coming again is something I'm loathed to live with.

I've filled out form after form over the years, declaring the income that I receive, and the bank is more than aware of my health. Yet as the years have passed, their stance has never changed: they want their money, plus more.

Only last week they wrote to me to say they've re-evaluated my situation and feel I should be able to increase my payments if I give them the money I'm given for personal care assistance—my bewilderment over their behaviour never ceases.

I know I will have to continue making payments to the bank out of the benefits I am given for food, care and shelter, until the day I die. And I wonder how much I have actually paid in total over the last twenty years, for what was meant to be a four-year loan for a car and two weeks away—thank goodness we enjoyed that holiday!

The bank plan to repossess everything in my home when I pass away, and I've been instructed to tell Sam and Melissa that they mustn't take anything from the flat for themselves. So, I literally leave nothing behind that my family are legally allowed to have to remember me by, which does sadden me.

I can't help but question how the bankers at the top of the pyramid sleep at night. Truly, I can't fathom how they can bring themselves to consciously reinforce a system like this. When disaster strikes we must still pay the banks—their lack of compassion astounds me.

When I consider the banking industry, I can't see any love at the heart of it, it all appears to be based upon a cold obsession with profit—as if they literally believe money is the most important thing in the world. Clearly, I'm no economist, but it appears clear that the global distribution of wealth is hellishly imbalanced, and maybe it's this lack of compassion or unhealthy worship of money that's doing us in. It's always felt to me as if the system we know enables the rich to get richer whilst the poor get poorer, and I wonder when the scales will finally tip in the favour of the masses.

I pray that our conscious evolution will bring forth the inner power necessary to uplift and reform the systems which support our societies. And I pray this happens rapidly, so everyone can live being treated humanely in every aspect of life.

CHAPTER THIRTY

ollowing my breakup with Aaron, Sam and Melissa were incredibly kind and took it upon themselves to search for a new home for me, close to where they live. They asked me to stay with them one weekend and surprised me by organising to visit a flat in a senior citizens' complex literally around the corner from their home. Their positivity and compassion brought tears to my eyes when I realised why we were all there in an airy, two-bedroom apartment—Sam teasing me, 'Well, we figured it would be handy if you lived here—we could really use a babysitter from time to time!'

We all laughed and I hugged the pair of them tightly, feeling so honoured that they would ask me to live near them; it was such a breath-taking moment. The last thing I wanted was to be a burden on Sam—he had his own life to lead and his family to raise. But just to be near him, to be close enough to watch my grandchildren grow up and be a part of their lives is the biggest privilege I've ever known.

Sam is now in his thirties; he's a qualified social worker, and he assures me that he feels fulfilled and inspired in his career. He works in a child protection unit, and when he's not at work making sure vulnerable children are safe, he's at home with a wife he loves, raising his own children and enjoying life with everything he's got. Sam is, without doubt, the most wonderful person I've ever met, and when I look at my life now, I think if the only reason I've existed was that so Sam could enter the world, then I'm more than happy with that.

So, four years ago, I moved to live in the countryside near Bristol, just around the corner from my family, who understand what love really is. I know I'm truly blessed to be a part of their lives.

I've been living peacefully for some time now, and I wake up every day knowing love and feeling centred. But around eighteen months ago, I was taken very ill, and it all happened very suddenly.

I had fallen asleep on the sofa in the afternoon and was woken by the sound of the phone ringing, so I pulled myself up to answer it and heard Sam's voice on the other end. I remember feeling surprised as he doesn't phone very much, I mostly see him in person, and as we spoke Sam told me, 'Mum, I thought you were babysitting this evening? We've been waiting for you for over half an hour. Are you OK?' And as he spoke it seemed that I had lost any recognition of what day or time it was.

Not knowing if I felt well or not, I replied, 'Oh... I'm so sorry... I fell asleep. Shall I come over now?'

As Sam spoke, I struggled to make any sense out of what was happening to me. I felt so peculiar.

Only a few seconds later, Sam said, 'Mum, you don't sound well. I'm going to call an ambulance for you. Go and unlock your front door while I'm still on the phone, and I'm coming straight over.' But before Sam and the paramedics arrived, I had slipped into a coma that took my consciousness to a different dimension for several weeks.

The hospital told Sam it was unlikely I would ever wake up, and I was completely unaware of my physical body or of the grief Sam had already started to process. I couldn't hear him talking to me at my bedside; and although my body lay in that hospital room, I swear, I wasn't there. During those weeks, I was a free spirit and I was outside of the Earth as we understand it to be.

I can picture it now, as clear as day, how I soared up beyond the stratosphere to a point from which I could turn back and look down upon the world and the existence we call Life. From outerspace, I saw the past, the present, and the future of Earth, all existing at once, as one entity. Its dimension was curved, shaped as an ellipse rather than a sphere. The past was to my left, the present in the middle, and the future to my right: it was all happening at once, and I grasped instantly that Time only exists as a human concept.

When I looked at the very distant past, I saw memories which I didn't recognise as my own—and I've contemplated since that maybe these scenes were showing me the past of my DNA.

In the present, through flashing images, I saw the state of the Earth exactly as it is, being exploited and destroyed in so many ways, yet I was also shown scenes of immense love, natural beauty, and compassion.

No matter what visions played, I felt comforted by an underlying and awe-inspiring sensation of innate security and harmony. And whilst the images that I saw in the future are near impossible for me to describe now that I'm back in my body, what I felt was undoubtedly peace, and I know that this is the energy which underpins our existence.

There is an abundance of work to be done to heal our planet from the damage that our species has caused, but I am left feeling certain that this amazing effort will be undertaken and it will be successful.

Through my spiritual voyage, I saw how these trying times are triggering us to collectively value and nurture Peace, Freedom, and Sustainability. It is a relative dimension that we inhabit, so, in order for us to recognise what Love is, its opposite must exist.

Joy is not distinguished as joy without the balance of sadness. Without inner turmoil, inner peace cannot be comprehended. Without opposing extremes, there is only Consciousness—and our dimension is about experiencing. To experience, we must witness the contrast. To know peace, you must understand war. To know freedom, you must understand oppression. And to comprehend the importance of sustainability and the consequences of our actions, we have had to witness nature dying at our hands. We are being shown the dark, so that we can see the light and consciously choose it as our true path.

Above all, I sensed a great feeling of tranquillity and unity. My being was in harmony with everything that exists, existed, or will exist. I was tuned into the frequency of the omnipresent Universal energy, and I was able to appreciate how we are all truly connected. We exist as part of the whole—just as there is a universe inside our bodies made up of trillions of cells, our being is part of our Universe and our energy is interlinked with every living thing. We are part of the same

Consciousness. There is only one I AM, and we are all it—through Life, we are experiencing our Self through billions of perspectives.

I'm not sure if I was sent back from that place or if I chose to come back, but suddenly, I was aware of my body again and I came around. Amazingly, I woke up when Sam and Melissa were visiting, so I opened my eyes to see them standing next to me with tears shimmering in theirs. I smiled as Sam took my hand, but when I tried to talk, I found only a whisper came out. It then dawned on me that I was in hospital, and as I looked at my body, I saw that I was hooked up to a variety of machines.

The first words I said (which must have seemed very strange at the time), weren't 'What happened?' or 'Hello' or anything like that—instead I smiled and said, 'Please tell Emily congratulations on her baby; she's beautiful.'

Emily was one of their best friends, and Sam and Melissa were both immediately concerned that the coma had sent me crazy, as Emily didn't have a baby nor was she pregnant. In my weak state, I urged them cheerfully to believe that she did have a baby; I told them it was a girl and asked for them to pass on my love, so they ended up just placating me and the subject was quickly changed.

A few weeks later, however, they told me that Emily and her husband had announced they were three months pregnant, and six months following that, they had a delightful baby girl in their arms.

Melissa was kind enough to show me a picture of their daughter, and when I saw it, it was a direct match to a vision I had seen in my coma. With joy lighting up my face, I simply said, 'Yes, that's her! I told you she was beautiful!'

It's funny, because they define being in a coma as experiencing a state of deep unconsciousness, but unconscious is far from how I would describe my being during those weeks. I was Superconscious… it was next level Consciousness… and it confirmed the Truth I had always yearned to understand.

When I was allowed to return home from hospital, I experienced a very strange sensation of not feeling quite right in my surroundings, and I do wonder if I came back into a very slightly different time continuum, where everything looked the same but was ever so subtly different.

I knew the flat I was in was my home, but it didn't really feel like mine, and I recognised my slippers which sat on the floor next to my bed, but they didn't feel like mine either. I believe I experienced a kind of friction in moving between dimensions, and for several weeks I went through an adjustment period where I had to get used to occupying my body, my home, and my possessions once again. It all felt rather surreal.

Since that time, I've had all sorts of spiritual encounters and I've met a lot of people who report having experienced similar things, so I'm sure our society is quietly evolving in this regard.

In recent years, I've had some astounding dreams which have been unlike anything I'd seen before. They've occurred every month or two, and during these episodes, I've felt like I've entered an entirely different dimension to that which I've previously known as the dream world. The dreams have been lucid, where I've talked rationally with people who I've loved and lost. I've talked with my dad and several of my friends, and it's felt like my loved ones have found a way to visit me through the subconscious world which can transcend death—every dream I've had like this has been wonderfully peaceful and reassuring.

I've also had dreams with premonitory insights into distressing situations involving people I know. But the messages always come with love, even when the gravity of the circumstance is intense.

One night, I dreamt of Jimmy being in serious trouble and an angel coming to me and telling me not to worry. The angel was the most beautiful creature you could ever imagine, and they said Jimmy was in their care and assured me that he would be fine. As soon as I got up the next morning, I phoned Yvette, and my goodness, she sounded awful. She told me Jimmy had been in a car crash and had been taken into hospital the day before— he was in a coma. Immediately my dream made sense to me, so with a very level head, I told her not to worry. I explained I was ringing as I'd received a message that the angels were looking after him, and sure enough, a few days later Jimmy was out of the coma and went on to make a full recovery.

As the months and years keep ticking by, I feel as if I've come to appreciate just how magical this world of ours is. It's as if Life wants to prove to me that there is more to our dimension than meets the eye; as if the Universe wants to confirm to me that we are more than just flesh and blood. And through all my supernatural experiences, I've come to believe that we have many more than five senses. I think in spiritual Consciousness, we can open up psychic and telepathic abilities, and as humanity is forever evolving, I do feel as if the switching on of these new senses or abilities will become our next stage in evolution.

During the last twenty years, I've kept on regularly reading Tarot cards for myself and for others, and I still cherish the deck that Aaron bought me. For decades, the cards have been my method of connecting with the Divine Creative energy to seek guidance from this higher power—and they've never failed me. However, in recent months, I've experienced a phenomenon where I already know which cards will be drawn before they're turned over.

When I meditate on the deck and tune in, I see pictures of the cards in my mind's eye, and when people ask me to read for them, I now find that I don't really need the cards as a mediator. I can look at the person's face, sense their energy, and see their cards all around them; often our physical environment will even directly match a scene shown on a card.

I understand the term clairvoyant literally translates to mean someone who sees clearly, and that definition resonates with me very much. It seems now that I have foresight naturally within me, and after a lifetime of inner turmoil, my view is now clear.

I've found my spiritual insights have come in various guises, and in addition to foresight, I've found that spirits themselves appear to be open to directly visiting me—so many things have happened that I can't explain with science. And as I know I'm not the only one who's experiencing such things, I wonder what it will take for us to collectively accept our spiritual senses and update our national curriculums to include them as facts?

Every time I encounter a spirit energy, I enter a state where I feel what's happening with my heart and soul, not my rational mind. I don't need to process or explain what's happening with my ego; I just witness it in complete awe and leave each encounter with more direct confirmation that there is life after death.

To give you an example of how strange some of these encounters feel, there was one day last year when I had nipped into the village centre to post a letter, and saw my close friend Barbara drive towards me. She beeped her horn repeatedly (even though she had my attention from the second I saw her car) and she waved fervently at me, wearing a big, broad smile, so I waved and smiled back.

Barbara was a black lady with a very distinctive African dress sense—she always wore a headdress—and there was no doubt in my mind that it was Barbara who I had seen that afternoon. Her face was easy to see, she was wearing her favourite scarf around her hair, and she was driving her white Skoda car.

I tell you no word of a lie, when I got home not ten minutes later, my phone rang, and I took a call from my good friend Janette telling me, 'Ana, I'm so sorry to tell you this, but Barbara passed away in hospital this morning.'

Janette and I used to have coffee with Barbara every couple of weeks, and bless her, she must have found my reply so odd, when I said, 'What? Who do you mean?'

She replied in a puzzled tone, 'I mean Barbara. Our Barbara. Barbara Scott.'

There was in fact only one Barbara who we knew, so my behaviour on that call couldn't have seemed more out of place to poor Janette. But with my mind reeling whilst I was completely spinning out, I replied, 'No, I'm sorry, Janette, but you've got that wrong. Barbara's not dead—I've just seen her in the village.'

It really was a crazy situation to be told how someone *I had just seen* had died earlier that day. And whilst I implored Janette to believe that Barbara was fine and had looked happy and healthy when I'd seen her, it turned out that Janette was right. Barbara had passed away, and I've since been left with a memory that doesn't fit in with reality as we know it. Now, you know I can't prove any of this, but I hope you hear me when I tell you this is my truth.

I do sense that death is starting to get close to me now, and as this is happening, I feel I'm already connecting to the next dimension. However, please be assured that I have no fear of dying—for I know that our soul energy carries on.

Before I lived in the flat where I am now in Bristol, an elderly lady (who was said to be a bit of a recluse) lived and died here, and as time's gone by, I've sometimes felt that lady's presence here with me. It's as if she still feels this flat is her home, but I've never felt any negativity from her. I smell her perfume, I get goose bumps feeling the air move gently around me for no reason, and in those times, I know she's here. But I'm fine with her, and it seems she's fine with me too. Her energy doesn't cause me any problems or unpleasantness; I simply accept her, and in doing so, I think we get on. I don't know why she isn't yet ready to fully move on to the next dimension; but whilst ever she wants to stay here, I respect her choice.

In daily life, I now potter around as best I can, but my health has deteriorated to the point where I'm unable to venture out and campaign for AIDS awareness like I used to. I can no longer clean my own house nor do my own shopping, so I've had to consciously subdue my fiercely independent nature, and be calm in the position where I know it's OK to accept help from others—as long as I am helpful in return.

But how can I help when I live within the confinement of a body that's so frail? The only way I have found to answer that is to feel in my heart that the love I have to give is a worthy contribution to society. I can feel love, I can create love, and I can give love—Love and Time are the assets that I now have to share—and I can only pray that my good intentions are in fact of service to others.

When my family, friends, and care workers come to see me, I always ask how they are, and I listen to their problems with an open mind and a non-judgmental heart. I consciously pour my love on to them in effort to lift their spirits and raise their vibrational level, so that hopefully they feel better when they leave than when they'd arrived. I don't ever want to drain anyone, and I don't want to take any energy from them that they don't want to give.

I babysit my two beautiful grandchildren twice a week when Sam and Melissa take a little time for themselves; I sometimes see friends for cup of tea, or natter on the phone with my siblings. But mostly I'm at home, and when I'm alone, I make full use of the internet and social media.

The experience of connecting with people all over the world with similar interests amazes me, and I find it wonderful how long-distance communication is so much easier in this digital age.

I'm a member of various spiritual and activist online groups, and I love how honesty pours out of these forums. It seems incredible to me that people who are complete strangers share their deepest thoughts and experiences so freely in search of the deeper meaning of life and the solutions to our global problems. In the solitude of my flat, I find myself now blessed with wonderful connections to so many others.

I love reading the passionate, insightful posts I see from people of all ages, and I enjoy posting words of advice or comfort whenever I see someone asking openly for spiritual guidance.

I've also been intrigued by the huge number of posts I've read from people who are exploring the idea of communal living and free towns—it seems that the desire to live in self-governing, independent communities is now stronger around the world than I've ever known before. And I've happily shared my experiences of life in Arcadia, hoping that the vision that we held in our commune can be of some inspiration to other freedom seekers.

Although I never stayed in touch with any of my Arcadian friends, I have researched what's happened in the commune since I left, and understand that Arcadia is still a living, breathing community, where now close to a thousand residents live, spread over the twenty acres of land. They've battled the police and overarching system for their way of living and still maintain their self-declared independence from the state.

While I will always look back fondly at my time in Arcadia—for it was an incredibly inspiring community—I am now of the opinion that we shouldn't have to leave the established towns and cities to experience freedom.

I feel there must be a way for existing communities to come together and declare themselves free, without having to start up from scratch elsewhere. And whilst I certainly don't profess to have all the answers, I do believe that the blue-prints required to set peace free already exist out there, and much work has already been done around the world to pave the way towards a state of free living.

It feels to me as if the next stage of our conscious evolution will see the jigsaw pieces of the greater good being finally recognised and valued by the masses and placed together with loving intention.

Personally, I feel that fear is the biggest problem that we're collectively dealing with. It's the worst virus that threatens us at every level of our society—from the billionaires to the penniless, fear can attack us all. Warping our spiritual nature, fear compels us to act selfishly and blinds us to the strength of the love that we're made with.

I know I spent a substantial amount of my life living in fear, but now I feel I've been able to rise up through this to a sustainably high vibrational level. And I think if everyone consciously developed their ability to live and act in alignment with love, not fear, then this world would change overnight.

I have all the proof I need to know that there is more than the dimension we live in, and I have come to feel sure that the reason I'm still alive is that my mission, up to now, has been incomplete. I've needed to do more to fulfil my destiny.

When I've seen so many wonderful people die before me, who appear to have been cheated out of life and called over well before their time, I've sometimes struggled to fathom why I'm still here. Despite everything life has thrown at me, I've been unable to die.

The specialists and consultants have been telling me I might have another year left for several years, but the end has never arrived, and I've been left thinking there *must* be a reason I'm still in this body. It seems to me that the Universe has had something more that it's wanted me to do—something more than just listening to and loving others in my community.

When I consider the Big Picture and my personal mission, I know that raising awareness of AIDS has been a key part of my life. But, now, when I wonder what my journey has prepared me to do, I see that I must expand my mission to encompass spirituality too—for I have been between dimensions, I've connected with spirits, and that is now a part of my truth that I have to tell.

In addition, to love and time, I know that my truth is the other asset that I have to share. And I believe that every time one of us tells our Truth, coming from a place of Love, we can help each other, comfort each other, inspire each other and evolve.

I feel that in writing to you, I am finally completing my life. In return for sharing all the memories and reflections that have whirled around my mind for so many decades, I sense that my spirit will be released, and I will be free of the body which is so difficult to manoeuvre these days.

I would like for you to rest assured that in these final days of my life—for I know, dear Reader, as this book approaches its end that the next dimension is now calling me—I feel comforted by the energy of the people I encounter on a daily basis. And I'm positive that a tidal wave of enlightenment is set to flow across the world.

I've made many, many friends during recent years, and it's been truly uplifting to encounter so many people who shine. I find that I am always surrounded by love. Even when I am alone, I feel it in the air and running through me.

With every day that passes, I adopt a stance of accepting everything and everyone around me without judging, and I remain peaceful in my being. Yes, there are things happening in modern society that I don't agree with and which I don't believe are in the best interest of our species or the Earth in its entirety. However, I'm sure my coma showed me that there is a way for us to rebalance our existence and it will be found.

It does concern me that recreational drugs are as rife now with the younger generations as they were in my day, and I know there are many, many people out there who turn to drugs for a release, not bothered in the slightest about any question of legality, just concerned with trying to change their vibration for a few hours.

In my opinion, drugs are simply a shortcut to temporary inner peace: a sticking plaster solution which we can use to try to bond together the fibres of our troubled lives.

When we take drugs, what we're saying is, "I'd like to feel different to how I'm naturally feeling right now." We want to feel calmer, or more relaxed for example, or we want to blur the pain of our past. We want to unwind quickly from a degree of mental stress. And drugs offer us such a release. We're not troubled by the emotional burdens we carry when we're high; they fade away into the background, and the drugs feel like our friend—sometimes they can feel like your only friend—the only way you know how to make it through another set of twenty-four hours.

When we become addicted to using drugs, we make a substance our ally: we appreciate the change of frequency it temporarily brings us, and we use it seeking to connect with a lighter version of ourselves that we prefer. You know I took more than my fair share of drugs, but with the help of Sunrise House, I learned that to live peacefully, it's critical that we heal the pain or tension that the drugs cover up. We must honestly address every mistake we've ever made, offload resentments that we've held onto, and make peace with ourselves. Showing ourselves kindness, we must believe that we are worthy of love, and find a way to naturally connect to our higher Self—which for me, came through meditation and love.

There are many aspects of our planetary existence that are unhealthy right now, and I know that everyone is wondering how we fix the issues that we collectively face. Sometimes our problems seem so huge we don't even know where to begin, but I know inner peace is possible, and world peace is possible too. As the pendulum swings, I believe world peace is now our only option—we've tried fighting, and I don't see that it creates anything except death and suffering.

I sense there is a goal in the air, which urges humanity to exist in harmony with nature. And now as my life comes to an end, I recognise that we've got a lot of work to do before we achieve that state. I've heard our species likened to a cancer of the planet, and while I understand that point of view, I do believe that spiritual consciousness is spreading like wild-fire, and that it is this energy that will rebalance our societies.

I'm convinced that if we all live our lives with positive intentions and wage peace for the greater good, then we can become a species who act as guardians of Earth, rather than exploiters. I've seen the future and I sense this is true. However, I know to achieve a state of conscious sustainability, we must apply ourselves to heal our planet, and we must do this together peacefully.

I have no doubt that now is the time for enlightened principles to flow through our societies, reforming industries and enabling individual, sovereign freedom to finally flourish.

So, my dear, that is my journey: a rather spectacular series of traumatic events, interspersed with moments of beauty, true love, and spiritual peace.

I believe that each one of us is equal and powerful in our own right, and that we are capable of incredible things, especially if we unite our efforts. We search the Earth for answers to our own unique life questions, and if we help each other to find the answers we yearn for, I know great things will come.

I do feel change has been a prominent theme in my life, and I know I have lived through an incredible transformation. I was once an abused scullery maid in Nottingham with no self-worth, and now I'm a fifty-six-year-old woman with a deep sense of inner security and a very positive outlook on the mystery of the Universe.

I have known what it is to be healthy and I've lived with a body that has changed beyond all recognition, so I now look like a very sick, elderly woman. I have encountered poverty and crime, and as you well know, I have never achieved financial wealth, a true career, nor fame. I have lived the life of a nobody. My existence has often been judged by others, and I've experienced the hardship of labels and discrimination. Yet despite never having material riches, I know in the love I have with my family, I have struck gold. I have nothing and everything at the same time. Centring myself in love and divine connection, I know bliss.

So, now, as my body is tired and my eyes are yearning to close one last time, I will leave you here and wish you well in your journey and all your endeavours. My time has now come and I really am so grateful that I was given enough time to write to you before I pass over.

Thank you for taking the time to read my life; I wish you nothing but love, peace, and happiness in yours.

When the Earth is sick and the animals and the plants are dying, there shall arise a new tribe.
This new tribe will be made up of all colours and creeds.
They will be called the Rainbow Warriors, and they will put their faith into actions not words.

— Hopi Prophecy

Acknowledgements

There are so many people that I would like to thank. Firstly, thank you to all of you who have read this book and given me your feedback during the seven years it's taken me to complete this novel. Your review and counsel has been so helpful and deeply appreciated at every step of the way.

To my dear friend and mentor, James Redfield, thank you for all the time you have invested in me, the guidance that you've given, and the wisdom you've shared with me. Thank you for helping me to deliver this book to the world. I appreciate your work more than words can say.

To my business partner and soul sister, Kelly Redfield, thank you for being the shining light that you are. Thank you for walking this path with me, side by side—with one shoe each! I can't wait to discover our adventures that lie ahead.

To my wonderful mum, thank you for the hours on end that you've spent reading the many versions of this book, and for your ever truthful red pen! Thank you for always being there for me, for the unconditional love you've always given, and for being my best friend.

To my beautiful friends, Roisin, Naomi, Leanne, Michelle, Amanda, Coquis, and Julie, thank you for being the wonderful ladies that you are. Thank you for taking the time to read this book and for sharing with me your heartfelt experience of discovering Ana's journey. Thank you for the friendship and love that you give, and for being a part of my life as we journey our paths, only ever a phone call away.

To my editors Holli Smith and Jenny Humphreys, thank you so much for all your assistance with helping me fine-tune my manuscript. You've both been an absolute pleasure to work with. You are super star editors, and I'm truly grateful for all the questions, corrections, and suggestions you gave me. Thank you!

To my Celestine Family, thank you for the community that we have created together which feels like home. Thank you for the light and love that you bring into the world, and all the positive energy you invest in our endeavours.

About The Author

Joanne Louise Hardy is a writer and management consultant, working as director of celestinevision. com, and advisor to James Redfield since 2017. Keenly interested in the Human Potential Movement, Joanne writes with the mission of contributing to our Conscious Evolution by exploring life situations, human emotions, and the path to enlightened living. Originally from Nottingham, England, Joanne now lives in rural France with her two daughters and two dogs.

We hope you enjoyed this Insighful Living book.
Insightful Living was founded by Kelly Redfield and
is run by a team who put every effort into serving
the greater good with endeavours to support humanity's
conscious evolution.
We offer books that we hope will speak to your soul,
as well as life coaching and mentoring services to support
you in breaking through to your most inspired life.

INSIGHTFUL LIVING
Mount Laurel, Alabama, USA

To be kept updated with future releases from
Joanne Louise Hardy, follow her on
Facebook or Instagram at /JoanneLouiseHardyAuthor

Printed in Great Britain
by Amazon

57669397R00213